Business Arbitration—

What You Need to

Know

by Robert Coulson
President
American Arbitration
Association

REVISED FIFTH EDITION

Revised Fifth Edition, October 1993

For information, write to the American Arbitration Association,
140 West 51st Street, New York, NY 10020–1203
Library of Congress Catalog Card Number: 85–48286
ISBN: 0–943001–25–0

Contents

PREFACE

Business Arbitration—What You Need to Know has been prepared to assist the reader in making use of alternative dispute resolution for commercial disputes, especially under the various rules of the American Arbitration Association. It contains a wealth of information on that subject. This book can help you prepare your case, eliminating uncertainty about dispute settlement procedures.

Arbitration is generally informal and businesslike—nothing to fear. Each party has the right to present its entire case. The law requires that the arbitrator hear any relevant evidence that is submitted and consider all of the arguments.

Most important business disputes are resolved privately, usually directly by the parties. When it is necessary to obtain an impartial decision, private arbitration is often the first choice. The facts and arguments can be submitted directly to the arbitrators so that a sound decision can be made. The American business community uses arbitration because it is a sensible way to resolve disputes.

Whether you are an arbitrator, an attorney, a business executive, or a private party, this book will help you to understand how arbitration can be used by you to better manage your own business controversies. It is not complicated. You do not need a legal education to understand how the process works. If you add arbitration to your personal skills, you will benefit in very practical ways.

Arbitration is not the only way to settle disputes privately. This edition covers some of the other options—negotiation, mediation, factfinding, and minitrial, among others. It is only when such techniques fail that arbitration need be initiated. Wherever possible, parties should settle their dispute between themselves.

As president of the American Arbitration Association, it has been my privilege to spend almost my entire professional life encouraging people to resolve their disputes privately. This book has been part of that effort.

CHAPTER 1

AN INTRODUCTION TO COMMERCIAL ARBITRATION

Conflict is a fact of business life, a necessary aspect of a market economy. Controversies originate for many reasons, including normal market competition and honest disagreements about rights. Disputes also arise from clashes between individuals. Americans are perfectly willing to assert their legal rights. The question is how? It is not always necessary to go to court.

A free and democratic society provides many systems for resolving controversies. People think of the courts as being primary, but, of course, they are not. Most disagreements are resolved informally, without the need for judicial intervention. Settlements are worked out privately, often without lawyers and usually without judges or juries.

In the United States, the growth of litigation has outrun our courts' ability to respond. Judges are finding it difficult to cope with the needs and demands of society. Most Americans no longer want to get involved in lawsuits. They are looking for alternative methods for resolving their disputes.

Voluntary procedures such as negotiation, mediation, conciliation, and arbitration are becoming our primary methods for settling disputes. These procedures are defined as alternative dispute resolution (ADR). The courts encourage this trend. In cases where the parties would benefit from a prompt decision, many judges will suggest mediation and arbitration as alternatives.

Commercial arbitration is not a single uniform system. There are many rules and procedures applicable to business disputes. Even under the same set of rules, arbitrators and parties may handle cases in different ways. Some hearings are more formal than others, depending on the controversy. The preferences of the participants can make a difference in the format. Arbitration, in fact, affords business the kind of flexibility it demands in other areas. This book can help you to arbitrate and to decide which kind of arbitration is right for your dispute.

WHAT IS ARBITRATION?

Arbitration is the submission of a disagreement to one or more impartial persons. Usually, the parties agree to abide by the arbitrator's decision. Because the decision is binding, arbitration differs from mediation or conciliation, where the third party brings the parties together to discuss settlement. It also differs from factfinding, where an impartial person studies the circumstances and makes a report. In most instances, arbitrators' decisions are private and only of interest to the parties involved. Few private arbitration awards come to the attention of the courts.

Arbitration is a system created by the parties themselves. When they have worked hard to settle a dispute but have failed, they can submit the remaining issues to arbitration. They can design their own arbitration procedure or refer to the well-tested rules of the American Arbitration Association. In any case, the process belongs to the parties.

THE AMERICAN ARBITRATION ASSOCIATION

The American Arbitration Association (AAA) is a public-service, not-for-profit, membership organization, founded in 1926 to encourage the use of arbitration and other techniques of voluntary dispute settlement. The AAA is based in New York City and has dispute settlement centers located in major cities throughout the United States. The Association provides education, training, and research on all forms of out-of-court dispute settlement. The AAA offers information on private dispute resolution and helps industries to design their own systems.

LEGISLATIVE HISTORY OF ARBITRATION

Private arbitration has gained widespread acceptance since the first modern arbitration laws were passed in the late 1920s. Congress passed the United States Arbitration Act (Federal Arbitration Act), which applies to most business controversies, in 1925. In 1955, the National Conference of Commissioners on Uniform State Laws adopted the Uniform Arbitration Act. Modern arbitration laws reflect the needs of the business community and the growing support for arbitration among lawyers and judges.

Winning the right to arbitrate future disputes has been a victory for business. The various state arbitration statutes are listed in the appendix. National policy favors arbitration, as reflected in the Federal Arbitration Act. Recent cases from both federal and state courts have expressed that support in strong terms.

Arbitration systems, like other voluntary institutions, are sensitive to changes in the law or to government intervention. In some cases, legislation may encourage arbitration by simplifying and reducing the issues between parties. Automobile no-fault laws are examples of this.

Many thousands of cases are arbitrated each year. Arbitration is popular with the American people. Rather than being a system of "second-class justice," it is the first choice of many people. Arbitration takes cases out of the courts. It saves public money. It puts the control of dispute settlement into the hands of the parties.

Arbitration has become an important part of the justice system. Encouraging arbitration prevents unnecessary litigation. Lawyers are generally supportive of arbitration.

ARBITRATING COMMERCIAL DISPUTES

Arbitration provides an alternative system of justice. Millions of contracts, insurance policies, leases, franchise and employment agreements, and other business and personal arrangements include arbitration clauses. Those clauses allow the parties to arbitrate disputes that may arise over the meaning or application of the language in the contract. Some of these clauses refer to the rules of the AAA. These rules are printed in this book. Ask any AAA regional office for the most up-to-date versions of these rules. They will be provided without charge and the AAA staff will be delighted to answer your questions about any aspect of the process.

Major arbitration systems in the United States have been created to resolve disputes in accordance with procedures that reflect the needs of a particular industry. Trade associations often take the lead in creating arbitration systems. Often, they participate in advisory committees that monitor the operation of the system and recruit arbitrators. Their members stand to gain by using arbitration rather than going to court. Association leaders like the idea of resolving their members' disputes without government interference. Arbitration can avoid publicity that might be detrimental to the entire industry.

THE ADVANTAGES OF ARBITRATION

Why do so many executives include arbitration clauses in their contracts?

Business firms prefer to have their disagreements decided by people who are experts. Arbitrators, unlike judges, can be chosen for their business experience. AAA panels include engineers, business consultants, accountants, and many other specialized experts, as well as attorneys.

The simplicity of arbitration is also an inducement. No company wants to have its funds tied up for extended periods of time. The arbitration process can move promptly, which is especially important in disputes over performance payments or between business partners who cannot agree about the division of assets.

Arbitration cases take place in a private, informal atmosphere where the parties feel comfortable. There is less chance that trade secrets will be disclosed to competitors or that a firm's reputation will be placed in jeopardy. In arbitration, confidentiality is honored.

Because the award is not subject to appeal, arbitration results in a final and binding decision. Most parties prefer that decisions be final, rather than face the prospect of extended appellate litigation. Americans want to stay out of court.

WHO USES ARBITRATION?

Many business disputes are resolved by arbitration. Some of the major uses are described in this book—for example, resolution of disputes in such fields as construction, insurance, and international trade. Many thousands of other controversies are arbitrated. Collection claims, individual employee grievances, partnership and private corporation problems, patent and licensing disputes, and disagreements between authors and publishers are a few examples. Many cases originate from the real estate industry, the securities industry, and from computer disputes.

The Construction Industry

The construction industry is a frequent user of arbitration. In earlier years, the industry used arbitration informally. This created problems, and, in 1965, a joint industry committee asked the AAA to create an improved system. A national panel of expert arbitrators was established.

Now the AAA's Construction Industry Arbitration Rules are found in most building contracts. The caseload has grown to thousands of cases annually. Many are claims by contractors for payment, but subcontractors, engineers, or architects may be involved. Several subcontractors may process claims against a prime contractor in one proceeding.

The AAA offers an expedited arbitration system for construction claims, which can result in faster processing and reduced costs. Mediation rules for the construction industry are designed to encourage settlement even before arbitration begins.

Disputes over alleged defects in new homes can be resolved under the insurance-backed limited warranty that is given to the purchaser of a new home by the builder. In these cases, the process takes place at the home site.

Chapter 2 describes how dispute resolution works in the construction industry.

The Textile and Apparel Industries

Years ago, leaders in the textile and apparel fields joined together to form what is now the General Arbitration Council of the Textile and Apparel Industries. It operates as part of the AAA. Many trade associations are represented on the council, which supervises the arbitration of textile and apparel cases. The arbitrators are active business executives. Most such cases are heard in New York City, where there is a pool of experienced textile arbitrators.

Arbitration in the textile/apparel industries is described in chapter 3.

Securities Arbitration

Arbitration has proven to be an extremely effective forum for resolving disputes arising from the thousands of securities transactions that take place each year. The AAA's Securities Arbitration Rules contain specific procedures for selection of arbitrators with appropriate securities expertise. In addition, an expedited system has been included in the rules for cases in which no party's claim exceeds $25,000, exclusive of interest and arbitration costs.

Securities Arbitration Rules are reproduced at the end of this chapter.

Lemon Law

Although a majority of states have laws protecting consumers of defective new and used motor vehicles, until recently, consumers have had only two options for seeking restitution—filing a lawsuit, or submitting a claim to a manufacturer's dispute resolution program. The new-generation lemon laws, enacted by a number of states—Connecticut, Florida, Georgia, Hawaii, Massachusetts, New York, and Washington among them—provide an alternative arbitral forum for these disputes. The AAA has been named an administrator of the independent lemon-law arbitration programs of Hawaii, Massachusetts, and New York.

Insurance Claims

One of the largest consumer arbitration systems, operating in many states, involves the determination of uninsured motorist claims. The claimant must prove both negligence and damages. Arbitration is used to decide liability and how much the company owes. Another AAA system resolves a wide variety of insurance claims by arbitration and mediation.

Arbitration also is used to resolve claims under many no-fault automobile laws. By eliminating the issue of negligence and the common-law right to compensation for pain and suffering, the injured person's claim is simplified.

The resolution of insurance claims is described in chapter 4.

International Trade

When business is carried out between parties from different countries, each party will want to avoid the other party's national courts. Arbitration makes it possible to create a self-contained system where such matters can be decided by impartial experts acting under the rules and procedures of an administrative agency. The American Arbitration Association administers such cases under whatever rules are selected by the parties and has issued special procedures for international cases.

International commercial arbitration is discussed in chapter 6.

Divorce Settlements

Marital separation agreements provide an example of the flexibility of ADR. Once a couple has agreed to discuss their separation, the last thing they should want to do is go to court. Impartial experts are assuming new roles as family mediators, helping couples to settle their problems and converting many potential lawsuits into uncontested applications for divorce. Also, arbitration clauses are commonly inserted in separation agreements.

Community Dispute Services

Criminal complaints and controversies between individuals in a community can often be handled in mediation and arbitration. People involved in those kinds of problems may be allowed to transfer their dispute to a community tribunal. An impartial third party appointed by a local mediation center can help the parties resolve their problems. This works well for people who have an ongoing relationship.

Centers have been established in many communities to deal with such conflicts. They have been widely accepted by courts and other local groups. Mediation and arbitration tribunals for community disputes have been created all over the country.

OTHER KINDS OF ALTERNATIVE DISPUTE RESOLUTION

Many ADR techniques are private. Others have been created by the courts. The primary method for resolving disputes is *negotiation*. Ninety–five percent of the cases filed in court are resolved without a trial. Most disputes are never filed in court; instead, lawyers and business executives constantly negotiate.

The *mini-trial* is a technique used by corporations involved in major controversies. The parties schedule a hearing, where trial attorneys make legal presentations to a panel consisting of top executives from each organization who, afterwards, attempt to negotiate a business solution. A neutral person presides. The neutral may serve as a mediator or give an advisory opinion after the hearing. For lawyers, the mini-trial provides an arena within which to demonstrate their skills as advocates. In a mini-trial, the clients' senior executive sits at the head of the table. The AAA has formulated procedures for mini-trials. These appear at the end of chapter 5.

Mediation is another alternative dispute resolution technique. A mediator meets with the parties and their representatives, attempting to arrange an acceptable settlement. A mediator has no authority to make decisions for the parties. Rather, a mediator helps them analyze the issues and exchange their perceptions about the relevant data, seeking a formula for compromise. Increasingly, attorneys are making use of professional mediation. The experience has been positive—over 80 percent of the disputes are settled.

Once parties agree to mediate, the procedure seems to take on a life of its own. Of the many claims mediated under AAA rules, only a few are not settled. The mediators are trained by the AAA. They receive a fee. Most cases take less than a day. The settlements must be satisfactory to both parties.

Another book in this series has been written about mediation, explaining how the process works; how mediators bring out the facts; how they caucus with the parties; and how they encourage settlement. If you are considering mediation, you should know how the process works.

Another technique is called *med-arb*. A neutral person is asked to mediate, but also can decide any issues the parties are unable to settle.

A mediator has no hold on the parties. Either party can disengage at any time. In arbitration, on the other hand, the third person is given the power to make a decision. Med–arb is a combination of both techniques.

COURT-ADMINISTERED ALTERNATIVE DISPUTE RESOLUTION

Arbitration has also been used by courts. For relatively small civil cases, some courts have installed court-administered arbitration. This can be done through enabling legislation or by court rule. Here, arbitration is mandatory for cases below a certain minimum dollar amount. After a case is filed in court, the parties are required to submit it to a panel of arbitrators, usually selected by rotation from a list provided by a local bar association. An arbitration hearing is held, after which the panel issues its award. Losing parties can request a trial *de novo* upon payment of certain fees.

Court-administered arbitration is imposed by the courts to encourage the settlement of relatively small cases. Many cases are settled, so that the courts avoid having to provide a trial.

For civil cases, other alternative systems are available. Some courts use referees, who are appointed to hear and decide a particular case or provide a preliminary hearing. They report back to the judge with findings of fact and conclusions of law. Other courts use masters for the same purpose. In a few states, by statute, parties can submit their dispute to a retired judge or attorney who serves as an arbitrator, except that the award is subject to appeal to the same extent as a court judgment. This system is called private adjudication or rent-a-judge. The arbitrator is given the power and authority of an active judge and may even hold the hearing in the courthouse. The parties pay the expenses of the process. Trial attorneys represent the parties as they would in court.

Another system is the summary jury trial. It consists of a short trial before a jury drawn from the regular panel list. The trial may be completed in a single day. A brief presentation is made by both attorneys, resulting in an advisory verdict. The verdict may be accepted by the parties, or can provide the basis for further settlement discussions. If it is rejected by either party, a normal jury trial can be obtained.

Mediation may also take place in court. A judge may engage in mediation as part of a settlement conference or an outside mediator may be used.

WHO ARE THE ARBITRATORS?

Relatively small cases are usually heard by a single arbitrator, while in more important matters parties may prefer a group decision by three arbitrators. That is up to the parties. If they can't agree, the AAA will decide for them. In this book, most references will be to a single arbitrator.

To provide the business community with neutral experts from many areas of specialization, the AAA maintains a national panel consisting of more than 55,000 people. Arbitrators are nominated by leaders in their industries or professions. They are added to the panel after the AAA has checked their qualifications and reputations.

Commercial arbitrators serve under the rules selected by the parties. Their conduct is guided by the Code of Ethics for Arbitrators in Commercial Disputes. The code is reproduced in the appendix of this book.

Arbitrators deserve respect and courtesy. In small cases, they may be serving without compensation. Parties can demonstrate their appreciation and serve their own best interests by presenting their cases in an expeditious and orderly way.

Guidelines for Handling Larger, Complex Commercial Arbitrations appear at the end of this chapter.

THE ROLE OF LAWYERS IN ARBITRATION

Under AAA rules, each party is guaranteed the right to be represented by an attorney. In commercial arbitration cases involving significant amounts of money or complex legal questions, lawyers usually represent each party. Professional representation is important in these cases. Presenting a case in arbitration involves the same skills of advocacy that lawyers need in litigation.

Some lawyers still think of courts as the exclusive forum for civil cases, particularly if they do not have an active commercial practice. In fact, only a small percentage of business claims are decided as a result of trials in court; 95 percent are settled. More commercial claims are arbitrated than are tried before juries.

Arbitration provides an alternative to the courthouse. Most business clients think that commercial arbitration is a sensible way to resolve disputes. Their attorneys tend to agree and, as they gain experience in arbitration, they see its practical benefits.

Court delays and inconveniences can be particularly frustrating to a busy lawyer. There has been a strong trend toward ADR. When selecting an attorney to represent you, be sure that this subject is discussed. Otherwise, you may get embroiled in unpleasant litigation.

BUSINESS PEOPLE CAN PARTICIPATE IN DISPUTE RESOLUTION

Executives should know how to negotiate. Bargaining is the key to justice in our society. Lawyers need such skills. So does everyone else.

In the world of trade and commerce, disputes are common, no matter how carefully a contract is written. Different perceptions lead to delayed shipments, complaints about quality of merchandise, claims of nonperformance, and similar misunderstandings. Even with good intentions, parties perform less than they promise.

Business controversies often concern the evaluation of facts and the interpretation of contract terms. Executives make these judgments every day. When differences arise out of day-to-day commercial affairs, they usually prefer to settle through arbitration, privately and informally, in a businesslike setting that encourages continued business relationships.

Like other business functions, arbitration calls for special knowledge. The executives who were involved in creating the disputed transaction may be participating in the settlement discussions and in arbitration. A business executive can help to prepare the case, select the arbitrator, and explain the evidence at the hearing. The inside lawyer in a business corporation can assist in the many parts of the process that fall outside the expertise of the executive. A member of the firm's legal staff may represent the company at the arbitration hearing. In many cases, an outside trial lawyer may be preferred.

THE ARBITRATION AGREEMENT

An agreement to arbitrate involves a binding commitment by both parties to resort to arbitration in the event that a dispute arises about the meaning or application of a contract.

American business people are free to enter into contracts. The extent of our private rights in this regard is unique, when compared with other countries. Here, contracts can be signed without prior government approval and without the payment of a tax. Freedom to contract without government interference is taken for granted.

Americans also have the right to enter into agreements to arbitrate future disputes under whichever impartial system they designate. The Federal Arbitration Act and modern state arbitration laws lend enforceability to such provisions. Only in rare instances will arbitration clauses not be enforced by the courts. Awards resulting from properly conducted arbitrations are recognized in all jurisdictions. Moreover, the Federal Arbitration Act enforces awards obtained in other countries.

The right to arbitrate is a fundamental part of our constitutional privilege to enter into contracts. Arbitration is an optional method of settlement. Parties have a right to cancel a contract without intervention by the courts. This privilege includes the right to fix the terms of such a cancellation and to submit those terms to an impartial arbitrator. The parties have the mutual right to interpret their own contract. This includes the right to authorize an impartial arbitrator to render such an interpretation for them.

In commercial relationships, parties are encouraged to arbitrate. Many arbitration clauses inserted in contracts refer to the AAA because the parties want their agreement to be self-executing. By giving authority to an impartial administrator, they avoid having to go to court.

In litigation, the emphasis is on procedure. The judicial machinery is designed to correct mistakes. The rules are supposed to protect the parties against errors, with appellate review playing an important role.

In arbitration, the parties rely upon their own ability to select a wise and impartial decision maker. They waive their right to have a judge second guess the arbitrator's decision. The emphasis is on the integrity and experience of the decision maker. Parties select arbitration because they desire an informed judgment, applied and obtained through a simplified hearing procedure. They intend the result to be final. The emphasis is on substance rather than procedure.

When an arbitration clause names the AAA, the parties rely upon the Association to provide effective and impartial administration in accordance with its rules. You should read those rules and, if you have questions, you should ask the AAA.

STANDARD ARBITRATION CLAUSE AND SUBMISSION AGREEMENT

By including an arbitration clause in contracts, business people can choose their own dispute settlement process. They can write their own arbitration clause, but most often it is sensible to use well-tested clauses printed in form contracts.

The AAA recommends the following arbitration clause for insertion in general commercial contracts:

> Any controversy or claim arising out of or relating to this contract, or the breach thereof, shall be settled by arbitration in accordance with the Commercial Arbitration Rules of the American Arbitration Association, and judgment upon the award rendered by the arbitrator(s) may be entered in any court having jurisdiction thereof.

Arbitration clauses are designed to meet the specific needs of the parties. Sometimes, a clause will refer to special rules. Among the AAA's rules are the Commercial Arbitration Rules (all-purpose procedures for business disputes), or, for specific industries, the Construction Industry Arbitration Rules, the Real Estate Valuation Arbitration Rules, the Arbitration Rules of the General Arbitration Council of the Textile and Apparel Industries, the Securities Arbitration Rules, and the International Arbitration Rules. These rules reflect modern arbitration practice. Prompt and inexpensive hearings can usually be obtained under these procedures.

Where parties do not have an arbitration clause in their contract or where the dispute does not involve a prior contract, a dispute can still be submitted to arbitration by using the following general form:

> We, the undersigned parties, hereby agree to submit to arbitration under the Commercial Arbitration Rules of the American Arbitration Association the following controversy: (cite briefly). We further agree that the above controversy be submitted to (one)(three) arbitrator(s) selected from the panels of arbitrators of the American Arbitration Association. We further agree that we will faithfully observe this agreement and the rules and that we will abide by and peform any award rendered by the arbitrator(s) and that a judgment of the court having jurisdiction may be entered upon the award.

STEP ONE: HOW TO INITIATE AN ARBITRATION

All that is required to begin the arbitration, regardless of how the parties agree to arbitrate, is notification to the AAA and the defending party. The AAA will supply appropriate forms free of charge. A case can also be initiated through ordinary correspondence, provided the essential information is included.

On receiving such a notification, the Association assigns the case to one of its staff members, a case administrator. From this point on, the administrator is at the disposal of the parties, assisting both sides until an award is rendered.

Questions may arise as to where the case will be administered or where the hearings will take place. Usually, that can be decided by the parties. If the place of arbitration has not been designated in the contract or agreed to by the parties, the AAA will designate the place in accordance with its rules.

In appropriate cases, the administrator may schedule a conference with the parties and their counsel to arrange for the exchange of information or to make arrangements for a convenient schedule of hearings.

STEP TWO: SELECTION OF THE ARBITRATOR

The parties are free to mutually agree on who will serve as their arbitrator, or to agree on some method for selecting one.

The AAA maintains a list of experienced experts from which arbitrators may be selected. Unless the parties have chosen a different method, the AAA uses the following procedure:

1. On receiving the demand for arbitration or the submission agreement and determining that arbitrators have not been identified, the administrator

sends each party a specially prepared list of proposed arbitrators with biographical information. In drawing up the list, the AAA is guided by the nature of the dispute.

2. Parties are allowed ten days to study the list, to cross off objectionable names, and to number the remaining names in order of preference. Additional information about the proposed arbitrators is available through the administrator. It is up to each party to investigate the people being suggested.

3. When the lists are returned, the administrator compares indicated preferences and notes the mutual choices. Where no mutually acceptable choice remains on a list, another list may be submitted at the request of the parties. If any party thinks that the wrong kinds of arbitrators have been listed, the matter should be discussed with the administrator.

4. If, despite efforts to arrive at a mutual choice, parties cannot agree upon an arbitrator, the AAA will make administrative appointments. No arbitrator whose name was crossed off by any party will be appointed.

STEP THREE: PREPARATION FOR THE HEARING

After an arbitrator is appointed, the case administrator consults the parties in order to schedule a mutually convenient day and time for the hearing. This information is shared with the arbitrator, who makes the date official. The administrator manages the arrangements for the hearing, relieving the arbitrator of that burden and eliminating the necessity for direct communication between the parties and the arbitrator except at the hearing. By discouraging communication with the arbitrator, except in the presence of the parties, there is no opportunity for one side to offer arguments or evidence that the other has no opportunity to rebut.

Because the arbitrator must reach a decision on the basis of the evidence presented at the hearing, it is essential that the parties and their attorneys carefully prepare their case. Here are a few practical suggestions:

1. Assemble all documents and papers you will need at the hearing. Make copies for the arbitrator and the other party. If some of the documents you need are in the other party's possession, ask that they be brought to the hearing. A checklist of your own documents and exhibits will be helpful in assuring an orderly presentation. Under most arbitration laws, the arbitrator has authority to subpoena documents and witnesses.

2. Interview all of your witnesses. Make certain the witnesses understand the whole case and the importance of their testimony. Coordinate their testimony so that your case will seem consistent and credible. Prepare your witnesses for cross-examination. If one of your witnesses requires an interpreter, make arrangements in advance.

3. If there is a possibility that additional witnesses, not on your regular list, may have to appear, alert them to be available and on call.

4. Make a written summary of what each witness will prove. This will be useful as a checklist at the hearing and will help ensure that nothing is overlooked.

5. Study the case from the other side's point of view. Be prepared to answer the opposition's evidence.

6. If it will be necessary for the arbitrator to visit a building site or warehouse for an inspection, make plans in advance. The arbitrator must be accompanied by representatives of both parties, unless specifically authorized by the parties to conduct the investigation without them present.

7. If a transcript of the testimony is needed, the parties requesting such transcript should make arrangements directly with the recording agency. The expense is borne by the parties requesting the service.

In large and complex cases, the arbitrators may provide for a preliminary hearing to identify the issues, to arrange for an exchange of documents, to identify witnesses, and to schedule hearings.

STEP FOUR: PRESENTATION OF THE CASE

Arbitration hearings are less formal than court trials. The parties and their attorneys sit on opposite sides of a conference table. Arbitrators are expected to hear all of the evidence that is relevant to the case. Because they must determine for themselves what is relevant, arbitrators are inclined to accept evidence that might not be allowed by judges. This does not mean, however, that all evidence is of equal weight or that irrelevant or repetitious evidence will not be rejected by the arbitrator. Arbitrators are not required to follow courtroom rules of evidence. In fact, an arbitrator may become impatient with a party that keeps making technical objections.

You should bear in mind that direct testimony of witnesses tends to be more persuasive than hearsay evidence, and that facts are better established by testimony and exhibits than by mere argument. Documentary evidence is often an essential part of any case. Most important is the contract itself, or the sections that have some bearing on the dispute. Documentary evidence may also include records of transactions between the parties, memoranda or correspondence, official minutes of meetings, medical reports, and progress-of-work reports. Every piece of documentary evidence should be properly identified and its authenticity established. The material should be physically presented to the arbitrator, and a copy made available to the other side. Key words, phrases, and sections of written documents can be underlined to focus the arbitrator's attention on the essential part. Properly presented documentary evidence can be most persuasive.

Parties usually depend on direct examination of witnesses for presentation of facts. After being identified and qualified, a witness is generally allowed to testify without interruption. Although leading questions may be permitted in arbitration, testimony is more effective when the witness relates facts from knowledge. Questions from counsel may be useful in emphasizing the points being made or in keeping a witness "on track."

Every witness is subject to cross-examination. Among the purposes of cross-examination are to bring out facts the witnesses may not have disclosed in direct testimony; to correct misstatements; to place facts in their true perspective; to reconcile apparent contradictions; and to attack the credibility of witnesses. In planning cross-examination, the objective to be achieved should be kept in mind. Cross-examination should sometimes be waived.

EVIDENCE AND PROOF

The arbitrator must provide a fair hearing, giving both parties sufficient opportunity to present their respective evidence and arguments. The AAA rules provide that "the arbitrator shall be the judge of the relevance and materiality of the evidence offered and conformity to legal rules of evidence shall not be necessary" (except where a statute or an arbitration agreement otherwise provides).

There are many reasons why evidentiary rules may not be suitable in arbitration. First, arbitration is intended to be an informal procedure. Second, the rules of evidence are essentially rules of exclusion. They were developed to prevent a jury from hearing or considering prejudicial or unreliable testimony and exhibits. In arbitration, however, a sophisticated person, selected by the parties for technical knowledge and good judgment, hears the case; such a person should be able to disregard evidence that is not relevant or reliable. Third, there may be a therapeutic value in allowing the parties to vent their feelings, or to "get things off their chests," even if the testimony has little probative value.

An award will not be overturned because of a liberal admission of evidence. On the other hand, refusal to hear relevant evidence may constitute grounds for vacating the award.

To say that conformity to the legal rules of evidence is not necessary does not mean that the lawyers are foreclosed from referring to them. The AAA rules recognize that arbitrators must make judgments about materiality and relevance and should not consider immaterial, irrelevant, or redundant testimony. The rules of evidence may help the arbitrator to decide such issues. Even if questionable evidence is ultimately admitted, an explanation of the legal rules of evidence may assist the arbitrator in deciding how much weight it should be given. For example, pointing up the likelihood of errors in hearsay evidence may warn the arbitrator not to place too much reliance upon it. The careful advocate will urge the arbitrator to guard against the unreliability of certain evidence.

The arbitrator should not allow testimony to stray too far afield or be influenced by prejudicial or unreliable testimony. The rules of evidence, flexibly applied, can assist the arbitrator in meeting this obligation. The general rule is to hear evidence that will help clarify the issues and to reach a resolution of the dispute. Even though arbitrators admit evidence or testimony over the objection of a party, they may be skeptical as to its probative value. The arbitrator can use the technical rules of evidence as aids or guidelines to help weigh the value of the evidence offered. In weighing such evidence, an arbitrator should be aware of the following terms:

1. Direct Evidence—Evidence that directly proves a fact, without an inference or presumption. If true, such evidence establishes the fact. Direct evidence from one witness may be sufficient for proof of any fact.

2. Circumstantial Evidence—Evidence that tends to establish the "principal fact" by proving other facts from which the principal fact can be inferred. The inference is founded on experience and observed facts, establishing a connection between the proven facts and the fact to be proven.

3. Relevant and Material Evidence—Evidence is relevant if it reasonably tends to prove or disprove the fact at issue. Evidence is material if it will influence the decision of the case.

4. Best Evidence—Primary evidence as distinguished from secondary; original as distiguished from copies. Best evidence favors the presentation of original documents instead of copies.

5. Hearsay Evidence—Hearsay is second-hand evidence. It is testimony of a statement made by someone other than the witness, repeated at the hearing to show the truth of the matters contained in it. The reliability of a statement rests upon the believability of the person who made the statement. Courts tend to exclude hearsay evidence because of the risk of inaccuracy in the repetition of the story and because there is no opportunity to cross-examine the person making the original statement. There are numerous exceptions to the hearsay rule. Records kept in the ordinary course of business are one such exception. The arbitrator may give hearsay little weight where the opposing party presents contradictory evidence that is subject to cross-examination. An affidavit is a type of hearsay evidence that is allowed by AAA rules. The rules caution the arbitrator to give an affidavit "only such weight as the arbitrator deems it entitled to after consideration of any objections made to its admission."

6. Parol Evidence—Testimony that seeks to explain the meaning of the contract. When a contract is intended to be the complete and final expression of the rights and duties of the parties, no evidence, oral or written, of prior understandings or negotiations is admissible to contradict or vary the terms of the agreement.

7. Opinion Evidence—Evidence of what the witness thinks about the facts in dispute, as distinguished from personal knowledge of the facts, is generally not admissible in court except where the witness is an expert in the field. The importance of opinion evidence depends on whether the opinion deals with a crucial issue in the case. When a witness is asked an opinion about an important issue and the other party objects, the arbitrator will rule on admissibility. Generally, an arbitrator will allow opinions but will limit the weight given to them according to the qualifications of the witness who expressed them. On the other hand, an arbitrator may bar a witness who is not an expert from giving an opinion on the ultimate question to be decided. Greater latitude is given in arbitration because the arbitrator is likely to be an experienced person, with special knowledge, who will not be improperly influenced by the opinions of witnesses.

8. Inference—A deduction of fact that may logically and reasonably be drawn from another fact or group of facts found or otherwise established in the matter. An inference is the result of reasoning based upon evidence.

9. Presumption—When a certain group of facts leads to a certain conclusion, the arbitrator may make a presumption.

10. Cumulative Evidence—A repetition of evidence that has been testified to previously. Evidence is not cumulative merely because it tends to establish the same ultimate fact. Cumulative evidence is additional evidence of the same kind to prove the same point. In order to conduct an orderly and expeditious hearing, an arbitrator may limit evidence that is repetitive and cumulative in nature. The arbitrator may encourage the attorney to move forward with the case.

11. Burden of Proof—There is no "burden of proof" in business arbitration. A party proves a case by providing sufficient evidence to convince the arbitrator on the relevant issues. Each party is expected to prove its case and, if the evidence does not support one of the claims submitted to arbitration, the arbitrator will simply deny that claim.

12. Leading Questions—Questions worded so that they suggest to witnesses the desired answers. The danger of leading questions is that the questioner, not the witness, is testifying. Leading questions may be time saving in matters that are not in dispute, or when asked during cross-examination. Leading questions about a basic matter asked of a witness, however, may be objectionable or improper and may be stopped by the arbitrator.

13. Objections—In arbitration, an advocate may make objections to exclude a particular question, to modify the manner of questioning, to change momentum, or to calm a witness who is testifying on cross-examination. An objection can also warn the arbitrator about the weakness of the evidence.

THE DUTY OF THE ARBITRATOR TO DISCLOSE

An arbitrator should have no interest, financial or otherwise, in the outcome of the case.

It is not unusual for an arbitrator, on being asked to serve, to discover some prior or present business connection with one of the parties. The Commercial Arbitration Rules require that neutral arbitrators "disclose to the AAA any circumstance likely to affect impartiality, including any bias or any financial or personal interest in the result of the arbitration or any past or present relationship with the parties or their representatives."

If the contact was so close as to be disqualifying, the arbitrator should decline to serve. When the parties cannot agree as to the seriousness of challenges, the AAA has to determine whether the arbitrator shall be disqualified. Not every business relationship will affect the enforcement of the award. In some situations, it will be enough for the arbitrator to disclose the connection before accepting the appointment.

When the parties and their witnesses assemble in the hearing room, the arbitrator may recall for the first time a relationship with a person involved. Disclosure at this time gives the parties an opportunity to waive their objections. Such a waiver will bar any subsequent objection to the award on the ground of bias.

THE POWER OF THE ARBITRATOR

An arbitrator is given substantial authority by the parties and by the law. Some of these powers are procedural: the right to issue subpoenas, to fix the date of hearing, to grant postponements (at the request of a party or on the arbitrator's initiative), to proceed with the hearing in the absence of a party who fails to appear after being notified. *Ex parte* awards can be enforced under federal and state laws as long as the agreement to arbitrate demonstrates the intent to allow such awards. If a contract specifies rules that permit hearings in the absence of a party, the resultant award will be valid and enforceable.

The arbitrator's authority is derived from the agreement of the parties and from the law. The authority to hear and decide any particular case exists only through the agreement of the parties to the dispute. The arbitrator must conform to standards of justice as expressed in both statutes and common law. These include obligations to attend all of the hearings, to listen to pertinent and material evidence, and to disclose any relationship with the parties. The arbitrator should be impartial in fact and in appearance. *An arbitrator should avoid any direct contact with the parties except at the hearing.*

At the hearing, the arbitrator should be fair to both parties. The adversaries will argue energetically for what they believe to be their rights. A vigorous tone, a strong objection to the arbitrator's acceptance of some evidence that may be damaging, an attempt by the claimant to increase the scope of the arbitrator's authority, and the resistance of the responding party to that attempt—all of these must be expected in arbitration. They are essential elements in the adversary process.

As a rule, arbitrators have no difficulty in maintaining order. An occasional emotional outburst or attempt to interrupt a witness during direct examination can be handled by the arbitrator with a reminder that the witness can be cross-examined later or that across-the-table bickering serves no useful purpose. Experienced arbitrators know that sometimes it is useful for the parties to "blow off steam" and find that the disputants can then proceed in an orderly fashion.

It is important that arbitrators not give any indication about how they will decide the case. They should not comment on the evidence or indicate their feelings about the merits of the case. They should avoid excessive cordiality with attorneys or parties.

The arbitrator is in charge of the hearing. Evidence must be taken in the presence of the parties. The parties and their attorneys have the right to be present at all times. The arbitrator may permit others to attend, with due regard for the parties' right of privacy. Arbitrators may require a witness to leave the hearing room during the testimony of other witnesses.

When the arbitrator is an expert and when the issue turns on an expert's judgment, it may seem logical for the arbitrator to resolve the matter by an examination. No difficulties are encountered when such an examination can be conducted in the hearing room with both parties present. When it is necessary to make an on-site inspection, the arbitrator should do so only with the knowledge of both parties, who have the right to accompany the arbitrator.

The arbitrator has broad powers to determine matters of fact and law as well as procedure. This authority must be exercised by the arbitrator alone, however; it may not be delegated to others. For example, the arbitrator should not seek clarification of a point of law by consulting an outside attorney. When some question of fact requires the services of an outside expert, such as a testing company or public accountants, the parties must give their permission. Parties may allow the arbitrator to engage such help, since this is not a delegation of authority. The ultimate decision still rests with the arbitrator. The arbitrator is not bound by the findings of any outside agency.

During the hearing, the parties or their lawyers may see an opportunity for settlement. They may ask for an adjournment to carry out further negotiations. The arbitrator should encourage such discussions but should take no part in them. It is permissible for the arbitrator to incorporate such a settlement in an award.

ELIMINATING DELAYS IN COMMERCIAL ARBITRATION

Arbitration is not always expeditious. One or both of the parties may not be interested in obtaining a prompt hearing. In some situations, it may appear that neither wants the matter processed with diligence.

A respondent against whom a money award is being claimed may resist arbitration, hoping to stave off the award. Inserting special language in the arbitration clause may increase a respondent's willingness to cooperate. For example, an escrow fund may be created so that the money in issue will be withdrawn from the operating funds of the respondent, pending the outcome. The deposit could be placed in an interest-bearing account subject to the arbitrator's award. Both parties may be more eager to reach a conclusion if the fund has been placed out of their grasp during the pendency of the arbitration.

Other sources of delay have also been identified. It may be difficult to obtain mutual acceptance of neutral arbitrators familiar with the trade practices in the industry but not closely identified with either party or their attorneys. Multiple disclosures and challenges to arbitrators may take time before a panel of acceptable, impartial arbitrators can be appointed. Discovery procedures can be an impediment, causing unnecessary delay before the attorneys are ready for their hearing. Discovery procedures are not customary in arbitration but can be arranged by the parties.

The professional staff of the AAA can help to expedite commercial arbitration cases. The AAA will schedule an administrative conference with the attorneys, in an effort to streamline the hearing procedure. It may be possible to avoid any need for discovery by encouraging stipulations as to the facts or by obtaining an agreement about how evidence will be presented. Parties can exchange documents prior to the hearing. Administrative conferences may also lead to negotiated settlements.

Expedited procedures are also available under the AAA's Commercial Arbitration Rules. These procedures can eliminate delays in arbitration by allowing notice by telephone, facilitating the arbitrator selection process, and reducing the time for making the award.

MEDIATION

Prior to submitting the matter to arbitration, the parties may wish to make one final attempt at mediation. Each of the AAA's offices maintains a list of experienced mediators who can schedule an initial meeting with the parties to ascertain whether mediation will be productive. Using the AAA mediation rules, such a meeting can take place promptly without delaying the initial steps of appointing an arbitrator and scheduling a hearing, and without payment of an additional administrative fee.

DISPOSING OF PAPERWORK

Expense can be avoided if the parties reduce the amount of paperwork. Transcripts and briefs can be eliminated. The AAA encourages parties to streamline their procedures. Purchasing an official transcript can be particularly expensive. In arbitration, transcripts are often a waste of money. In many cases, the arbitrator and the attorneys can rely on their own notes.

CONTROL OF SCHEDULING

In complex commercial arbitration cases, it may be difficult to schedule blocks of time when the arbitrators and the lawyers will be available. At the prearbitration conference, an effort should be made to arrange such dates. The parties should determine whether an arbitrator can devote sufficient consecutive time for hearing the case. Arbitration cases can advance rapidly if both the parties and the arbitrators will commit themselves to such a schedule. The AAA encourages the participants to begin hearings promptly, to take a minimal lunch period, and to continue as long as possible in the afternoon.

In lengthy cases, there is some risk that an arbitrator may be called away or become disabled. Or an arbitrator may be challenged because of an undisclosed relationship with one of the parties. Under the law, it may be necessary to replace the arbitrator and reschedule hearings. Once a panel of arbitrators has been selected, the parties should conclude their case as quickly as possible.

Parties who include arbitration clauses in their contract should encourage their counsel to move expeditiously. The AAA can help. Arbitrators are told that an important part of their responsibility is to expedite the process by keeping pressure on the advocates. The administrator does everything possible to persuade attorneys to honor their scheduled hearings. A fee is imposed for postponing a hearing. Ultimately, the speed and efficiency of the arbitration process rest in the hands of the parties. The parties and their attorneys should not delay the arbitration.

THE HEARING PROCEDURE

The moving party ordinarily proceeds first with its case, followed by the respondent. This order may be varied, however, when the arbitrator thinks it appropriate. Each party must try to convince the arbitrator of the correctness of its position. When both parties have had an opportunity to present their full case, the hearing will be closed. Do not allow yourself to be rushed. If you are participating in an arbitration for the first time, you should proceed carefully, asking for time to present your case.

Parties should present their case to the arbitrator in an orderly and logical manner. This usually includes the following steps:

1. An opening statement that briefly describes the controversy and indicates what is to be proved. Such a statement helps the arbitrator understand the relevance of testimony to be presented.

2. A discussion of the remedy sought. This is important because the arbitrator's remedial power is conferred by the agreement of the parties. This may include statutory remedies covered by the contract. Each party should try to show that the relief it wants can be granted within the arbitrator's authority.

3. An orderly introduction of witnesses to clarify the nature of the controversy and to identify relevant documents and exhibits. Cross-examination of witnesses can be revealing, but each party should plan to establish its own case through the direct testimony of its own witnesses.

4. A closing statement, which should include a summary of evidence and arguments and a refutation of points made by the opposition. The arbitrator will give both sides equal time for a closing statement. This occasion should be used to summarize the relevant facts and to emphasize the issue and the decision the arbitrator is being asked to make.

Because arbitration is somewhat informal, statements may be permitted during all phases of the hearing. There may be times, however, when the arbitrator will ask parties to concentrate on presenting evidence, putting off arguments until later. In any event, all arguments should be stated fully. Above all, your presentation should be accurate and credible. Exaggeration, concealing of facts, introduction of legal technicalities with the object of delaying the proceedings, or general disregard of ordinary rules of courtesy and decorum are likely to have an adverse effect upon arbitrators.

After both sides have had an equal opportunity to present their evidence, the arbitrator will declare the hearing closed. Under AAA rules, the arbitrator then has thirty days within which to render the award, unless the agreement provides otherwise.

THE ARBITRATION AWARD

The award is the arbitrator's decision on the matters submitted for consideration. It should completely resolve the dispute. Each party has agreed beforehand to abide by the decision. Most responsible parties comply with arbitration awards. The purpose of the award is to dispose of the issues, finally and conclusively.

Some judges have been tempted to review arbitrators' awards, particularly as to legal issues. That is not possible under the American system. By referring the issues to an arbitrator, the parties have agreed to a final and nonreviewable award. Final arbitration is not compatible with judicial review. An occasional mistake by an arbitrator, left uncorrected by the courts, is the price that must be paid for a healthy system of binding arbitration.

Most arbitration agreements provide for *binding* arbitration. Many parties might be unwilling to use arbitration without assurance that the decision would be final. Review of awards by a court would be contrary to the parties' expectations. Arbitration laws support this concept by providing very limited grounds for overturning an arbitration award.

Arbitrators are not required to write opinions explaining the reasons for their decisions. As a general rule, AAA commercial awards consist of a brief decision on a single sheet of paper. Written opinions can be dangerous because they identify targets for the losing party to attack.

One judge offered the following instruction to arbitrators:

> The thing we must look at is the face of the award itself, and see whether it is in excess of the powers of the arbitrator. . . . Although technical precision is not required in an award of arbitrators, I would urgently suggest that arbitrators follow the form of award provided by the American Arbitration Association. In the event they feel impelled by some uncontrollable urge, literary fluency, good conscience, or mere garrulousness to express themselves about a case they have tried, the opinion should be a separate document and not part of the award itself.

The AAA does not encourage such opinions. In some cases, both parties want an opinion. Then the AAA has no objection. Usually, however, the parties look to an arbitrator for a decision, not an explanation.

The arbitrator has no duty to inform the parties about the arbitration award. Instead, the AAA delivers copies of the award to the parties. Once the arbitrator has signed the award, the arbitrator has no further connection with the case and should not become involved in any court action that may follow. In fact, the arbitrator should not discuss the award or respond to a request for clarification. Any such requests should be brought to the attention of the AAA. The arbitrator's obligation to maintain confidence about the affairs of the parties continues indefinitely.

WHAT TO DO AFTER THE AWARD

If the award is in your favor, you should celebrate. Then, ask your adversary to comply with the award. If a losing party voluntarily performs pursuant to the terms of the award, nothing further is necessary. In cases of noncompliance, the winning party can move for a judgment confirming the award. Usually, a losing party will comply. Where the prevailing party requests the award, the award will almost always be confirmed.

If the award is not in your favor and you think that it is invalid, you can move for vacatur of the award. There are three grounds for vacating awards:

(1) arbitrator misconduct, such as corruption, fraud, or bias, (2) a showing that the arbitrator exceeded his or her authority, or (3) the failure to meet statutory requirements of due process. Included within the latter category are awards that contravene public policy.

Judicial review concerns itself only with defects in the arbitration procedure, not with the merits of the case. Arbitration laws draw narrow limits around the court's authority to review awards. The Federal Arbitration Act is typical, providing the following grounds for vacating an award:

§ 10. Same; vacation; grounds; rehearing

In either of the following cases the United States court in and for the district wherein the award was made may make an order vacating the award upon the application of any party to the arbitration—

(a) Where the award was procured by corruption, fraud, or undue means.

(b) Where there was evident partiality or corruption in the arbitrators, or either of them.

(c) Where the arbitrators were guilty of misconduct in refusing to postpone the hearing, upon sufficient cause shown, or in refusing to hear evidence pertinent and material to the controversy; or of any other misbehavior by which the rights of any party have been prejudiced.

(d) Where the arbitrators exceeded their powers, or so imperfectly executed them that a mutual, final, and definite award upon the subject matter submitted was not made.

(e) Where an award is vacated and the time within which the agreement required the award to be made has not expired the court may, in its discretion, direct a rehearing by the arbitrators.

Many state arbitration laws provide similar grounds for modifying an award. These narrow statutory grounds result in relatively few motions to vacate or modify arbitration awards.

Because commercial arbitrators do not write opinions explaining the reasons for their decisions, it may be difficult to determine whether arbitrators exceeded their powers. An undisclosed error of judgment is virtually immune from attack.

It is sometimes said that arbitrators are not bound by the law in reaching their decisions. This is misleading. Commercial arbitrators are carefully briefed by each lawyer as to the applicable law. At the same time, attorneys argue the practical considerations that should be weighed by the arbitrator.

It is improper for an arbitrator to refuse to listen to such arguments. Arbitrators must carefully consider the legal arguments, even though they are not required to make findings on legal issues.

Many commercial arbitrators are business people who regard their service as a contribution to their industry. They are not professional arbitrators. They are community leaders who are giving their time and their wisdom to their fellow citizens. If these arbitrators were required to produce comprehensive findings of fact and conclusions of law, the role of the commercial arbitrator would be changed considerably. These kinds of people only continue to participate in the process, making their services available, if courts will exercise restraint in reviewing awards. Private arbitration, the right to design the system the parties prefer, is fragile. It could be destroyed if courts demanded the right to review the substance of arbitrators' awards.

After an award has been issued, the power of the arbitrator ends. The arbitrator has no further authority to modify an award, unless the parties mutually agree to reopen the proceeding. The arbitrator is *functus officio* (having no further power or authority to act in the matter). In cases where the parties agree to seek further clarification of an award or an interpretation of a disputed ruling, the agreement must be in writing. Such a request should be filed with the AAA, which then makes necessary arrangements with the arbitrator. These requests are rare and, if the arbitrator refuses to explain the award, the parties have no further recourse.

PARTY-APPOINTED ARBITRATION—THE DRAWBACKS

Under some arbitration agreements, each party appoints one arbitrator; these two arbitrators then select a third member of the panel. This system is a holdover from the days when administrative agencies were not available. There are many problems with such a scheme. For example, it is not clear whether the party-appointed arbitrator is expected to be impartial. Also, the system creates impasses because either party can refuse to proceed. The moving party must then resort to the courts. Another problem is that a compromise award may be rendered by the neutral arbitrator for the sake of obtaining a majority. When parties discover that such a system has been designated in their agreement, they sometimes authorize the third arbitrator to act alone. Because of the obvious weaknesses in the party-appointed system, it has been dying out in the United States.

In New Jersey, courts have even held that a party-appointed arbitrator is required to disclose any relationships with that party that might create an appearance of bias. In one case, a party-appointed arbitrator failed to report such a connection and the award was vacated.

Parties are well advised to avoid the party-appointed system, using a single neutral arbitrator or a totally neutral panel.

CONCLUSION

Business executives are losing patience with courts that take years to achieve results and leave both parties exhausted by delays and legal expenses. They prefer to use alternative dispute resolution. They are finding that commercial arbitration and mediation are sensible ways to resolve business disputes.

The following chapters and collected materials inform the reader about some of the specialized business dispute resolution systems. Landmark law cases on commercial arbitration are summarized. Various procedural rules and the Code of Ethics are printed in full. Bibliographies list the books and articles that describe this rapidly expanding field.

Alternative dispute resolution is built on the belief that business people can profit by a simple and understandable system for obtaining impartial decisions. Arbitration has maintained its purpose and vitality. Each year, the AAA sees an increasing use of arbitration.

COMMERCIAL ARBITRATION RULES

As Amended and Effective on May 1, 1992

1. Agreement of Parties—The parties shall be deemed to have made these rules a part of their arbitration agreement whenever they have provided for arbitration by the American Arbitration Association (hereinafter AAA) or under its Commercial Arbitration Rules. These rules and any amendment of them shall apply in the form obtaining at the time the demand for arbitration or submission agreement is received by the AAA. The parties, by written agreement, may vary the procedures set forth in these rules.

2. Name of Tribunal—Any tribunal constituted by the parties for the settlement of their dispute under these rules shall be called the Commercial Arbitration Tribunal.

3. Administrator and Delegation of Duties—When parties agree to arbitrate under these rules, or when they provide for arbitration by the AAA and an arbitration is initiated under these rules, they thereby authorize the AAA to administer the arbitration. The authority and duties of the AAA are prescribed in the agreement of the parties and in these rules, and may be carried out through such of the AAA's representatives as it may direct.

4. National Panel of Arbitrators—The AAA shall establish and maintain a National Panel of Commercial Arbitrators and shall appoint arbitrators as provided in these rules.

5. Regional Offices—The AAA may, in its discretion, assign the administration of an arbitration to any of its regional offices.

6. Initiation under an Arbitration Provision in a Contract—Arbitration under an arbitration provision in a contract shall be initiated in the following manner:

(a) The initiating party (hereinafter claimant) shall, within the time period, if any, specified in the contract(s), give written notice to the other party (hereinafter respondent) of its intention to arbitrate (demand), which notice shall contain a statement setting forth the nature of the dispute, the amount involved, if any, the remedy sought, and the hearing locale requested, and

(b) shall file at any regional office of the AAA three copies of the notice and three copies of the arbitration provisions of the contract, together with the appropriate filing fee as provided in the schedule.

The AAA shall give notice of such filing to the respondent or respondents. A respondent may file an answering statement in duplicate with the AAA within ten days after notice from the AAA, in which event the respondent shall at the same time send a copy of the answering statement to the claimant. If a counterclaim is asserted, it shall contain a statement setting forth the nature of the counterclaim, the amount involved, if any, and the remedy sought. If a counterclaim is made, the appropriate fee provided in the schedule shall be forwarded to the AAA with the answering statement. If no answering statement is filed within the stated time, it will be treated as a denial of the claim. Failure to file an answering statement shall not operate to delay the arbitration.

7. Initiation under a Submission—Parties to any existing dispute may commence an arbitration under these rules by filing at any regional office of the AAA three copies of a written submission to arbitrate under these rules, signed by the parties. It shall contain a statement of the matter in dispute, the amount involved, if any, the remedy sought, and the hearing locale requested, together with the appropriate filing fee as provided in the schedule.

8. Changes of Claim—After filing of a claim, if either party desires to make any new or different claim or counterclaim, it shall be made in writing and filed with the AAA, and a copy shall be mailed to the other party, who shall have a period of ten days from the date of such mailing within which to file an answer with the AAA. After the arbitrator is appointed, however, no new or different claim may be submitted except with the arbitrator's consent.

9. Applicable Procedures—Unless the AAA in its discretion determines otherwise, the Expedited Procedures shall be applied in any case where no disclosed claim or counterclaim exceeds $50,000, exclusive of interest and arbitration costs. Parties may also agree to using the Expedited Procedures in cases involving claims in excess of $50,000. The Expedited Procedures shall be applied as described in Sections 53 through 57 of these rules, in addition to any other portion of these rules that is not in conflict with the Expedited Procedures.

All other cases shall be administered in accordance with Sections 1 through 52 of these rules.

10. Administrative Conference, Preliminary Hearing, and Mediation Conference—At the request of any party or at the discretion of the AAA, an administrative conference with the AAA and the parties and/or their representatives will be scheduled in appropriate cases to expedite the arbitration proceedings. There is no administrative fee for this service.

In large or complex cases, at the request of any party or at the discretion of the arbitrator or the AAA, a preliminary hearing with the parties and/or their representatives and the arbitrator may be scheduled by the arbitrator to specify the issues to be resolved, to stipulate to uncontested facts, and to consider any other matters that will expedite the arbitration proceedings. Consistent with the expedited nature of arbitration, the arbitrator may, at the preliminary hearing, establish (i) the extent of and schedule for the production of relevant documents and other information, (ii) the identification of any witnesses to be called, and (iii) a schedule for further hearings to resolve the dispute. There is no administrative fee for the first preliminary hearing.

With the consent of the parties, the AAA at any stage of the proceeding may arrange a mediation conference under the Commercial Mediation Rules, in order to facilitate settlement. The mediator shall not be an arbitrator appointed to the case. Where the parties to a pending arbitration agree to mediate under the AAA's rules, no additional administrative fee is required to initiate the mediation.

11. Fixing of Locale—The parties may mutually agree on the locale where the arbitration is to be held. If any party requests that the hearing be held in a specific locale and the other party files no objection thereto within ten days after notice of the request has been sent to it by the AAA, the locale shall be the one requested. If a party objects to the locale requested by the other party, the AAA shall have the power to determine the locale and its decision shall be final and binding.

12. Qualifications of an Arbitrator—Any neutral arbitrator appointed pursuant to Section 13, 14, 15, or 54, or selected by mutual choice of the parties or their appointees, shall be subject to disqualification for the reasons specified in Section 19. If the parties specifically so agree in writing, the arbitrator shall not be subject to disqualification for those reasons.

Unless the parties agree otherwise, an arbitrator selected unilaterally by one party is a party-appointed arbitrator and is not subject to disqualification pursuant to Section 19.

The term "arbitrator" in these rules refers to the arbitration panel, whether composed of one or more arbitrators and whether the arbitrators are neutral or party appointed.

13. Appointment from Panel—If the parties have not appointed an arbitrator and have not provided any other method of appointment, the arbitrator shall be appointed in the following manner: immediately after the filing of the demand or submission, the AAA shall send simultaneously to each party to the dispute an identical list of names of persons chosen from the panel.

Each party to the dispute shall have ten days from the transmittal date in which to strike any names objected to, number the remaining names in order of preference, and return the list to the AAA. If a party does not return the list within the time specified, all persons named therein shall be deemed acceptable. From among the persons who have been approved on both lists, and in accordance with the designated order of mutual preference, the AAA shall invite the acceptance of an arbitrator to serve. If the parties fail to agree on any of the persons named, or if acceptable arbitrators are unable to act, or if for any other reason the appointment cannot be made from the submitted lists, the AAA shall have the power to make the appointment from among other members of the panel without the submission of additional lists.

14. Direct Appointment by a Party—If the agreement of the parties names an arbitrator or specifies a method of appointing an arbitrator, that designation or method shall be followed. The notice of appointment, with the name and address of the arbitrator, shall be filed with the AAA by the appointing party. Upon the request of any appointing party, the AAA shall submit a list of members of the panel from which the party may, if it so desires, make the appointment.

If the agreement specifies a period of time within which an arbitrator shall be appointed and any party fails to make the appointment within that period, the AAA shall make the appointment.

If no period of time is specified in the agreement, the AAA shall notify the party to make the appointment. If within ten days thereafter an arbitrator has not been appointed by a party, the AAA shall make the appointment.

15. Appointment of Neutral Arbitrator by Party-Appointed Arbitrators or Parties—If the parties have selected party-appointed arbitrators, or if such arbitrators have been appointed as provided in Section 14, and the parties have authorized them to appoint a neutral arbitrator within a specified time and no appointment is made within that time or any agreed extension, the AAA may appoint a neutral arbitrator, who shall act as chairperson.

If no period of time is specified for appointment of the neutral arbitrator and the party-appointed arbitrators or the parties do not make the appointment within ten days from the date of the appointment of the last party-appointed arbitrator, the AAA may appoint the neutral arbitrator, who shall act as chairperson.

If the parties have agreed that their party-appointed arbitrators shall appoint the neutral arbitrator from the panel, the AAA shall furnish to the party-appointed arbitrators, in the manner provided in Section 13, a list selected from the panel, and the appointment of the neutral arbitrator shall be made as provided in that section.

16. Nationality of Arbitrator in International Arbitration—Where the parties are nationals or residents of different countries, any neutral arbitrator shall, upon the request of either party, be appointed from among the nationals of a country other than that of any of the parties. The request must be made prior to the time set for the appointment of the arbitrator as agreed by the parties or set by these rules.

17. Number of Arbitrators—If the arbitration agreement does not specify the number of arbitrators, the dispute shall be heard and determined by one arbitrator, unless the AAA, in its discretion, directs that a greater number of arbitrators be appointed.

18. Notice to Arbitrator of Appointment—Notice of the appointment of the neutral arbitrator, whether appointed mutually by the parties or by the AAA, shall be sent to the arbitrator by the AAA, together with a copy of these rules, and the signed acceptance of the arbitrator shall be filed with the AAA prior to the opening of the first hearing.

19. Disclosure and Challenge Procedure—Any person appointed as neutral arbitrator shall disclose to the AAA any circumstance likely to affect impartiality, including any bias or any financial or personal interest in the result of the arbitration or any past or present relationship with the parties or their representatives. Upon receipt of such information from the arbitrator or another source, the AAA shall communicate the information to the parties and, if it deems it appropriate to do so, to the arbitrator and others. Upon objection of a party to the continued service of a neutral arbitrator, the AAA shall determine whether the arbitrator should be disqualified and shall inform the parties of its decision, which shall be conclusive.

20. Vacancies—If for any reason an arbitrator is unable to perform the duties of the office, the AAA may, on proof satisfactory to it, declare the office vacant. Vacancies shall be filled in accordance with the applicable provisions of these rules.

In the event of a vacancy in a panel of neutral arbitrators after the hearings have commenced, the remaining arbitrator or arbitrators may continue with the hearing and determination of the controversy, unless the parties agree otherwise.

21. Date, Time, and Place of Hearing—The arbitrator shall set the date, time, and place for each hearing. The AAA shall send a notice of hearing to the parties at least ten days in advance of the hearing date, unless otherwise agreed by the parties.

22. Representation—Any party may be represented by counsel or other authorized representative. A party intending to be so represented shall notify the other party and the AAA of the name and address of the representative at least three days prior to the date set for the hearing at which that person is first to appear. When such a representative initiates an arbitration or responds for a party, notice is deemed to have been given.

23. Stenographic Record—Any party desiring a stenographic record shall make arrangements directly with a stenographer and shall notify the other parties of these arrangements in advance of the hearing. The requesting party or parties shall pay the cost of the record. If the transcript is agreed by the parties to be, or determined by the arbitrator to be, the official record of the proceeding, it must be made available to the arbitrator and to the other parties for inspection, at a date, time, and place determined by the arbitrator.

24. Interpreters—Any party wishing an interpreter shall make all arrangements directly with the interpreter and shall assume the costs of the service.

25. Attendance at Hearings—The arbitrator shall maintain the privacy of the hearings unless the law provides to the contrary. Any person having a direct interest in the arbitration is entitled to attend hearings. The arbitrator shall otherwise have the power to require the exclusion of any witness, other than a party or other essential person, during the testimony of any other witness. It shall be discretionary with the arbitrator to determine the propriety of the attendance of any other person.

26. Postponements—The arbitrator for good cause shown may postpone any hearing upon the request of a party or upon the arbitrator's own initiative, and shall also grant such postponement when all of the parties agree.

27. Oaths—Before proceeding with the first hearing, each arbitrator may take an oath of office and, if required by law, shall do so. The arbitrator may require witnesses to testify under oath administered by any duly qualified person and, if it is required by law or requested by any party, shall do so.

28. Majority Decision—All decisions of the arbitrators must be by a majority. The award must also be made by a majority unless the concurrence of all is expressly required by the arbitration agreement or by law.

29. Order of Proceedings and Communication with Arbitrator—A hearing shall be opened by the filing of the oath of the arbitrator, where required; by the recording of the date, time, and place of the hearing, and the presence of the arbitrator, the parties, and their representatives, if any; and by the receipt by the arbitrator of the statement of the claim and the answering statement, if any.

The arbitrator may, at the beginning of the hearing, ask for statements clarifying the issues involved. In some cases, part or all of the above will have been accomplished at the preliminary hearing conducted by the arbitrator pursuant to Section 10.

The complaining party shall then present evidence to support its claim. The defending party shall then present evidence supporting its defense. Witnesses for each party shall submit to questions or other examination. The arbitrator has the discretion to vary this procedure but shall afford a full and equal opportunity to all parties for the presentation of any material and relevant evidence.

Exhibits, when offered by either party, may be received in evidence by the arbitrator.

The names and addresses of all witnesses and a description of the exhibits in the order received shall be made a part of the record.

There shall be no direct communication between the parties and a neutral arbitrator other than at oral hearing, unless the parties and the arbitrator agree otherwise. Any other oral or written communication from the parties to the neutral arbitrator shall be directed to the AAA for transmittal to the arbitrator.

30. Arbitration in the Absence of a Party or Representative—Unless the law provides to the contrary, the arbitration may proceed in the absence of any party or representative who, after due notice, fails to be present or fails to obtain a postponement. An award shall not be made solely on the default of a party. The arbitrator shall require the party who is present to submit such evidence as the arbitrator may require for the making of an award.

31. Evidence—The parties may offer such evidence as is relevant and material to the dispute and shall produce such evidence as the arbitrator may deem necessary to an understanding and determination of the dispute. An arbitrator or other person authorized by law to subpoena witnesses or documents may do so upon the request of any party or independently.

The arbitrator shall be the judge of the relevance and materiality of the evidence offered, and conformity to legal rules of evidence shall not be necessary. All evidence shall be taken in the presence of all of the arbitrators and all of the parties, except where any of the parties is absent in default or has waived the right to be present.

32. Evidence by Affidavit and Posthearing Filing of Documents or Other Evidence—The arbitrator may receive and consider the evidence of witnesses by affidavit, but shall give it only such weight as the arbitrator deems it entitled to after consideration of any objection made to its admission.

If the parties agree or the arbitrator directs that documents or other evidence be submitted to the arbitrator after the hearing, the documents or other evidence shall be filed with the AAA for transmission to the arbitrator. All parties shall be afforded an opportunity to examine such documents or other evidence.

33. Inspection or Investigation—An arbitrator finding it necessary to make an inspection or investigation in connection with the arbitration shall direct the AAA to so advise the parties. The arbitrator shall set the date and time and the AAA shall notify the parties. Any party who so desires may be present at such an inspection or investigation. In the event that one or all parties are not present at the inspection or investigation, the arbitrator shall make a verbal or written report to the parties and afford them an opportunity to comment.

34. Interim Measures—The arbitrator may issue such orders for interim relief as may be deemed necessary to safeguard the property that is the subject matter of the arbitration, without prejudice to the rights of the parties or to the final determination of the dispute.

35. Closing of Hearing—The arbitrator shall specifically inquire of all parties whether they have any further proofs to offer or witnesses to be heard. Upon receiving negative replies or if satisfied that the record is complete, the arbitrator shall declare the hearing closed. If briefs are to be filed, the hearing shall be declared closed as of the final date set by the arbitrator for the receipt of briefs. If documents are to be filed as provided in Section 32 and the date set for their receipt is later than that set for the receipt of briefs, the later date shall be the date of closing the hearing. The time limit within which the arbitrator is required to make the award shall commence to run, in the absence of other agreements by the parties, upon the closing of the hearing.

36. Reopening of Hearing—The hearing may be reopened on the arbitrator's initiative, or upon application of a party, at any time before the award is made. If reopening the hearing would prevent the making of the award within the specific time agreed on by the parties in the contract(s) out of which the controversy has arisen, the matter may not be reopened unless the parties agree on an extension of time. When no specific date is fixed in the contract, the arbitrator may reopen the hearing and shall have thirty days from the closing of the reopened hearing within which to make an award.

37. Waiver of Oral Hearing—The parties may provide, by written agreement, for the waiver of oral hearings in any case. If the parties are unable to agree as to the procedure, the AAA shall specify a fair and equitable procedure.

38. Waiver of Rules—Any party who proceeds with the arbitration after knowledge that any provision or requirement of these rules has not been complied with and who fails to state an objection in writing shall be deemed to have waived the right to object.

39. Extensions of Time—The parties may modify any period of time by mutual agreement. The AAA or the arbitrator may for good cause extend any period of time established by these rules, except the time for making the award. The AAA shall notify the parties of any extension.

40. Serving of Notice—Each party shall be deemed to have consented that any papers, notices, or process necessary or proper for the initiation or continuation of an arbitration under these rules; for any court action in connection therewith; or for the entry of judgment on any award made under these rules may be served on a party by mail addressed to the party or its representative at the last known address or by personal service, in or outside the state where the arbitration is to be held, provided that reasonable opportunity to be heard with regard thereto has been granted to the party.

The AAA and the parties may also use facsimile transmission, telex, telegram, or other written forms of electronic communication to give the notices required by these rules.

41. Time of Award—The award shall be made promptly by the arbitrator and, unless otherwise agreed by the parties or specified by law, no later than thirty days from the date of closing the hearing, or, if oral hearings have been waived, from the date of the AAA's transmittal of the final statements and proofs to the arbitrator.

42. Form of Award—The award shall be in writing and shall be signed by a majority of the arbitrators. It shall be executed in the manner required by law.

43. Scope of Award—The arbitrator may grant any remedy or relief that the arbitrator deems just and equitable and within the scope of the agreement of the parties, including, but not limited to, specific performance of a contract. The arbitrator shall, in the award, assess arbitration fees, expenses, and compensation as provided in Sections 48, 49, and 50 in favor of any party and, in the event that any administrative fees or expenses are due the AAA, in favor of the AAA.

44. Award upon Settlement—If the parties settle their dispute during the course of the arbitration, the arbitrator may set forth the terms of the agreed settlement in an award. Such an award is referred to as a consent award.

45. Delivery of Award to Parties—Parties shall accept as legal delivery of the award the placing of the award or a true copy thereof in the mail addressed to a party or its representative at the last known address, personal service of the award, or the filing of the award in any other manner that is permitted by law.

46. Release of Documents for Judicial Proceedings—The AAA shall, upon the written request of a party, furnish to the party, at its expense, certified copies of any papers in the AAA's possession that may be required in judicial proceedings relating to the arbitration.

47. Applications to Court and Exclusion of Liability—(a) No judicial proceeding by a party relating to the subject matter of the arbitration shall be deemed a waiver of the party's right to arbitrate.

(b) Neither the AAA nor any arbitrator in a proceeding under these rules is a necessary party in judicial proceedings relating to the arbitration.

(c) Parties to these rules shall be deemed to have consented that judgment upon the arbitration award may be entered in any federal or state court having jurisdiction thereof.

(d) Neither the AAA nor any arbitrator shall be liable to any party for any act or omission in connection with any arbitration conducted under these rules.

48. Administrative Fees—As a not-for-profit organization, the AAA shall prescribe filing and other administrative fees to compensate it for the cost of providing administrative services. The fees in effect when the demand for arbitration or submission agreement is received shall be applicable.

The filing fee shall be advanced by the initiating party or parties, subject to final apportionment by the arbitrator in the award.

The AAA may, in the event of extreme hardship on the part of any party, defer or reduce the administrative fees.

49. Expenses—The expenses of witnesses for either side shall be paid by the party producing such witnesses. All other expenses of the arbitration, including required travel and other expenses of the arbitrator, AAA representatives, and any witness and the cost of any proof produced at the direct request of the arbitrator, shall be borne equally by the parties, unless they agree otherwise or unless the arbitrator in the award assesses such expenses or any part thereof against any specified party or parties.

50. Neutral Arbitrator's Compensation—Unless the parties agree otherwise, members of the National Panel of Commercial Arbitrators appointed as neutrals will serve without compensation for the first day of service.

Thereafter, compensation shall be based on the amount of service involved and the number of hearings. An appropriate daily rate and other arrangements will be discussed by the administrator with the parties and the arbitrator. If the parties fail to agree to the terms of compensation, an appropriate rate shall be established by the AAA and communicated in writing to the parties.

Any arrangement for the compensation of a neutral arbitrator shall be made through the AAA and not directly between the parties and the arbitrator.

51. Deposits—The AAA may require the parties to deposit in advance of any hearings such sums of money as it deems necessary to cover the expense of the arbitration, including the arbitrator's fee, if any, and shall render an accounting to the parties and return any unexpended balance at the conclusion of the case.

52. Interpretation and Application of Rules—The arbitrator shall interpret and apply these rules insofar as they relate to the arbitrator's powers and duties. When there is more than one arbitrator and a difference arises among them concerning the meaning or application of these rules, it shall be decided by a majority vote. If that is not possible, either an arbitrator or a party may refer the question to the AAA for final decision. All other rules shall be interpreted and applied by the AAA.

Expedited Procedures

53. Notice by Telephone—The parties shall accept all notices from the AAA by telephone. Such notices by the AAA shall subsequently be confirmed in writing to the parties. Should there be a failure to confirm in writing any notice hereunder, the proceeding shall nonetheless be valid if notice has, in fact, been given by telephone.

54. Appointment and Qualifications of Arbitrator—The AAA shall submit simultaneously to each party an identical list of five proposed arbitrators drawn from the National Panel of Commercial Arbitrators, from which one arbitrator shall be appointed.

Each party may strike two names from the list on a peremptory basis. The list is returnable to the AAA within seven days from the date of the AAA's mailing to the parties.

If for any reason the appointment of an arbitrator cannot be made from the list, the AAA may make the appointment from among other members of the panel without the submission of additional lists.

The parties will be given notice by telephone by the AAA of the appointment of the arbitrator, who shall be subject to disqualification for the reasons specified in Section 19. Within seven days, the parties shall notify the AAA, by telephone, of any objection to the arbitrator appointed. Any objection by a party to the arbitrator shall be confirmed in writing to the AAA with a copy to the other party or parties.

55. Date, Time, and Place of Hearing—The arbitrator shall set the date, time, and place of the hearing. The AAA will notify the parties by telephone, at least seven days in advance of the hearing date. A formal notice of hearing will also be sent by the AAA to the parties.

56. The Hearing—Generally, the hearing shall be completed within one day, unless the dispute is resolved by submission of documents under Section 37. The arbitrator, for good cause shown, may schedule an additional hearing to be held within seven days.

57. Time of Award—Unless otherwise agreed by the parties, the award shall be rendered not later than fourteen days from the date of the closing of the hearing.

SUPPLEMENTARY PROCEDURES FOR LARGE, COMPLEX DISPUTES

Effective on March 1, 1993

1. Applicability—(a) The Supplementary Procedures for Large, Complex Disputes (hereinafter "Procedures") shall apply to all cases administered by the American Arbitration Association (hereinafter "AAA") under any of its rules in which the claim or counterclaim of any party is at least $1,000,000 exclusive of interest, costs and fees or is undetermined, and in which either (1) all parties have elected to have the Procedures apply to the resolution of their dispute or (2) a court or governmental agency of competent jurisdiction has determined that a dispute should be resolved before the AAA pursuant to the Procedures. Parties may also agree to using the Supplementary Procedures for Large, Complex Disputes in cases involving claims under $1,000,000. The Procedures are designed to complement the rules selected by the parties to govern their dispute. To the extent that there is any variance between such rules and these Procedures, the Procedures shall control. Any such cases are herein referred to as "Large, Complex Cases."

(b) The parties to any arbitration proceeding that is to be subject to the Procedures may, by consent of all parties, agree to eliminate, modify or alter any of the Procedures, and, in such case, the Procedures as so modified or altered shall apply to that particular case.

2. Administrative Conference—Prior to the dissemination of a list of potential arbitrators, the AAA shall, unless it determines the same to be unnecessary, conduct an administrative conference with the parties or their attorneys or other representatives, either in person or by conference call, at the discretion of the AAA. Such administrative conference shall be conducted for the following purposes and for such additional purposes as the parties or the AAA may deem appropriate:

(a) to obtain additional information about the nature and magnitude of the dispute and the anticipated length of hearing and scheduling;

(b) to discuss the views of the parties about the technical and other qualifications of the arbitrators; and

(c) to consider, with the parties, whether mediation or other nonadjudicative methods of dispute resolution might be appropriate.

3. Arbitrators—(a) Large, Complex Cases shall be heard and determined by either one or three arbitrators, as may be agreed upon by the parties. If the parties are unable to agree upon the number of arbitrators, then one arbitrator shall hear and determine the case unless the AAA shall determine otherwise.

(b) The AAA shall appoint arbitrators as agreed by the parties. If they are unable to agree on a method of appointment, the AAA shall appoint arbitrators as provided in the rules under which the case is being administered.

(c) Compensation for the arbitrators shall be based upon the magnitude and complexity of the case and shall be arranged by the AAA with the parties and the arbitrators prior to the commencement of the arbitration hearings. If the parties fail to agree to the terms of compensation, an appropriate rate shall be established by the AAA.

4. Preliminary Hearing—As promptly as practicable after the selection of the arbitrators, a preliminary hearing shall be held among the parties or their attorneys or other representatives and the arbitrators. With the consent of the arbitrators and the parties, the preliminary hearing may (1) be conducted by the Chair of the panel of arbitrators rather than all the arbitrators and/or (2) be conducted by telephone conference call rather than in person or (3) be omitted. At the preliminary hearing the matters that may be considered shall include, without limitation by specification, (a) service of a detailed statement of claims, damages and defenses, a statement of the issues asserted by each party and positions with respect thereto, and any legal authorities the parties may wish to bring to the attention of the arbitrators; (b) stipulations to uncontested facts; (c) exchange and premarking of those documents which each party believes may be offered at the hearing; (d) the identification and availability of witnesses, including experts, and such matters with repect to witnesses including their biographies and expected testimony as may be appropriate; (e) whether, and the extent to which, any sworn statements and/or depositions shall be permitted; (f) whether a stenographic or other official record of the proceedings shall be maintained; and (g) the possibility of utilizing mediation or other nonadjudicative methods of dispute resolution.

5. Management of Proceedings—(a) Arbitrators shall take such steps as they may deem necessary or desirable to avoid delay and to achieve a just, speedy and cost-effective resolution of Large, Complex Cases.

(b) Parties shall cooperate in the exchange of documents, exhibits and information within such party's control if the arbitrators consider such production to be consistent with the goal of achieving a just, speedy and cost-effective resolution of a Large, Complex Case.

(c) The parties may conduct such discovery as may be agreed to by all the parties provided, however, that the arbitrators may provide for or place such limitations on the conduct of such discovery as the arbitrators may deem appropriate.

(d) At the request of a party, the arbitrators may order the conduct of the deposition of, or the propounding of interrogatories to, such persons who may possess information determined by the arbitrators to be necessary to a determination of a Large, Complex Case and who will not be available to testify at the hearings.

6. Form of Award—If requested by all parties, the award of the arbitrators shall be accompanied by a statement of the reasons upon which such award is based. If requested by one party the arbitrators may, in their discretion, issue such a statement.

7. Interest, Fees and Costs—The award of the arbitrators may include (a) interest at such rate and from such date as the arbitrators may deem appropriate (b) an apportionment between the parties of all or part of the fees and expenses of the AAA and the compensation and expenses of the arbitrators; and (c) an award of attorneys' fees if all parties have requested or authorized such an award.

Panel Qualification Criteria

1. Experience and Competence—(a) Fifteen-year business or professional practice involving complex legal or business matters; (b) Extensive experience in dispute resolution; (c) Strong academic background and professional/business credentials preferred; (d) Scholarship and continuing education preferred.

2. Neutrality—(a) Commitment to impartiality and objectivity; (b) Freedom from national or cultural prejudice; (c) Independence and open mindedness.

3. Judicial Capacity—(a) Dispute-management skills; (b) Judicial temperament: impartiality, patience, courtesy; (c) Talent for adjudication, negotiation, and conciliation.

4. Reputation—(a) Highest respect of Bar and/or business community; (b) Integrity, patience, courtesy.

5. Commitment and Availability—(a) A willingness to serve if nominated, and general availability to serve in accordance with the needs of the parties; (b) Ability to devote time and effort to major disputes; (c) Successful completion of an advanced AAA panelist training course.

6. Quality Control—(a) Careful attention paid to selecting panelists to meet the needs of the particular dispute and the desires of the parties; (b) Periodic review of the panel.

SECURITIES ARBITRATION RULES

As Amended and Effective on May 1, 1993

1. Agreement of Parties—The parties shall be deemed to have made these rules a part of their arbitration agreement whenever they have provided for arbitration by the American Arbitration Association (hereinafter AAA) or under its Securities Arbitration Rules. These rules and any amendment of them shall apply in the form obtaining at the time the demand for arbitration or submission agreement involving a securities or commodity futures dispute is received by the AAA.

2. Name of Tribunal—Any tribunal constituted by the parties for the settlement of their dispute under these rules shall be called the Securities Arbitration Tribunal.

3. Administrator and Delegation of Duties—When parties agree to arbitrate under these rules, or when they provide for arbitration by the AAA and an arbitration is initiated under these rules, they thereby authorize the AAA to administer the arbitration. The authority and duties of the AAA are established in the agreement of the parties and in these rules, and may be carried out through such of the AAA's representatives as it may direct. The AAA may, in its discretion, assign the administration of an arbitration to any of its regional offices.

4. National Panel of Arbitrators—The AAA shall establish and maintain a National Panel of Securities Arbitrators and shall appoint arbitrators as provided in these rules.

5. Initiation under an Arbitration Provision in a Contract—Arbitration under an arbitration provision in a contract shall be initiated in the following manner.

(a) The initiating party (hereinafter claimant) shall, within the time period, if any, specified in the contract(s), give written notice to the other party (hereinafter respondent) of its intention to arbitrate (demand), which notice shall contain a statement setting forth the nature of the dispute, the amount involved, if any, the remedy sought, and the hearing locale requested, and

(b) shall file at any regional office of the AAA three copies of the notice and three copies of the arbitration provisions of the contract, together with the appropriate filing fee as provided in the schedule. The AAA shall give notice of such filing to the respondent or respondents.

6. Answers and Third-Party Claims—A respondent may file an answering statement in duplicate with the AAA within 20 days from the commencement of administration, simultaneously sending a copy of the answering statement to the claimant. A party may also file an answer to a changed or new claim, as provided in Section 8. If no answering statement is filed within the time period stated above, it will be treated as a general denial of the claim.

If a counterclaim is asserted, it shall contain a statement setting forth the nature of the counterclaim, the amount involved, if any, and the remedy sought. If a counterclaim is made, the appropriate fee provided in the schedule shall be forwarded to the AAA with the answering statement.

If a respondent fails to file an answering statement within the time period stated above, the claimant may serve respondent with a written request for an answering statement. A respondent who fails to file an answer within 10 days of such a request may, in the discretion of the arbitrator, be barred from presenting any matter, argument or defense (other than a general denial) that could have been raised in an answering statement, but an arbitrator may not enter an award against a party without hearing evidence to support the making of an award. Arbitrators should endeavor to rule on requests to bar such matters prior to the hearing.

The demand or answer may assert a third-party claim against another party, if the third party is obliged to arbitrate the subject of that party's claim under these rules. The arbitrator is authorized to resolve any dispute over such joinder.

7. Initiation under a Submission—Parties to any existing dispute may start an arbitration under these rules by filing at any regional office of the AAA three copies of a written submission to arbitrate under these rules, signed by the parties. It shall contain a statement of the matter in dispute, the amount involved, if any, the remedy sought, and the hearing locale requested, together with the appropriate filing fee as provided in the schedule.

8. Changes of Claim—After filing of a claim, if either party desires to make any new or different claim or counterclaim, it shall be made in writing and filed with the AAA. Simultaneously, a copy must be sent to the other party, who shall have a period of 10 days from the date of such transmittal within which to file an answer with the AAA. After the arbitrator is appointed, however, no new or different claim may be submitted except with the arbitrator's consent.

9. Applicable Procedures—Unless the AAA in its discretion determines otherwise, the Expedited Procedures shall be applied in any case where no disclosed claim or counterclaim exceeds $25,000, exclusive of interest and arbitration costs. Parties may also agree to use the Expedited Procedures in cases involving claims in excess of $25,000. The

Expedited Procedures shall be applied as described in Sections 51 through 55 of these rules, in addition to any other portion of these rules that is not in conflict with the Expedited Procedures.

All other cases shall be administered in accordance with Sections 1 through 50 of these rules.

10. Administrative Conference, Preliminary Hearing, and Mediation Conference—At the request of any party or at the discretion of the AAA, an administrative conference with the AAA and the parties and/or their representatives will be scheduled in appropriate cases to expedite the arbitration proceedings. There is no administrative fee for this service.

At the request of any party or at the discretion of the arbitrator or the AAA, a preliminary hearing with the parties and/or their representatives and the arbitrator may be scheduled by the arbitrator to specify issues to be resolved, to stipulate to uncontested facts, to schedule hearings to resolve the dispute, and to consider other matters that will expedite the arbitration proceedings. There is no administrative fee for the first preliminary hearing.

Unless the parties agree otherwise, the AAA at any stage of the proceeding may arrange a mediation conference under the Commercial Mediation Rules, in order to facilitate settlement. The mediator shall not be an arbitrator appointed to the case. Where the parties to a pending arbitration agree to mediate under the AAA's rules, no additional administrative fee is required to initiate the mediation.

11. Exchange of Information—Consistent with the expedited nature of arbitration, the arbitrator may establish (i) the extent of and schedule for production of documents and other information and (ii) identification of witnesses to be called. The arbitrator is authorized to resolve any dispute over this information exchange.

12. Fixing of Locale—The parties may agree on the locale where the arbitration is to be held. If any party requests that the hearing be held in a specific locale and the other party files no objection thereto within 20 days after notice of the request has been sent to it by the AAA, the locale shall be the one requested. If a party objects to the locale requested by the other party, the AAA shall have the power to determine the locale and its decision shall be final and binding.

13. Qualifications of an Arbitrator—Any neutral arbitrator appointed pursuant to Section 14, 15, 16, or 52, or selected by mutual choice of the parties or their appointees, shall be subject to disqualification for the reasons specified in Section 20. If the parties agree in writing, the arbitrator shall not be subject to disqualification for those reasons.

Unless the parties agree otherwise, an arbitrator selected unilaterally by one party is a party-appointed arbitrator and is not subject to disqualification pursuant to Section 20.

The term "arbitrator" in these rules refers to the arbitration panel, whether composed of one or more arbitrators and whether the arbitrators are neutral or party appointed. An affiliated arbitrator as provided in Sections 14 and 18 is one who has or has had direct involvement in or relationship with the securities brokerage industry for a minimum of three years if now employed in that industry or for a minimum of five years if no longer so employed. Involvement in or relationship with would include (a) employment at a brokerage firm in a professional capacity, whether employed in sales, management, support or trading, or (b) employment as counsel, accountant or other professional who devotes a majority of his or her efforts to brokerage or brokerage-related matters. Persons out of the industry for more than 10 years are not affiliated. Persons whose firms or direct family members derive significant income from securities brokerage or brokerage-related matters, but who do not qualify as affiliated arbitrators as defined above, may not serve as arbitrators.

14. Appointment from Panel—If the parties have not appointed an arbitrator and have not provided any other method of appointment, the arbitrator shall be appointed in the following manner: immediately after the filing of the demand or submission, the AAA shall send simultaneously to each party to the dispute two lists of names and biographical information of persons chosen from the panel. The first list, from which one arbitrator will be appointed, will contain names of arbitrators affiliated with the securities industry. The second list, from which two arbitrators will be appointed, will contain names of arbitrators not affiliated with the securities industry. Additional biographical information on proposed arbitrators may be available from the AAA and will be furnished to a party upon request.

Each party to the dispute has 20 days from the transmittal date in which to strike any names objected to, number the remaining names in order of preference, and return the list to the AAA. If a party does not return the list within the time specified, all persons shall be deemed acceptable. From among the persons who have been approved on both lists and in accordance with the designated order of mutual preference, the AAA shall invite the arbitrator(s) who will serve.

If appointments cannot be made from the submitted list, the AAA will submit to the parties a final list of proposed arbitrators, consisting of a limited number of names. Each separately appearing party may strike on a peremptory basis one name for each arbitrator to be appointed, and return the list to the AAA within 10 days from the date of the AAA's transmittal to the parties. The AAA shall make the appointment(s) from the name(s) remaining on the list.

15. Direct Appointment by a Party—If the agreement of the parties names an arbitrator or specifies a method of appointing an arbitrator, that designation or method shall be followed. The notice of appointment, with the name and address of the arbitrator, shall be filed with the AAA by the appointing party. Upon the request of any appointing party, the AAA shall submit a list of members of the panel from which the party may, if it so desires, make the appointment.

If the agreement specifies a period of time within which an arbitrator shall be appointed and any party fails to make the appointment within that period, the AAA shall make the appointment.

If no period of time is specified in the agreement, the AAA shall notify the party to make the appointment. If, within 20 days, an arbitrator has not been appointed by a party within the specified period, the AAA shall make the appointment.

16. Appointment of Neutral Arbitrator by Party-Appointed Arbitrators or Parties—If the parties have selected party-appointed arbitrators, or if such arbitrators have been appointed as provided in Section 15, and the parties have authorized them to appoint a neutral arbitrator within a specified time and no appointment is made within that time or any agreed extension, the AAA may appoint a neutral arbitrator, who shall act as chairperson.

If no period of time is specified for appointment of the neutral arbitrator and the party-appointed arbitrators or the parties do not make the appointment within 10 days from the date of the appointment of the last party-appointed arbitrator, the AAA may appoint the neutral arbitrator, who shall act as chairperson.

If the parties have agreed that their party-appointed arbitrators shall appoint the neutral arbitrator from the panel, the AAA shall furnish to the party-appointed arbitrators a list selected from the panel, and the appointment of the neutral arbitrator shall be made as provided in Section 14.

17. Nationality of Arbitrator in International Arbitration—Where the parties are nationals or residents of different countries, any neutral arbitrator shall, upon the request of any party, be appointed from among the nationals of a country other than that of any of the parties. The request must be made prior to the time set for the appointment of the arbitrator as agreed by the parties or set by these rules.

18. Number of Arbitrators—Where the claim of any party exceeds $25,000, the dispute shall be heard and determined by three arbitrators. Unless the parties otherwise agree, the majority shall be arbitrators not affiliated with the securities industry. All other disputes shall be heard and determined by one arbitrator not affiliated with the securities industry, as provided in Section 52.

19. Notice to Arbitrator of Appointment—Notice of the appointment of the neutral arbitrator, whether appointed by agreement of the parties or by the AAA, shall be sent to the arbitrator by the AAA, together with a copy of these rules. The signed acceptance of the arbitrator shall be filed with the AAA prior to the opening of the first hearing.

20. Disclosure and Challenge Procedure—Any person appointed as neutral arbitrator shall disclose to the AAA any circumstance likely to affect impartiality, including any bias or any financial or personal interest in the result of the arbitration or any past or present relationship with the parties or their representatives. Upon receipt of such information from the arbitrator or another source, the AAA shall communicate the information to the parties and, if it deems it appropriate to do so, to the arbitrator and others. Upon objection of a party to the continued service of a neutral arbitrator, the AAA shall determine whether the arbitrator should be disqualified and shall inform the parties of its decision, which shall be conclusive.

21. Vacancies—If for any reason an arbitrator is unable to perform the duties of the office, the AAA may, on proof satisfactory to it, declare the office vacant. Vacancies shall be filled in accordance with the applicable provisions of these rules.

In the event of a vacancy in a panel of arbitrators after the hearings have commenced, unless the parties agree otherwise, the vacancy shall be filled as provided above, and the newly constituted panel shall determine whether all or part of any prior hearing shall be repeated.

22. Date, Time and Place of Hearing—The arbitrator shall set the date, time and place for each hearing. The AAA shall send a notice of hearing to the parties at least 10 days in advance of the hearing date, unless otherwise agreed by the parties.

23. Representation—Any party may be represented by counsel or other authorized representative. A party intending to be represented shall notify the other party and the AAA of the name, address and telephone number of the representative at least three days prior to the date set for the hearing at which that person is first to appear. When a representative initiates an arbitration or responds for a party, notice of representation is deemed to have been given.

24. Stenographic Record—Any party desiring a stenographic record shall make arrangements directly with a stenographer and shall notify the other parties of these arrangements in advance of the hearing. The requesting party or parties shall pay the cost of the record.

If the transcript is agreed by the parties to be, or determined by the arbitrator to be, the official record of the proceeding, it must be made available to the arbitrator and to the other parties for inspection, at a date, time, and place determined by the arbitrator.

25. Interpreters—Any party wishing an interpreter shall make all arrangements directly with the interpreter and shall assume the costs of the service.

26. Attendance at Hearings; Experts—The arbitrator shall maintain the privacy of the hearings unless the law provides to the contrary. Any person having a direct interest in the arbitration is entitled to attend hearings. Although expert witnesses are generally permitted to attend the hearing, the arbitrator shall have the power to require the exclusion of any witness, other than a party or other essential person, during the testimony of any other witness. It shall be discretionary with the arbitrator to determine the propriety of the attendance of any other person.

27. Postponements—The arbitrator for good cause shown may postpone any hearing upon the request of a party or upon the arbitrator's own initiative, and shall grant a postponement when all of the parties agree.

28. Oaths—Before proceeding with the first hearing, each arbitrator may take an oath of office and, if required by law, shall do so. The arbitrator may require witnesses to testify under oath administered by any duly qualified person and, if it is required by law or requested by any party, shall do so.

29. Majority Decision—All decisions of the arbitrators must be by a majority. The award must also be made by a majority unless the concurrence of all is expressly required by the arbitration agreement or by law.

30. Order of Proceedings and Communication with Arbitrator—A hearing shall be opened by the filing of the oath of the arbitrator, where required; by the recording of the date, time and place of the hearing, and the presence of the arbitrator, the parties and their representatives, if any; and by the receipt by the arbitrator of the statement of the claim and the answering statement, if any.

The arbitrator may, at the beginning of the hearing, ask for statements clarifying the issues involved. In some cases, part or all of the above will have been accomplished at the preliminary hearing conducted by the arbitrator pursuant to Section 10.

The complaining party shall then present evidence to support its claim. The defending party shall then present evidence supporting its defense. Witnesses for each party shall submit to questions or other examination. The arbitrator has the discretion to vary this procedure but shall afford a full and equal opportunity to all parties for the presentation of any material and relevant evidence.

Exhibits, when offered by either party, may be received in evidence by the arbitrator.

The names and addresses of all witnesses and a description of the exhibits in the order received shall be made a part of the record.

There shall be no direct communication between the parties and a neutral arbitrator other than at oral hearing, unless the parties and the arbitrator agree otherwise. Any other oral or written communication from the parties to the neutral arbitrator shall be directed to the AAA for transmittal to the arbitrator.

31. Arbitration in the Absence of a Party or Representative—Unless the law provides to the contrary, the arbitration may proceed in the absence of any party or representative who, after due notice, fails to be present or fails to obtain a postponement. An award shall not be made solely on the default of a party. The arbitrator shall require the party who is present to submit such evidence as the arbitrator may require for the making of an award.

32. Evidence—The parties may offer evidence that is relevant and material to the dispute, and shall produce such evidence as the arbitrator deems necessary to an understanding and determination of the dispute. An arbitrator or other person authorized by law to subpoena witnesses or documents may do so upon the request of any party or independently.

The arbitrator shall be the judge of the relevance and materiality of the evidence offered, and conformity to legal rules of evidence shall not be necessary. All evidence shall be taken in the presence of all of the arbitrators and all of the parties, except where any of the parties is absent in default or has waived the right to be present.

33. Evidence by Affidavit and Posthearing Filing of Documents or Other Evidence—The arbitrator may receive and consider the evidence of witnesses by affidavit, but shall give it only such weight as the arbitrator deems it entitled to after consideration of any objection made to its admission.

If the parties agree or the arbitrator directs that documents or other evidence be submitted to the arbitrator after the hearing, the documents or other evidence shall be filed with the AAA for transmission to the arbitrator. All parties shall be afforded an opportunity to examine such documents or other evidence.

34. Inspection or Investigation—An arbitrator finding it necessary to make an inspection or investigation in connection with the arbitration shall direct the AAA to so advise the parties. The arbitrator shall set the date and time and the AAA shall notify the parties. Any party who so desires may be present at such an inspection or investigation. In the event that one or all parties are not present at the inspection or investigation, the arbitrator shall make a verbal or written report to the parties and afford them an opportunity to comment.

35. Interim Measures—The arbitrator may direct whatever interim measures are deemed necessary with respect to the dispute, including measures for the conservation of property, without prejudice to the rights of the parties or to the final determination of the dispute. Such interim measures may be taken in the form of an interim award and the arbitrator may require security for the costs of such measures.

36. Closing of Hearing—The arbitrator shall specifically inquire of all parties whether they have any further proofs to offer or witnesses to be heard. Upon receiving negative replies or if satisfied that the record is complete, the arbitrator shall declare the hearing closed.

If briefs are to be filed, the hearing shall be declared closed as of the final date set by the arbitrator for the receipt of briefs. If documents are to be filed as provided in Section 33 and the date set for their receipt is later than that set for the receipt of briefs, the later date shall be the date of closing the hearing. The time limit within which the arbitrator shall endeavor to make the award shall start to run, in the absence of other agreements by the parties, upon the closing of the hearing.

37. Reopening of Hearing—The hearing may be reopened on the arbitrator's initiative, or upon application of a party, at any time before the award is made. If reopening the hearing would prevent the making of the award within the specific time agreed on by the parties in the contract(s) out of which the controversy has arisen, the matter may not be reopened unless the parties agree on an extension of time. When no specific date is fixed in the contract, the arbitrator may reopen the hearing and shall have thirty days from the closing of the reopened hearing within which to make an award.

38. Waiver of Oral Hearing—Where each party's claim does not exceed $5,000, exclusive of interest and costs, the dispute shall be resolved by submission of documents, unless any party requests an oral hearing, or the arbitrator determines that an oral hearing is necessary. The parties may also provide, by written agreement, for the waiver of oral hearings in any case. If the parties are unable to agree as to the procedure, the AAA shall specify a fair and equitable procedure.

39. Waiver of Rules—Any party who proceeds with the arbitration after knowledge that any provision or requirement of these rules has not been complied with and who fails to state an objection in writing shall be deemed to have waived the right to object.

40. Extensions of Time—The parties may modify any period of time by mutual agreement. The AAA or the arbitrator may for good cause extend any period of time established by these rules, except the time for making the award. The AAA shall notify the parties of any extension.

41. Serving of Notice—Each party shall be deemed to have consented that any papers, notices, or process necessary or proper for the initiation or continuation of an arbitration under these rules; for any court action in connection therewith; or for the entry of judgment on any award made under these rules may be served on a party by mail addressed to the party or its representative at the last known address or by personal service, in or outside the state where the arbitration is to be held, provided that reasonable opportunity to be heard with regard thereto has been granted to the party.

The AAA and the parties may also use facsimile transmission, telex, telegram or other written forms of electronic communication to give the notices required by these rules.

42. The Award—(a) The arbitrator shall endeavor to issue the award promptly and, unless otherwise agreed by the parties, within 30 days from the date of closing of the hearing or, if oral hearings have been waived, from the date of the AAA's transmittal of the final statements and proofs to the arbitrator.

(b) The award shall be in writing, shall be signed by a majority of the arbitrators, and shall be executed in the manner required by law. The award shall contain the names of the parties and representatives, if any, a summary of the issues, including type(s) of any security or product in controversy, the damages and/or other relief requested and awarded, a statement of any other issues resolved, a statement regarding the disposition of any statutory claim, the names of arbitrators, the date when the case was filed, the date of the award, the number and dates of hearings, the location of the hearings, and the signatures of the arbitrators concurring in or dissenting from the award.

(c) The arbitrator may grant any remedy or relief that the arbitrator deems just and equitable and within the scope of the agreement of the parties, including, but not limited to, specific performance of a contract. The arbitrator shall, in the award, assess arbitration fees, expenses, and compensation as provided in Sections 46, 47, and 48 in favor of any party and, in the event that any administrative fees or expenses are due the AAA, in favor of the AAA.

(d) If the parties settle their dispute during the course of the arbitration, the arbitrator may, upon the written agreement of those parties, set forth the terms of the agreed settlement in an award. Such an award is called a consent award.

(e) Parties shall accept as legal delivery of the award the placing of the award or a true copy thereof in the mail addressed to a party or its representative at the last known address, personal service of the award, or the filing of the award in any other manner that is permitted by law.

(f) An award issued under these rules shall be publicly available provided that the names of the parties will not be publicly available.

43. Correction of Award—Within 20 days after the transmittal of an award, any party, upon notice to the other parties, may request that the arbitrator correct any clerical, typographical, technical or computational error in the award. The arbitrator is not empowered to redetermine the merits of any claim already decided.

The other parties shall be given 10 days to respond to the request. The arbitrator shall dispose of the request within 20 days after transmittal by the AAA to the arbitrator of the request and any response thereto.

44. Release of Documents for Judicial Proceedings—The AAA shall, upon the written request of a party, furnish to the party, at its expense, certified copies of any papers in the AAA's possession that may be required in judicial proceedings relating to the arbitration.

45. Applications to Court and Exclusion of Liability—(a) No judicial proceeding by a party relating to the subject matter of the arbitration shall be deemed a waiver of the party's right to arbitrate.

(b) Neither the AAA nor any arbitrator in a proceeding under these rules is a necessary party in judicial proceedings relating to the arbitration.

(c) Parties to these rules shall be deemed to have consented that judgment upon the arbitration award may be entered in any federal or state court having jurisdiction thereof.

(d) Neither the AAA nor any arbitrator shall be liable to any party for any act or omission in connection with any arbitration conducted under these rules.

46. Administrative Fees—As a not-for-profit organization, the AAA shall prescribe filing and other administrative fees to compensate it for the cost of providing administrative services. The fees in effect when the demand for arbitration or submission agreement is received shall be applicable.

The filing fee shall be advanced by the initiating party or parties, subject to final apportionment by the arbitrator in the award.

The AAA may, in the event of extreme hardship on the part of any party, defer or reduce the administrative fees.

47. Expenses—Unless the parties agree otherwise, all expenses of the arbitration, including required travel and other expenses of the arbitrator and AAA representatives, and the cost of any proof produced at the direct request of the arbitrator, shall be borne equally by the parties, subject to final allocation by the arbitrator as provided in Section 42(c).

48. Neutral Arbitrator's Compensation—Unless the parties agree otherwise, members of the National Panel of Securities Arbitrators will receive compensation for the first and second days of service at the rate of $400 per day per arbitrator, advanced equally by the parties.

For service thereafter, an appropriate daily rate and other arrangements will be discussed by the administrator with the parties prior to the appointment of the arbitrator. If the parties fail to agree to the terms of compensation, an appropriate rate will be established by the AAA and communicated in writing to the parties.

49. Deposits—The AAA may require the parties to deposit in advance of any hearings such sums of money as it deems necessary to cover the expense of the arbitration, including the arbitrator's fee, if any, and shall render an accounting to the parties and return any unexpended balance at the conclusion of the case.

50. Interpretation and Application of Rules—The arbitrator shall interpret and apply these rules insofar as they relate to the arbitrator's powers and duties. When there is more than one arbitrator and a difference arises among them concerning the meaning or application of these rules, it shall be decided by a majority vote. If that is not possible, either an arbitrator or a party may refer the question to the AAA for final decision. All other rules shall be interpreted and applied by the AAA.

Expedited Procedures

51. Notice by Telephone—The parties shall accept all notices from the AAA by telephone. Such notices by the AAA shall subsequently be confirmed in writing to the parties. Should there be a failure to confirm in writing any notice hereunder, the proceeding shall nonetheless be valid if notice has, in fact, been given by telephone.

52. Appointment and Qualifications of Arbitrator—The AAA shall submit simultaneously to each party an identical list of five proposed arbitrators drawn from the National Panel of Securities Arbitrators, from which one arbitrator shall be appointed. The arbitrators contained on the list will not be affiliated with the securities industry.

Each party may strike two names from the list on a peremptory basis. The list is returnable to the AAA within 20 days from the date of the AAA's transmittal to the parties.

If for any reason the appointment of an arbitrator cannot be made from the list, the AAA may make the appointment from among other members of the panel without the submission of additional lists.

The parties will be given notice by telephone by the AAA of the appointment of the arbitrator, who shall be subject to disqualification for the reasons specified in Section 20. Within seven days, the parties shall notify the AAA, by telephone, of any objection to the arbitrator appointed. Any objection by a party to the arbitrator shall be confirmed in writing to the AAA with a copy to the other party or parties.

53. Date, Time, and Place of Hearing—The arbitrator shall set the date, time, and place of the hearing. The AAA will notify the parties by telephone, at least seven days in advance of the hearing date. A formal notice of hearing will also be sent by the AAA to the parties.

54. The Hearing—Generally, the hearing shall be completed within one day, unless the dispute is resolved by submission of documents under Section 38. The arbitrator, for good cause shown, may schedule an additional hearing to be held within seven days.

55. Time of Award—Unless otherwise agreed by the parties, the arbitrator shall endeavor to render the award not later than 14 days from the date of the closing of the hearing.

BIBLIOGRAPHY

American Arbitration Association, *Commercial Arbitration Rules As Amended and Effective on May 1, 1992* (New York: American Arbitration Association)

_____, *Commercial Mediation Rules As Amended and Effective on January 1, 1992* (New York: American Arbitration Association)

_____, *A Guide for Commercial Arbitrators.* (New York: American Arbitration Association; February, 1993)

_____, *A Guide to Arbitration for Business People* (New York: American Arbitration Association; May, 1992)

_____, *Securities Arbitration Rules As Amended and Effective on May 1, 1993* (New York: American Arbitration Association)

_____, *Supplementary Procedures for Large, Complex Disputes Effective on February 1, 1993* (New York: American Arbitration Association)

Arbitration & the Law: AAA General Counsel's Annual Reports (New York: American Arbitration Association, since 1981)

Cooley, John W., "Arbitration vs. Mediation—It's Time to Settle the Differences" in *Chicago Bar Record*, Volume 66, Number 4 (January/February, 1985): 204–221

Domke, Martin, *Domke on Commercial Arbitration (the Law and Practice of Commercial Arbitration)*, Edited by Gabriel M. Wilner (Wilmette, IL: Callaghan, 1984 with a 1990 Supplement)

Friedman, George H., "Commercial Arbitration" in Benjamin M. Becker, Bernard Savin, David Becker, and David L. Gibberman, *Legal Checklists*, (Wilmette, IL: Callaghan, 1990): 5-4:1–5-4:10

Hart, B. C., "Alternative Dispute Resolution: Negotiation, Mediation, and Minitrial" in *Federation of Insurance and Corporate Counsel Quarterly*, Volume 37, Number 2 (Winter, 1987): 113–131

Lawyers' Arbitration Letter (New York: American Arbitration Association, Quarterly since 1960)

Levy, Gerald M., Editor, *Arbitration of Real Estate Valuation Disputes* (New York: American Arbitration Association, 1987)

Meyerowitz, Steven A., "The Arbitration Alternative" in *American Bar Association Journal*, Volume 71 (1985): 78–80

Oehmke, Thomas, *Commercial Arbitration* (Rochester: Lawyers Co-operative Publishing, 1987)

Robbins, David E., "Securities Arbitration: Preparation and Presentation" in *The Arbitration Journal*, Volume 42, Number 2 (June, 1987): 3–14

Rodman, Robert M., *Commercial Arbitration with Forms* (St. Paul: West Publishing, 1984)

Williston, Samuel A., *A Treatise on the Law of Contracts*, Volume 16, Edited by Walter H. E. Jaeger (Rochester: Lawyers Co-operative Publishing, 1976 with a 1989 Supplement)

THE CONSTRUCTION INDUSTRY

A HISTORY OF CONSTRUCTION ARBITRATION

Arbitration of construction disputes is not a new concept. As early as 1871, arbitration was introduced into standard-form construction agreements, and attorneys representing architects, contractors, and engineers were using arbitration. When the American Institute of Architects (AIA) began using printed forms, arbitration clauses were part of its recommended owner–architect contracts. The procedures outlined in the AIA's article 40 of "The General Conditions of the Contract for the Construction of Buildings" provided for arbitration in accordance with either the AIA rules, which specified a party-appointed system, or the Commercial Arbitration Rules of the American Arbitration Association.

The choice of a party-appointed system or arbitration under AAA rules may have seemed ideal because it gave the parties an option, but this dual option created difficulties in initiating a claim. Neither procedure was completely satisfactory. In practice, party-appointed panels caused lengthy delays. And to some construction industry professionals, the AAA commercial rules were undesirable because the AAA had not yet recruited a nationwide panel of expert construction arbitrators.

In 1964, an AIA–AGC (Associated General Contractors) liaison committee studied the problem. After reviewing their members' experience under both systems, the committee recommended the adoption of the AAA as the sole administrator, but suggested that the committee help the AAA develop procedures and panels of arbitrators custom-tailored to the construction industry. By 1965, the National Construction Industry Arbitration Committee (NCIAC) included representatives of the following organizations: the American Consulting Engineers Council (then the Consulting Engineers Council); the American Institute of Architects; Associated General Contractors; Associated Specialty Contractors, Inc. (then the Council of Mechanical Specialty

57

Contracting Industries); and the National Society of Professional Engineers. After a thorough study, Construction Industry Arbitration Rules were adopted providing a uniform nationwide procedure for the construction industry. A specialized panel, made up of industry experts, was selected by local advisory committees. More than 30,000 arbitrators, representing all segments of the industry, now serve on the AAA's national construction panel, and there are over 100 different categories represented on that panel.

The construction industry rules are recommended for use throughout the building and construction industry. In 1990, the NCIAC changed its name to the National Construction Dispute Resolution Committee (NCDRC) and its membership includes the American Society of Civil Engineers; the American Society of Interior Designers; the American Society of Landscape Architects; the American Subcontractors Association; Associated Builders and Contractors, Inc.; the Business Roundtable; the Construction Specifications Institute; the National Association of Home Builders; and the National Utility Contractors Association. These 14 national construction associations participate in sponsoring this arbitration system.

THE ARBITRATION CLAUSE

The modern construction project—with its multiplicity of participants, complex procedures, and new techniques and materials—requires careful planning, bid documents, and contracts. The potential for controversy is always present. Including a reliable arbitration clause in an agreement can help to resolve these disputes more quickly and efficiently. The ingredients of a properly formulated arbitration clause are:, (1) a delineation of which disputes are arbitrable; (2) reference to a standard procedure under which the arbitration will be conducted; and (3) a commitment that the parties will be bound by the ultimate award. A frequently used contract provision is found in AIA Document A201 (1987), subparagraph 4.5.1 of the General Conditions:

> Any controversy or Claim arising out of or related to the Contract, or the breach thereof, shall be settled by arbitration in accordance with the Construction Industry Arbitration Rules of the American Arbitration Association, and judgment upon the award rendered by the arbitrator or arbitrators may be entered in any court having jurisdiction thereof, except controversies or Claims relating to aesthetic effect and except those waived as provided for in Subparagraph 4.3.5. Such controversies or Claims upon which the Architect has given notice and rendered a decision as provided in Subparagraph 4.4.4 shall be subject to arbitration upon written demand of either party. Arbitration may be commenced when 45 days have passed after a Claim has been referred to the Architect as provided in Paragraph 4.3 and no decision has been referred to the arbitrators.

By referring to the AAA's Construction Industry Arbitration Rules, a well-tested procedure is available to the parties, backed up by an experienced administrative agency.

Participants in a construction project should check the arbitration clauses in their various interlocking contracts. For example, the AIA's Standard Form of Agreement between Owner and Contractor (Document A101) provides that the General Conditions of the Contract will be applicable to other contract documents. The arbitration provision between a prime contractor and a subcontractor, however, may not be identical to the provision in the General Conditions, although sometimes the arbitration clause between the owner and the prime contractor will "flow down" to the subcontractor. The AIA subcontract form (Document A401, 1987) provides an example of this type of clause commonly used by the industry:

> 6.1 Any controversy or claim between the Contractor and the Subcontractor arising out of or related to this Subcontract, or the breach thereof, shall be settled by arbitration, which shall be conducted in the same manner and under the same procedure as provided in the Prime Contract with respect to claims between the Owner and the Contractor, except that a decision by the Architect shall not be a condition precedent to arbitration. If the Prime Contract does not provide for arbitration or fails to specify the manner and procedure for arbitration, it shall be conducted in accordance with the Construction Industry Arbitration Rules of the American Arbitration Association currently in effect unless the parties mutually agree otherwise.

SPECIAL PROVISIONS

Sometimes a construction contract should be tailor-made. For instance, some public works contracts specify that, although the hearing must be held within the jurisdiction involved, the arbitrators may not be from that area; or the parties might designate that claims over a certain dollar amount must be heard by a panel of three arbitrators; or they might specify the qualifications and backgrounds of the individuals on their panel. Arbitration is flexible. Even where the parties specify the construction rules, they can add special provisions.

Consider the case of an owner and a contractor who had enjoyed a long and profitable working relationship. When they encountered a disagreement that they could not resolve through negotiations, they decided to design a special arbitration procedure. Their contract provided that damages for delay would be borne by the contractor. But they were unable to negotiate the amount of liability. In order to facilitate the process, they agreed that the hearing should take no more than one day. They also instructed the arbitrator to issue the award within seven days from the date of the hearing. Finally, they agreed to use a method called "final-offer arbitration." At the close of the hearing, each party gives its "final offer" to the arbitrator, who selects one of the offers, based on the merits of the case. No compromise is permitted.

Because the arbitration process is flexible, the parties can devise a system that they believe will be fair and will not damage their working relationship. An arbitration clause may specify the location of hearings, the qualifications of the arbitrator, provisions for discovery procedures, or expedited hearing schedules.

The parties control the process. They should discuss these procedural issues. With the aid of their lawyers, the parties should design a convenient and appropriate procedure. This can be done at a prearbitration conference with a representative of the AAA.

The AAA administers arbitration cases in accordance with the parties' arbitration agreement. In most cases, administrative details need not be described in the contract. By using a standard arbitration clause specifying the AAA's Construction Industry Arbitration Rules, the parties can obtain an orderly and expeditious arbitration. Even where parties do not use a printed form contract, they may refer to the Construction Industry Arbitration Rules by using the following clause in their contract:

> Any controversy or claim arising out of or relating to this contract, or the breach thereof, shall be settled by arbitration in accordance with the Construction Industry Arbitration Rules of the American Arbitration Association, and judgment upon the award rendered by the arbitrator(s) may be entered in any court having jurisdiction thereof.

ENFORCEABILITY OF ARBITRATION CLAUSES

The construction industry has been in the vanguard of lobbying for modern arbitration legislation. Prior to the passage of modern laws, many courts refused to enforce agreements to arbitrate future disputes under building contracts. In the absence of a statute, the courts looked to the common law decisions of England. And, at the time of the American Revolution, the English courts were refusing to enforce arbitration agreements in contracts because they "ousted the courts of jurisdiction."

Although this did not mean that arbitration was not being used by parties, it did mean that a party could refuse to arbitrate and thus force the contractor into court. During the 1920s, public policy began to shift in favor of arbitration. Courts were already becoming crowded, and legislators became convinced that arbitration offered a suitable tribunal for determination of business disputes.

Contractual arbitration reduced the burden on court calendars. Legislation to encourage arbitration was urged by the construction industry. Modern laws first appeared in the important commercial states. At the same time, a movement to pass a national arbitration law began to take shape.

In general, construction projects involve interstate movement of materials and personnel. Disputes are therefore arbitrated under federal law and are covered by the Federal Arbitration Act. Under this act, a written arbitration provision in a contract involving "commerce" is "valid, irrevocable, and enforceable." Federal policy favors arbitration. When a question arises about whether an issue is subject to arbitration, a court will enforce a contract clause providing for arbitration. For the construction contract that involves interstate commerce, there need be little concern about state arbitration statutes that are not compatible with modern arbitration practice. The federal law will apply, and that law supports arbitration.

Even for purely *intra*state construction contracts, most state arbitration laws enforce arbitration clauses. Even under common law, the parties always have the right to submit an existing dispute to arbitration. The courts will enforce the arbitrator's award. Most state laws now enforce arbitration clauses. References are contained in the appendix.

MOTIONS TO STAY

Attempts to compel arbitration against a resisting party involve a showing that there is an agreement to arbitrate, that an arbitrable dispute exists, and that the other party has been notified of the demand for arbitration. If the opposing party initiates litigation, a motion can be filed to stay that proceeding on the ground that the lawsuit is in violation of the arbitration clause. In rendering a decision on arbitrability, the courts will look to the arbitration clause and not to the merits of the dispute.

Once a construction claim has been filed for administration, the AAA acknowledges receipt and sends both parties a list of potential arbitrators. If the respondent objects to the arbitration, the AAA will ask both parties for their comments. If the contract refers to the AAA, it will continue to administer the case and will so advise the parties. If the matter is not contested in court, the arbitrator can decide the arbitrability issue at the first hearing.

The AAA always follows court orders. Unless a court orders the Association to stop proceedings or the parties agree otherwise, the AAA will continue with the administration of the case while a motion is pending. If the moving party obtains a temporary stay from the courts, the arbitration will be held in abeyance until the motion to stay is resolved. Sometimes, a moving party will appeal a lower court's decision. Again, the AAA will proceed unless both parties agree to suspend administration or until a temporary stay is granted pending the appeal by the court.

There is no need to make the Association a party to such litigation. The construction rules state that "Neither the AAA nor any arbitrator in a proceeding under these rules is a necessary party in judicial proceedings relating to the arbitration." Parties should keep the case administrator advised of pending litigation. A copy of any court order should be forwarded promptly to the AAA, and it will immediately comply.

HOW TO INITIATE AN ARBITRATION

When a construction contract contains an arbitration clause, either party may initiate a claim by filing an AAA demand form or a letter that contains the required information. The demand should be accompanied by the appropriate filing fee. The demand for arbitration should describe the dispute in enough detail so that the AAA can select appropriate names from its panel of arbitrators.

THE ADMINISTRATIVE CONFERENCE— HOW IT HELPS THE PARTIES

The Construction Industry Arbitration Rules provide for an administrative conference at the request of the parties or at the discretion of the AAA. Such conferences are useful in complex cases where several days of hearings are anticipated.

Various administrative details are also discussed. A list of items that can be raised at the administrative conference includes: the parties' estimate of the number of hearings that will be required; the desired timetable for scheduling hearings; the terms of arbitrator compensation; the arrangements for an on-site inspection; hearing-room size; description of claims and counterclaims; exchange of witness lists and brief outline of testimony; arrangements for the exchange and marking of exhibits; whether briefs are to be submitted; and any other special arrangements in connection with the arbitration.

Parties are not always able to reach agreement on every point raised, but the administrative conference facilitates the arbitration process. Many construction cases involve testimony and documents that are complicated and difficult to organize. Anything that can be done to simplify the parties' presentations will help ensure a better understanding of the case. Many a case has been settled at an administrative conference, as the attorneys and principals take advantage of this opportunity to share their perceptions with one another.

SELECTING AN ARBITRATOR

The specialized arbitration panel constitutes one of the major advantages that arbitration enjoys over litigation. The parties have the opportunity to select individuals who understand the construction industry. There is no need to "educate the bench." The arbitrator will understand the case.

Every effort is made by the AAA to ensure that the list sent to the parties contains experienced arbitrators—practical experts with good reputations in their fields—who are acceptable to all parties. The demand form asks for the industry category of each party (subcontractor, contractor, architect, engineer, or owner). The claimant's description of the dispute in the demand, and the respondent's answering statement should contain enough information for the Association to suggest an appropriate list of potential arbitrators. The more information supplied about the nature of the dispute, the better prepared the AAA will be to compile a suitably balanced list. Each arbitrator card in the AAA's construction panel contains information about the individual's educational background, specialization, membership in professional associations, and years of experience. This information is included on the list that is sent to the parties. If more information is requested, it will be supplied by the AAA.

If multiple hearings will be required, the AAA should be notified in advance so it can submit a list of arbitrators available to serve for as long as necessary. Parties are also encouraged to allocate consecutive dates so that the matter can proceed without delays in the hearing process. In addition, when returning the lists of preferred selections, parties should also return the calendar forms and witness lists. These reduce the possibility of administrative delay, since the AAA can more easily determine whether prospective arbitrators are willing to serve on the case.

CHALLENGING THE ARBITRATOR FOR BIAS

Many people in the construction industry are acquainted with one another. Individuals selected as arbitrators may discover that they know people involved in the dispute. The construction rules require a neutral arbitrator to disclose "any circumstance likely to affect his or her impartiality." This would include a personal or financial relationship, past or present, with any party, counsel, or witness. Any such information should be communicated by the AAA to the parties, who are asked for their comments. Sometimes, a party will challenge the arbitrator, who may then be asked to resign. In cases where the grounds seem insubstantial, the AAA may decide that the arbitrator should continue to serve. A 1981 New Jersey case imposed the same disclosure obligations on party-appointed arbitrators.

Where such determinations have been tested in the courts, the standard applied is whether the arbitrator had an interest in the proceeding that was "direct, definite and capable of demonstration rather than remote, uncertain or speculative." The courts recognize that, in some situations, people in an industry do business together. The AAA tries to avoid the possibility that an award will be vacated because of a claim of bias.

WHERE SHOULD THE CASE BE HEARD?

The location of the hearing is seldom a problem in construction arbitration. If the parties anticipate that this issue might arise, however, they should so specify in their contract. Occasionally, if the locale has not been designated, one party may wish the hearing to take place near its office and the other may want it at the site.

If the arbitration clause does not specify a place of hearing and the parties cannot agree, the AAA must decide. Both parties will be requested to explain their reasons, and a determination will then be made by the AAA. Under the construction arbitration rules, this decision is final. Factors that are considered when making a decision on locale include: (1) location of the parties; (2) location of witnesses and documents; (3) location of the work site; (4) relative cost to the parties; (5) laws applicable to the contract; (6) previous court actions; and (7) availability of the most appropriate panels. The location requested by the filing party is given a preference.

THE POWERS OF THE ARBITRATOR

An arbitrator has broad powers under the Construction Industry Arbitration Rules. These include the authority to: consider amendments to the claim or counterclaim; decide questions of arbitrability; schedule, close, and reopen hearings; determine whether any person not directly involved may attend the hearing; grant or deny hearing adjournments; and conduct an arbitration in the absence of a party after due notice. Where authorized to do so by law, the arbitrator may subpoena witnesses or documents independently or at the request of a party. The arbitrator can also receive, consider, and weigh any evidence including evidence of witnesses by affidavit; conduct a viewing of the project site; order the safeguarding of any property subject to the dispute during the pendency of the arbitration hearings; grant interest on the award; or assess arbitrator fees and expenses equally or in favor of any party. The authority of the arbitrator is extensive, but only as to those issues designated by the parties.

CONSOLIDATING CLAIMS

A troublesome procedural issue involves the consolidation of construction arbitration claims. This is a major subject of debate within the industry. Some contend that consolidation of claims would avoid inconsistent results. Others reply that multiparty cases serve only to complicate the process and lead to unnecessary delays. Court opinions vary. Some of the factors that may be considered by a court when reaching a decision on a particular case are: (1) the arbitration clauses; (2) the similarity of issues between the various parties; (3) the similar method of selecting arbitrators in the various contracts; and (4) the participation in the selection of arbitrators that preceded the motion to consolidate. Some jurisdictions are liberal in granting consolidation where common issues are involved. Others seem to favor separate arbitrations.

The National Construction Dispute Resolution Committee has considered whether the construction rules should provide for consolidation. That decision has been left to the parties. Consolidation may be accomplished by stipulation or by a provision in the arbitration agreement. At the present time, the AIA's owner–architect agreement prohibits consolidation or joinder without the written consent of all parties. On the other hand, agreements between owners and prime contractors often provide that subcontractor claims in the same construction project may be consolidated in the owner–contractor arbitration. Some subcontractor agreements contain provisions allowing consolidation of two or more related controversies involving the contractor, the subcontractor, or other persons having contractual relations with the contractor.

The AAA administers each case as filed unless directed by the courts to do otherwise. If all parties agree to consolidate a case or to split up a case, the AAA will follow their direction. Where a demand for arbitration is filed against multiple parties, the case will be initiated that way. If one of the respondents objects and there are separate contracts, the claims will be separated unless a party obtains an order of consolidation. When the parties named in the demand are signatories to the same contract, the AAA will combine the claims. The parties control their own contractual system. The AAA's role is to try to determine what services have been authorized. The AAA attempts to process the case subject to direction from the courts.

EXPEDITED CONSTRUCTION ARBITRATION PROCEDURES

Expedited procedures are also available under AAA rules. These procedures are applied in any case where the total claim of any party does not exceed $50,000, exclusive of interest and arbitration costs. If both parties agree, expedited procedures may also be applied to cases involving claims of more than $50,000.

As a time-saving device, all notices and announcements are transmitted by the AAA to the parties by telephone and are subsequently confirmed in writing. The AAA also notifies the parties by telephone of the appointment of the arbitrator.

The date, time, and place of hearing are set by the arbitrator. The AAA will notify parties of these decisions by telephone seven days before the hearing, and will follow up with a Formal Notice of Hearing sent to each party.

The hearing and presentations of the parties are generally completed within one day. An additional hearing may be scheduled by the arbitrator, if necessary, to be held within five days. The award shall be rendered not later than five business days from the closing of the hearing, unless otherwise agreed to by the parties.

MEDIATION

It may be preferable for the parties to negotiate their own settlement without having to devote the time and effort required in arbitration.

Sometimes, parties hesitate to initiate direct discussions. Mediation can encourage parties to institute discussions or to narrow their differences. Mediation involves the use of a third party to help the parties in reaching a mutual settlement.

The AAA's voluntary construction mediation program provides for the appointment of a mediator "with expertise in the area of the dispute and knowledge of the mediation process." The AAA has established a panel of trained mediators. When drawing up a construction contract, parties can refer to the AAA's mediation program by agreeing to attempt mediation before going to arbitration. The following clause can be used:

> The parties hereby submit their dispute to mediation under the Construction Industry Mediation Rules of the American Arbitration Association. The requirement of filing a notice of claim shall be suspended until the conclusion of the mediation process.

In addition, the agreement can designate the mediator and any other details of the process.

Mediation is a voluntary process. The parties can withdraw and proceed to arbitration at any time. The rules provide that nothing that transpires during the mediation proceeding will prejudice the position of any of the parties to the dispute, whether in arbitration or in court.

If the mediation is successful, agreement is accomplished by the parties themselves. The mediator cannot force a settlement but, by encouraging meetings, can guide the parties and assist the negotiations. The mediator can help the parties to clarify issues and to set priorities, meeting with each party separately when joint sessions have reached an impasse. A mediator may "shuttle" back and forth between the parties, bringing them together whenever further discussions would be productive.

The AAA's mediation procedures are flexible. Mediation can take place at the project site or at any location agreeable to the parties, or the AAA will make its hearing rooms available. The National Construction Dispute Resolution Committee encourages industry professionals to make use of mediation as a means of bringing about settlements. There will be no additional administrative fee if the parties to an existing arbitration wish to mediate.

CONCLUSION

The construction industry serves every segment of our society. By providing a modern mechanism for the resolution of construction contract disputes, arbitration is making a valuable contribution to a dynamic industry. As they gain wider acceptance, mediation and other alternative dispute resolution techniques may play an equally significant role in bringing about settlements and reducing the frequency of disputes on the construction site.

CONSTRUCTION INDUSTRY ARBITRATION RULES

As Amended and Effective on Jaunuary 1, 1993

1. Agreement of Parties—The parties shall be deemed to have made these rules a part of their arbitration agreement whenever they have provided for arbitration by the American Arbitration Association (hereinafter AAA) or under its Construction Industry Arbitration Rules. These rules and any amendment of them shall apply in the form obtaining at the time the demand for arbitration or submission agreement is received by the AAA. The parties, by written agreement, may vary the procedures set forth in these rules.

2. Name of Tribunal—Any tribunal constituted by the parties for the settlement of their dispute under these rules shall be called the Construction Industry Arbitration Tribunal.

3. Administrator and Delegation of Duties—When parties agree to arbitrate under these rules, or when they provide for arbitration by the AAA and an arbitration is initiated under these rules, they thereby authorize the AAA to administer the arbitration. The authority and duties of the AAA are prescribed in the agreement of the parties and in these rules, and may be carried out through such of the AAA's representatives as it may direct.

4. National Panel of Arbitrators—In cooperation with the National Construction Industry Dispute Resolution Committee, the AAA shall establish and maintain a National Panel of Construction Industry Arbitrators and shall appoint arbitrators as provided in these rules.

5. Regional Offices—The AAA may, in its discretion, assign the administration of an arbitration to any of its regional offices.

6. Initiation under an Arbitration Provision in a Contract—Arbitration under an arbitration provision in a contract shall be initiated in the following manner:

(a) The initiating party (hereinafter claimant) shall, within the time period, if any, specified in the contract(s), give written notice to the other party (hereinafter respondent) of its intention to arbitrate (demand), which notice shall contain a statement setting forth the nature of the dispute, the amount involved, if any, the remedy sought, and the hearing locale requested, and

(b) shall file at any regional office of the AAA three copies of the notice and three copies of the arbitration provisions of the contract, together with the appropriate filing fee as provided in the schedule.

The AAA shall give notice of such filing to the respondent or respondents. A respondent may file an answering statement in duplicate with the AAA within ten days after notice from the AAA, in which event the respondent shall at the same time send a copy of the answering statement to the claimant. If a counterclaim is asserted, it shall contain a statement setting forth the nature of the counterclaim, the amount involved, if any, and the remedy sought. If a counterclaim is made, the appropriate fee provided in the schedule shall be forwarded to the AAA with the answering statement. If no answering statement is filed within the stated time, it will be treated as a denial of the claim. Failure to file an answering statement shall not operate to delay the arbitration.

7. Initiation under a Submission—Parties to any existing dispute may commence an arbitration under these rules by filing at any regional office of the AAA three copies of a written submission to arbitrate under these rules, signed by the parties. It shall contain a statement of the matter in dispute, the amount involved, if any, the remedy sought, and the hearing locale requested, together with the appropriate filing fee as provided in the schedule.

8. Changes of Claim—After filing of a claim, if either party desires to make any new or different claim or counterclaim, it shall be made in writing and filed with the AAA, and a copy shall be mailed to the other party, who shall have a period of ten days from the date of such mailing within which to file an answer with the AAA. After the arbitrator is appointed, however, no new or different claim may be submitted except with the arbitrator's consent.

9. Applicable Procedures—Unless the AAA in its discretion determines otherwise, the Expedited Procedures shall be applied in any case where no disclosed claim or counterclaim exceeds $50,000, exclusive of interest and arbitration costs. Parties may also agree to using the Expedited Procedures in cases involving claims in excess of $50,000. The Expedited Procedures shall be applied as described in Sections 53 through 57 of these rules, in addition to any other portion of these rules that is not in conflict with the Expedited Procedures.

All other cases shall be administered in accordance with Sections 1 through 52 of these rules.

10. Administrative Conference, Preliminary Hearing, and Mediation Conference—At the request of any party or at the discretion of the AAA, an administrative conference with the AAA and the parties and/or their representatives will be scheduled in appropriate cases to expedite the arbitration proceedings. There is no administrative fee for this service.

In large or complex cases, at the request of any party or at the discretion of the arbitrator or the AAA, a preliminary hearing with the parties and/or their representatives and the arbitrator may be scheduled by the arbitrator to specify the issues to be resolved, to stipulate to uncontested facts, and to consider any other matters that will expedite the arbitration proceedings. Consistent with the expedited nature of arbitration, the arbitrator may, at the preliminary hearing, establish (i) the extent of and schedule for the production of relevant documents and other information, (ii) the identification of any witnesses to be called, and (iii) a schedule for further hearings to resolve the dispute. There is no administrative fee for the first preliminary hearing.

With the consent of the parties, the AAA at any stage of the proceeding may arrange a mediation conference under the Construction Industry Mediation Rules, in order to facilitate settlement. The mediator shall not be an arbitrator appointed to the case. Where the parties to a pending arbitration agree to mediate under the AAA's rules, no additional administrative fee is required to initiate the mediation.

11. Fixing of Locale—The parties may mutually agree on the locale where the arbitration is to be held. If any party requests that the hearing be held in a specific locale and the other party files no objection thereto within ten days after notice of the request has been sent to it by the AAA, the locale shall be the one requested. If a party objects to the locale requested by the other party, the AAA shall have the power to determine the locale and its decision shall be final and binding.

12. Qualifications of an Arbitrator—Any neutral arbitrator appointed pursuant to Section 13, 14, 15, or 54, or selected by mutual choice of the parties or their appointees, shall be subject to disqualification for the reasons specified in Section 19. If the parties specifically so agree in writing, the arbitrator shall not be subject to disqualification for those reasons.

Unless the parties agree otherwise, an arbitrator selected unilaterally by one party is a party-appointed arbitrator and is not subject to disqualification pursuant to Section 19.

The term "arbitrator" in these rules refers to the arbitration panel, whether composed of one or more arbitrators and whether the arbitrators are neutral or party appointed.

13. Appointment from Panel—If the parties have not appointed an arbitrator and have not provided any other method of appointment, the arbitrator shall be appointed in the following manner: immediately after the filing of the demand or submission, the AAA shall send simultaneously to each party to the dispute an identical list of names of persons chosen from the panel.

Each party to the dispute shall have ten days from the transmittal date in which to strike any names objected to, number the remaining names in order of preference, and return the list to the AAA. If a party does not return the list within the time specified, all persons named therein shall be deemed acceptable. From among the persons who have been approved on both lists, and in accordance with the designated order of mutual preference, the AAA shall invite the acceptance of an arbitrator to serve. If the parties fail to agree on any of the persons named, or if acceptable arbitrators are unable to act, or if for any other reason the appointment cannot be made from the submitted lists, the AAA shall have the power to make the appointment from among other members of the panel without the submission of additional lists.

14. Direct Appointment by a Party—If the agreement of the parties names an arbitrator or specifies a method of appointing an arbitrator, that designation or method shall be followed. The notice of appointment, with the name and address of the arbitrator, shall be filed with the AAA by the appointing party. Upon the request of any appointing party, the AAA shall submit a list of members of the panel from which the party may, if it so desires, make the appointment.

If the agreement specifies a period of time within which an arbitrator shall be appointed and any party fails to make the appointment within that period, the AAA shall make the appointment.

If no period of time is specified in the agreement, the AAA shall notify the party to make the appointment. If within ten days thereafter an arbitrator has not been appointed by a party, the AAA shall make the appointment.

15. Appointment of Neutral Arbitrator by Party-Appointed Arbitrators or Parties—If the parties have selected party-appointed arbitrators, or if such arbitrators have been appointed as provided in Section 14, and the parties have authorized them to appoint a neutral arbitrator within a specified time and no appointment is made within that time or any agreed extension, the AAA may appoint a neutral arbitrator, who shall act as chairperson.

If no period of time is specified for appointment of the neutral arbitrator and the party-appointed arbitrators or the parties do not make the appointment within ten days from the date of the appointment of the last party-appointed arbitrator, the AAA may appoint the neutral arbitrator, who shall act as chairperson.

If the parties have agreed that their party-appointed arbitrators shall appoint the neutral arbitrator from the panel, the AAA shall furnish to the party-appointed arbitrators, in the manner provided in Section 13, a list selected from the panel, and the appointment of the neutral arbitrator shall be made as provided in that section.

16. Nationality of Arbitrator in International Arbitration—Where the parties are nationals or residents of different countries, any neutral arbitrator shall, upon the request of either party, be appointed from among the nationals of a country other than that of any of the parties. The request must be made prior to the time set for the appointment of the arbitrator as agreed by the parties or set by these rules.

17. Number of Arbitrators—If the arbitration agreement does not specify the number of arbitrators, the dispute shall be heard and determined by one arbitrator, unless the AAA, in its discretion, directs that a greater number of arbitrators be appointed.

18. Notice to Arbitrator of Appointment—Notice of the appointment of the neutral arbitrator, whether appointed mutually by the parties or by the AAA, shall be sent to the arbitrator by the AAA, together with a copy of these rules, and the signed acceptance of the arbitrator shall be filed with the AAA prior to the opening of the first hearing.

19. Disclosure and Challenge Procedure—Any person appointed as neutral arbitrator shall disclose to the AAA any circumstance likely to affect impartiality, including any bias or any financial or personal interest in the result of the arbitration or any past or present relationship with the parties or their representatives. Upon receipt of such information from the arbitrator or another source, the AAA shall communicate the information to the parties and, if it deems it appropriate to do so, to the arbitrator and others. Upon objection of a party to the continued service of a neutral arbitrator, the AAA shall determine whether the arbitrator should be disqualified and shall inform the parties of its decision, which shall be conclusive.

20. Vacancies—If for any reason an arbitrator is unable to perform the duties of the office, the AAA may, on proof satisfactory to it, declare the office vacant. Vacancies shall be filled in accordance with the applicable provisions of these rules.

In the event of a vacancy in a panel of neutral arbitrators after the hearings have commenced, the remaining arbitrator or arbitrators may continue with the hearing and determination of the controversy, unless the parties agree otherwise.

21. Date, Time, and Place of Hearing—The arbitrator shall set the date, time, and place for each hearing. The AAA shall send a notice of hearing to the parties at least ten days in advance of the hearing date, unless otherwise agreed by the parties.

22. Representation—Any party may be represented by counsel or other authorized representative. A party intending to be so represented shall notify the other party and the AAA of the name and address of the representative at least three days prior to the date set for the hearing at which that person is first to appear. When such a representative initiates an arbitration or responds for a party, notice is deemed to have been given.

23. Stenographic Record—Any party desiring a stenographic record shall make arrangements directly with a stenographer and shall notify the other parties of these arrangements in advance of the hearing. The requesting party or parties shall pay the cost of the record. If the transcript is agreed by the parties to be, or determined by the arbitrator to be, the official record of the proceeding, it must be made available to the arbitrator and to the other parties for inspection, at a date, time, and place determined by the arbitrator.

24. Interpreters—Any party wishing an interpreter shall make all arrangements directly with the interpreter and shall assume the costs of the service.

25. Attendance at Hearings—The arbitrator shall maintain the privacy of the hearings unless the law provides to the contrary. Any person having a direct interest in the arbitration is entitled to attend hearings. The arbitrator shall otherwise have the power to require the exclusion of any witness, other than a party or other essential person, during the testimony of any other witness. It shall be discretionary with the arbitrator to determine the propriety of the attendance of any other person.

26. Postponements—The arbitrator for good cause shown may postpone any hearing upon the request of a party or upon the arbitrator's own initiative, and shall also grant such postponement when all of the parties agree.

27. Oaths—Before proceeding with the first hearing, each arbitrator may take an oath of office and, if required by law, shall do so. The arbitrator may require witnesses to testify under oath administered by any duly qualified person and, if it is required by law or requested by any party, shall do so.

28. Majority Decision—All decisions of the arbitrators must be by a majority. The award must also be made by a majority unless the concurrence of all is expressly required by the arbitration agreement or by law.

29. Order of Proceedings and Communication with Arbitrator—A hearing shall be opened by the filing of the oath of the arbitrator, where required; by the recording of the date, time, and place of the hearing, and the presence of the arbitrator, the parties, and their representatives, if any; and by the receipt by the arbitrator of the statement of the claim and the answering statement, if any.

The arbitrator may, at the beginning of the hearing, ask for statements clarifying the issues involved. In some cases, part or all of the above will have been accomplished at the preliminary hearing conducted by the arbitrator pursuant to Section 10.

The complaining party shall then present evidence to support its claim. The defending party shall then present evidence supporting its defense. Witnesses for each party shall submit to questions or other examination. The arbitrator has the discretion to vary this procedure but shall afford a full and equal opportunity to all parties for the presentation of any material and relevant evidence.

Exhibits, when offered by either party, may be received in evidence by the arbitrator.

The names and addresses of all witnesses and a description of the exhibits in the order received shall be made a part of the record.

There shall be no direct communication between the parties and a neutral arbitrator other than at oral hearing, unless the parties and the arbitrator agree otherwise. Any other oral or written communication from the parties to the neutral arbitrator shall be directed to the AAA for transmittal to the arbitrator.

30. Arbitration in the Absence of a Party or Representative—Unless the law provides to the contrary, the arbitration may proceed in the absence of any party or representative who, after due notice, fails to be present or fails to obtain a postponement. An award shall not be made solely on the default of a party. The arbitrator shall require the party who is present to submit such evidence as the arbitrator may require for the making of an award.

31. Evidence—The parties may offer such evidence as is relevant and material to the dispute and shall produce such evidence as the arbitrator may deem necessary to an understanding and determination of the dispute. An arbitrator or other person authorized by law to subpoena witnesses or documents may do so upon the request of any party or independently.

The arbitrator shall be the judge of the relevance and materiality of the evidence offered, and conformity to legal rules of evidence shall not be necessary. All evidence shall be taken in the presence of all of the arbitrators and all of the parties, except where any of the parties is absent in default or has waived the right to be present.

32. Evidence by Affidavit and Posthearing Filing of Documents or Other Evidence—The arbitrator may receive and consider the evidence of witnesses by affidavit, but shall give it only such weight as the arbitrator deems it entitled to after consideration of any objection made to its admission.

If the parties agree or the arbitrator directs that documents or other evidence be submitted to the arbitrator after the hearing, the documents or other evidence shall be filed with the AAA for transmission to the arbitrator. All parties shall be afforded an opportunity to examine such documents or other evidence.

33. Inspection or Investigation—An arbitrator finding it necessary to make an inspection or investigation in connection with the arbitration shall direct the AAA to so advise the parties. The arbitrator shall set the date and time and the AAA shall notify the parties. Any party who so desires may be present at such an inspection or investigation. In the event that one or all parties are not present at the inspection or investigation, the arbitrator shall make a verbal or written report to the parties and afford them an opportunity to comment.

34. Interim Measures of Protection—(a) At the request of any party, the tribunal may take whatever interim measures it deems necessary with respect to the dispute, including measures for the conservation of property.

(b) Such interim measures may be taken in the form of an interim award and the tribunal may require security for the costs of such measures.

35. Closing of Hearing—The arbitrator shall specifically inquire of all parties whether they have any further proofs to offer or witnesses to be heard. Upon receiving negative replies or if satisfied that the record is complete, the arbitrator shall declare the hearing closed. If briefs are to be filed, the hearing shall be declared closed as of the final date set by the arbitrator for the receipt of briefs. If documents are to be filed as provided in Section 32 and the date set for their receipt is later than that set for the receipt of briefs, the later date shall be the date of closing the hearing. The time limit within which the arbitrator is required to make the award shall commence to run, in the absence of other agreements by the parties, upon the closing of the hearing.

36. Reopening of Hearing—The hearing may be reopened on the arbitrator's initiative, or upon application of a party, at any time before the award is made. If reopening the hearing would prevent the making of the award within the specific time agreed on by the parties in the contract(s) out of which the controversy has arisen, the matter may not be reopened unless the parties agree on an extension of time. When no specific date is fixed in the contract, the arbitrator may reopen the hearing and shall have thirty days from the closing of the reopened hearing within which to make an award.

37. Waiver of Oral Hearing—The parties may provide, by written agreement, for the waiver of oral hearings in any case. If the parties are unable to agree as to the procedure, the AAA shall specify a fair and equitable procedure.

38. Waiver of Rules—Any party who proceeds with the arbitration after knowledge that any provision or requirement of these rules has not been complied with and who fails to state an objection in writing shall be deemed to have waived the right to object.

39. Extensions of Time—The parties may modify any period of time by mutual agreement. The AAA or the arbitrator may for good cause extend any period of time established by these rules, except the time for making the award. The AAA shall notify the parties of any extension.

40. Serving of Notice—Each party shall be deemed to have consented that any papers, notices, or process necessary or proper for the initiation or continuation of an arbitration under these rules; for any court action in connection therewith; or for the entry of judgment on any award made under these rules may be served on a party by mail addressed to the party or its representative at the last known address or by personal service, in or outside the state where the arbitration is to be held, provided that reasonable opportunity to be heard with regard thereto has been granted to the party.

The AAA and the parties may also use facsimile transmission, telex, telegram, or other written forms of electronic communication to give the notices required by these rules.

41. Time of Award—The award shall be made promptly by the arbitrator and, unless otherwise agreed by the parties or specified by law, no later than thirty days from the date of closing the hearing, or, if oral hearings have been waived, from the date of the AAA's transmittal of the final statements and proofs to the arbitrator.

42. Form of Award—The award shall be in writing and shall be signed by a majority of the arbitrators. It shall be executed in the manner required by law.

43. Scope of Award—The arbitrator may grant any remedy or relief that the arbitrator deems just and equitable and within the scope of the agreement of the parties, including, but not limited to, specific performance of a contract. The arbitrator shall, in the award, assess arbitration fees, expenses, and compensation as provided in Sections 48, 49, and 50 in favor of any party and, in the event that any administrative fees or expenses are due the AAA, in favor of the AAA.

44. Award upon Settlement—If the parties settle their dispute during the course of the arbitration, the arbitrator may set forth the terms of the agreed settlement in an award. Such an award is referred to as a consent award.

45. Delivery of Award to Parties—Parties shall accept as legal delivery of the award the placing of the award or a true copy thereof in the mail addressed to a party or its representative at the last known address, personal service of the award, or the filing of the award in any other manner that is permitted by law.

46. Release of Documents for Judicial Proceedings—The AAA shall, upon the written request of a party, furnish to the party, at its expense, certified copies of any papers in the AAA's possession that may be required in judicial proceedings relating to the arbitration.

47. Applications to Court and Exclusion of Liability—(a) No judicial proceeding by a party relating to the subject matter of the arbitration shall be deemed a waiver of the party's right to arbitrate.

(b) Neither the AAA nor any arbitrator in a proceeding under these rules is a necessary party in judicial proceedings relating to the arbitration.

(c) Parties to these rules shall be deemed to have consented that judgment upon the arbitration award may be entered in any federal or state court having jurisdiction thereof.

(d) Neither the AAA nor any arbitrator shall be liable to any party for any act or omission in connection with any arbitration conducted under these rules.

48. Administrative Fees—As a not-for-profit organization, the AAA shall prescribe filing and other administrative fees to compensate it for the cost of providing administrative services. The fees in effect when the demand for arbitration or submission agreement is received shall be applicable.

The filing fee shall be advanced by the initiating party or parties, subject to final apportionment by the arbitrator in the award.

The AAA may, in the event of extreme hardship on the part of any party, defer or reduce the administrative fees.

49. Expenses—The expenses of witnesses for either side shall be paid by the party producing such witnesses. All other expenses of the arbitration, including required travel and other expenses of the arbitrator, AAA representatives, and any witness and the cost of any proof produced at the direct request of the arbitrator, shall be borne equally by the parties, unless they agree otherwise or unless the arbitrator in the award assesses such expenses or any part thereof against any specified party or parties.

50. Neutral Arbitrator's Compensation—Unless the parties agree otherwise, members of the National Panel of Construction Industry Arbitrators appointed as neutrals will serve without compensation for the first day of service.

Thereafter, compensation shall be based on the amount of service involved and the number of hearings. An appropriate daily rate and other arrangements will be discussed by the administrator with the parties and the arbitrator. If the parties fail to agree to the terms of compensation, an appropriate rate shall be established by the AAA and communicated in writing to the parties.

Any arrangement for the compensation of a neutral arbitrator shall be made through the AAA and not directly between the parties and the arbitrator.

51. Deposits—The AAA may require the parties to deposit in advance of any hearings such sums of money as it deems necessary to cover the expense of the arbitration, including the arbitrator's fee, if any, and shall render an accounting to the parties and return any unexpended balance at the conclusion of the case.

52. Interpretation and Application of Rules—The arbitrator shall interpret and apply these rules insofar as they relate to the arbitrator's powers and duties. When there is more than one arbitrator and a difference arises among them concerning the meaning or application of these rules, it shall be decided by a majority vote. If that is not possible, either an arbitrator or a party may refer the question to the AAA for final decision. All other rules shall be interpreted and applied by the AAA.

Expedited Procedures

53. Notice by Telephone—The parties shall accept all notices from the AAA by telephone. Such notices by the AAA shall subsequently be confirmed in writing to the parties. Should there be a failure to confirm in writing any notice hereunder, the proceeding shall nonetheless be valid if notice has, in fact, been given by telephone.

54. Appointment and Qualifications of Arbitrator—The AAA shall submit simultaneously to each party an identical list of five proposed arbitrators drawn from the National Panel of Construction Industry Arbitrators, from which one arbitrator shall be appointed.

Each party may strike two names from the list on a peremptory basis. The list is returnable to the AAA within seven days from the date of the AAA's mailing to the parties.

If for any reason the appointment of an arbitrator cannot be made from the list, the AAA may make the appointment from among other members of the panel without the submission of additional lists.

The parties will be given notice by telephone by the AAA of the appointment of the arbitrator, who shall be subject to disqualification for the reasons specified in Section 19. Within seven days, the parties shall notify the AAA, by telephone, of any objection to the arbitrator appointed. Any objection by a party to the arbitrator shall be confirmed in writing to the AAA with a copy to the other party or parties.

55. Date, Time, and Place of Hearing—The arbitrator shall set the date, time, and place of the hearing. The AAA will notify the parties by telephone, at least seven days in advance of the hearing date. A formal notice of hearing will also be sent by the AAA to the parties.

56. The Hearing—Generally, the hearing shall be completed within one day, unless the dispute is resolved by submission of documents under Section 37. The arbitrator, for good cause shown, may schedule an additional hearing to be held within seven days.

57. Time of Award—Unless otherwise agreed by the parties, the award shall be rendered not later than fourteen days from the date of the closing of the hearing.

BIBLIOGRAPHY

Acret, James, *Construction Arbitration Handbook* (Colorado Springs: Shepard's/ McGraw-Hill, 1985 with a 1991 Supplement)

American Arbitration Association, *Construction Contract Disputes: How They Can Be Resolved* (New York: American Arbitration Association, 1992)

———, *Construction Industry Arbitration Rules As Amended and Effective on January 1, 1993* (New York: American Arbitration Association)

———, *Construction Industry Mediation Rules As Amended and Effective on January 1, 1992* (New York: American Arbitration Association)

———, *A Guide for Construction Industry Arbitrators* (New York: American Arbitration Association; February, 1993)

———, *Guidelines for Expediting Larger, Complex Construction Arbitrations* (New York: American Arbitration Association, 1988)

———, *An Outline of the Law and Practice of Arbitration under the Construction Industry Arbitration Rules of the American Arbitration Association* (New York: American Arbitration Association, 1991)

American Institute of Architects, *Architect's Handbook of Professional Practice* (Washington, DC: American Institute of Architects, Serial)

Arbitration & the Law: AAA General Counsel's Annual Report (New York: American Arbitration Association, since 1981)

Association of Engineering Firms Practicing in the Geosciences, *ADR: Alternative Dispute Resolution for the Construction Industry* (Silver Spring, MD: Association of Engineering Firms Practicing in the Geosciences, 1988)

Coulson, Robert, "Dispute Management under Modern Construction Systems" in *Law and Contemporary Problems*, Volume 46, Number 1 (Winter, 1983): 127–135

Currie, Overton A., and William E. Dorris, "Understanding Construction Contracts: A Myriad of Special Clauses" in *The Arbitration Journal*, Volume 41, Number 1 (March, 1986): 3–16

Curtis, Gordon H., "How to Deal with Building Disputes" in *The National Law Journal* (September 3, 1984): 13

Cushman, Robert F., Editor, *The McGraw-Hill Construction Business Handbook: A Practical Guide to Accounting, Credit, Finance, Insurance, and Law for the Construction Industry* (New York: McGraw-Hill, 1978)

Cushman, Robert F., and Kenneth M. Cushman, Editors, *Construction Litigation: Representing the Owner* (New York: John Wiley and Sons, 1984 with a 1988 Supplement)

Cushman, Robert F., John D. Carter, and Alan Silverman, Editors, *Construction Litigation: Representing the Contractor* (New York: John Wiley and Sons, 1986 with a 1988 Supplement)

Cushman, Robert F., Michael S. Simon, and McNeil Stokes, *The Construction Industry Formbook: A Practical Guide to Reviewing and Drafting Forms for the Construction Industry* (Colorado Springs: Shepard's, 1979 with a 1989 Supplement)

Donner, Henry J., Stanley B. Edelstein, and Michael J. Gallagher, "Third Circuit Limits Construction Arbitration Rights" in *The Construction Lawyer*, Volume 7, Number 2 (April, 1987): 9

Gnaedinger, John P., "Mediation-Arbitration: Keeping Conflicts Out of Court" in *The Construction Specifier* (May, 1985): 52–55

Groton, James P., "A Guide to Improving Construction Contracts" in *The Arbitration Journal*, Volume 41, Number 2 (June, 1986): 21–24

_____. "Should an Owner Sign an Arbitration Agreement in a Construction Contract?" in *The Arbitration Journal*, Volume 43, Number 3 (September, 1988): 55–58

Hinchey, John W., "Payment and Performance Bond Coverage and Claims" in *The Arbitration Journal*, Volume 41, Number 2 (June, 1986): 25–33

Hoellering, Michael F., "Arbitration, Mediation and Minitrial in the Construction Setting" in *American Bar Association, General Practice Section Construction Law Committee, Program: Construction Law—A Short Course for Drafting to Litigation* (New York: American Bar Association, 1986)

_____, "Construction Arbitration: The Latest Developments" *International Construction Law Review*, Volume 4, Number 3 (July, 1987): 202–212

Ladino, Michael J., "What's Good and Bad About Arbitration?" in *Consulting/Specifying Engineer*, Volume 4, Number 4 (October 1988): 29–31

Marcus, Paula, "Building a Construction Contract That Works: The Owner's Role" in *The Arbitration Journal*, Volume 44, Number 1 (March, 1989): 3–14

_____ and George Marcus, "Fact-Based Mediation for the Construction Industry" in *The Arbitration Journal*, Volume 42, Number 3 (September, 1987): 6–14

Morgerman, Gary, "Arbitration and Construction: Mediation Recommended over Litigation" in *New York Construction News*, Volume 35, Number 7 (September 21, 1987): 10

Myers, James J., "International Construction Dispute Resolutions and New Alternatives" in *The Construction Lawyer*, Volume 6, Number 3 (April, 1986): 1, 13–25

Newhall, Christine, "Arbitration and Mediation of Construction Contract Disputes" in *The Construction Accounting Manual* (Boston: Warren, Gorham and Lamont, 1988 Cumulative Supplement): 17A1–17A36

Oehmke, Thomas, *Construction Arbitration* (New York: Clark Boardman Callahan, 1990 with a 1991 Supplement)

Opalinski, Christopher R., "A Model Owner's Disputes Provision" in *The Construction Specifier* (February, 1988): 23–26

Rubin, Robert A., and Lisa A. Banick, "Alternative Methods to Resolve Construction Disputes" in *Consulting/Specifying Engineer* (August, 1989): 31–34

————, *Resolving Construction Disputes: Alternative Methods* (San Francisco: Construction Management Association of America, 1986)

Siegfried, Steven M., "Arbitration in the Construction Industry" in *The Practical Real Estate Lawyer*, Volume 4, Number 3 (May, 1988): 47–62

Simon, Michael S., *Construction Claims and Liability* (New York: John Wiley and Sons, 1989)

Sweet, Justin, *Sweet on Construction Industry Contracts: Major AIA Documents* (New York: John Wiley and Sons, 1987, with a 1989 Supplement)

Watts, Thomas J., "Issues Related to Construction Claims" in *Cost Engineering*, Volume 29, Number 8 (August, 1987): 30–40

Werderitsch, Anthony J., "Construction Disputes: A Negotiated Resolution" in *American Association of Construction Engineers* (1986): N.2.1–N.2.6

Young, Vicki M., "Update on A.A.A. Rules for Construction Industry" in *The New York Law Journal* (May 17, 1989)

CHAPTER 3

THE TEXTILE AND APPAREL INDUSTRIES

Fashion and technology play an important role in the textile and apparel trades. When business executives and designers guess correctly about the public's preference for the coming season, almost anything sells. The industry prospers. When the consumer demand moves elsewhere, the picture changes. Mills, converters, and cutters drown in unsold goods. Manufacturers glare at unpaid accounts. Controversies multiply, insolvency beckons.

How can such controversies best be settled? Who should decide whether a fabric was rejected because quality standards had not been met or because the purchaser bought similar goods elsewhere at a lower price? When are goods only somewhat inferior, but still salable? Who is to fix a fair price?

HISTORY OF TEXTILE ARBITRATION

In 1920, the New York legislature enacted the first modern arbitration law in the United States. This was particularly important to the industry because arbitration in the textile and apparel industries are almost always heard in New York City.

Arbitration has been an important part of the textile industry for many years. Almost a century ago, the industry concluded that its disagreements did not belong in court. The issues were often technical, calling for knowledge and expertise that could not be found among judges or jurors.

Several historical strands contributed to the present system. The New England Cotton Manufacturers Association was formed in 1854, now known as the Northern Textile Association. In the South, the American Cotton Manufacturers Association took shape. These groups represented the northern and southern cotton mills. Their members sold their products through sales firms based in New York, organized through the Association of Cotton Textile Merchants of New York since 1918. These firms were based in and around Worth Street in lower New York City. The famous Worth Street

Rules were an attempt to ensure quality, uniformity, and reliable performance. A committee on arbitration formed by the textile merchants showed that it was possible for an industry to regulate its own commercial standards through voluntary, contractual methods.

The history of arbitration was similar in wool, silk, yarn, and man-made fibers. Each of these industries first created its own system of contracts and arbitration procedures, and then joined with the industry-wide General Arbitration Council (GAC) of the Textile and Apparel Industries. For example, in 1971, the National Association of Wool Manufacturers merged into the Association of Textile Manufacturers Institute (ATMI), one of the leading members of the GAC. The National Federation of Textiles, which had established an arbitration bureau for silk and rayon trade disputes, joined the other segments of the industry in the ATMI and became part of the GAC. A similar merger took place with the American Yarn Spinners Association.

Encouraged by the New York law, the industry's interest in voluntary arbitration grew rapidly. After the General Arbitration Council of the Textile Industry was formed in 1930, the caseload increased. In 1958, the Arbitration Bureau of the National Federation of Textiles was merged into the General Arbitration Council. Some contracts in the textile and apparel industries provided for arbitration under the AAA's commercial rules. In May 1964, the GAC became a division of the AAA, making use of its hearing rooms, research facilities, and administrative skills. The GAC retains a separate identity so that arbitrations can still be administered under its rules. Parties to disputes involving cloth and yarn mills, converters, dyers, printers, garment manufacturers, and any other aspect of the industry now have a choice—they can arbitrate under GAC rules or AAA commercial rules. In either case, the AAA staff and services are available.

BRINGING A DISPUTE TO ARBITRATION

In the textile and apparel industries, most documents contain a "future-dispute clause." These are found on the face of contracts, purchase orders, and confirmation-of-order forms. These clauses refer to the Arbitration Rules of the General Arbitration Council of the Textile and Apparel Industries or to the AAA's Commercial Arbitration Rules.

Some arbitration clauses give the party bringing the matter to arbitration the option of selecting either the GAC or the AAA, and read as follows:

> Any controversy or claim arising under or in relation to this contract shall be governed and controlled by the laws of the State of New York, and shall be settled by arbitration which shall be held in the City of New York in accordance with the laws of the State of New York and the rules then obtaining of the

American Arbitration Association, as the party first referring the matter to arbitration shall elect. The parties hereto consent to the personal jurisdiction and venue of the Supreme Court of the State of New York, County of New York, and of the United States District Court for the Southern District of New York and further consent that any process, notice of motion, or other application to the court or a judge thereof may be served outside the State of New York by registered or certified mail or by personal service, provided that a reasonable time for appearance is allowed.

The textile department of the AAA's New York regional office administers all kinds of textile and apparel disputes. This department administers cases under both GAC and AAA rules.

THE BATTLE OF THE FORMS

The arbitration clause in the purchase order does not always match the clause in the confirmation form. Although both parties may wish to arbitrate, they may not agree on the procedure. In those situations, the parties can still designate their choice by filling out a "submission agreement," setting forth the issue in dispute and containing the following language:

We, the undersigned parties, hereby agree to submit to arbitration under the rules of [the AAA or the GAC] the following controversy: (state briefly). We further agree that the above controversy be submitted to the arbitrator(s) selected from the panels of the General Arbitration Council of the Textile and Apparel Industries. We further agree that we will faithfully observe this agreement and the rules, that we will abide by and perform any award rendered by the arbitrator(s), and that a judgment of the court having jurisdiction may be entered upon the award.

A problem can arise if the parties have not agreed to arbitrate. A 1978 case in the Court of Appeals in New York, *Marlene Industries Corp.* v. *Carnac Textiles*, 45 N.Y.2d 327, 380 N.E.2d 239, 408 N.Y.S.2d 410 (1978), concerned such a situation. The parties entered into an oral agreement for the purchase and sale of some fabric. Marlene sent a printed purchase order to Carnac that did not contain an arbitration clause and stated that its terms could not be superseded by an unsigned contract. Carnac sent an Acknowledgment of Order with the usual arbitration clause. Neither party signed the other's document. The fabric was delivered. Some was accepted and paid for, some was rejected.

When Carnac commenced arbitration under the terms of its form, Marlene moved in court to stay the arbitration. The lower court and intermediate appellate courts ordered the arbitration to proceed, noting that arbitration was the norm in the industry. But the Court of Appeals reversed the lower courts. Ignoring the long history of arbitration in the textile industry, the court held that an arbitration clause was a material alteration in a contract of sale that could not be inferred without a clear agreement.

More recent court decisions, however, have helped limit the *Marlene* doctrine, even in cases involving unsigned documents. Among these are *Schubtex, Inc.* v. *Allen Snyder, Inc.*, 49 N.Y.2d 1, 399 N.E.2d 1154, 424 N.Y.S.2d 133 (1980), and *Ernest J. Michel & Co.* v. *Anabasis Trade, Inc.*, 50 N.Y.2d 951, 409 N.E.2d 931, 431 N.Y.S.2d 459 (1980). Even where arbitration was not agreed to by both parties, the court in *Schubtex* suggested that, in appropriate cases, an agreement to arbitrate could be inferred "from a course of past conduct or the custom and practice in the industry."

This exception was brought to the fore in *Michel*, a case involving seven confirmation contracts (with arbitration clauses), one of which was signed by the buyer and returned to the seller. The court affirmed the order compelling arbitration, stating that an "agreement to arbitrate was manifested" by the buyer's acceptance and confirmation of one of the seven order forms.

Where there is an agreement to arbitrate, either party can file a demand for arbitration. The AAA commercial rules specify that one copy of the demand be served on the other party, and that copies be filed with the Association together with the appropriate filing fee. The GAC rules state that the party initiating the arbitration must serve a copy of the demand for arbitration and the documents containing the arbitration agreement to the other party, and that copies of the demand and agreement be sent, with the fee, to the Council.

THE PANEL OF ARBITRATORS

Textile arbitrators are drawn from more than twenty branches of the textile and apparel industries, including mill workers, garment manufacturers, finishers, credit executives, converters, purchasing agents, retailers, wholesalers, and executives in other specialized fields. They generally do business with many people within the industry. Textile arbitrators serve on a voluntary basis, and view their service as a contribution to their industry. Cases usually require no more than one day of hearing. From time to time, however, a lengthy case may require particularly dedicated service from a panel. Arbitrators are highly regarded by their peers in the textile industry.

SELECTING AN ARBITRATOR

In textile/apparel cases administered under the AAA's commercial rules, the policy is now to assign three arbitrators if the claim exceeds $75,000. This is somewhat different than the GAC rules, which require three arbitrators where the amount in dispute is greater than $50,000, exclusive of interest and arbitration costs. Disputes involving less than the threshold amount are assigned one arbitrator.

Single-Arbitrator Cases

In a single-arbitrator case, an identical list of proposed arbitrators is submitted to the parties, who are allowed ten days to indicate their preferences and return the list. A party can strike names off this list. Extensions of time may be granted for good cause. If a party does not return its list on time, all names are deemed acceptable. The Association compares the lists returned by the parties and then attempts to appoint a mutually acceptable arbitrator from among the remaining names. If no names are agreeable to both parties or if the acceptable candidates cannot serve, the Association may send another list or may appoint an arbitrator from its panel, other than one whose name had appeared on the list.

In single-arbitrator cases, the person selected to hear the dispute is not selected from the segment of the industry of either party. Thus, a sole arbitrator in a case between an apparel manufacturer and a textile mill would not be from such a manufacturer or a mill.

Three-Arbitrator Panels

When three arbitrators are to be selected, the procedures differ. The AAA rules provide for selection of all three arbitrators by the parties, initially from lists or, if that proves impossible, by administrative appointment. Under the GAC rules, the first two arbitrators are selected from an initial list of names from the parties' own segment of the industry. The chairperson is selected by the first two appointments, who are furnished a list of proposed arbitrators. The third arbitrator can be administratively appointed if the first two arbitrators cannot agree on a name contained on the list or if the persons they select are unable to serve. Attorneys and accountants are not eligible to serve as arbitrators. Only people active in the industry are acceptable.

CHALLENGING AN ARBITRATOR FOR BIAS

If a party has a factual objection to the continued service of an arbitrator, the AAA or the General Arbitration Council can decide whether to remove that arbitrator on the basis of a challenge. Factual objections may include the arbitrator's past or present business or personal relationships with the parties or their attorneys. Arbitrators as well as the parties and their attorneys are urged to disclose any such relationships promptly. The Code of Ethics for

Arbitrators in Commercial Disputes and the applicable rules reflect the leading court decisions on this subject; they should be studied to see what kinds of relationships must be disclosed. In general, anything that might indicate potential bias should be disclosed.

THE ARBITRATION HEARING

Although informal, arbitration hearings in the textile field are not without structure. Parties to arbitration cases have the right to be represented by counsel. This was not always the case. When arbitration was first adopted by industry groups, it was conceived as a merchants' tribunal. But as issues became more complicated, often depending upon complex legal and contractual considerations, the parties saw the need for professional representation. A sophisticated arbitration bar has emerged, and today most textile parties make use of the highly skilled lawyers who practice textile arbitration.

THE TYPICAL CASE

In the typical case, when the parties arrive at the hearing place, they are introduced to the arbitrators, who will have been briefed by an AAA administrator. Sometimes attorneys will submit an opening brief or memorandum to assist the arbitrators in following the case. The chairperson will swear in those witnesses who intend to testify. The hearing then follows a familiar pattern of opening statements, introduction of the initiating documents, examination and cross-examination of witnesses, presentation of exhibits, and final summations. The parties "bring the case to the arbitrator," presenting such evidence and arguments as they deem pertinent. In cases involving the quality of fabric, it may be necessary for the panel to inspect the goods.

THE AWARD

After the parties have completed their presentation, the arbitrator must declare the hearings closed. Under the AAA's commercial rules, the award must be sent to the parties within thirty calendar days after the closing of the hearings. The GAC rules provide for five business days in an expedited case, and ten business days in a regular case. If the arbitration board consists of more than one arbitrator, a majority decision is required.

The award must fall within the limits of the arbitration agreement and must decide each claim and counterclaim submitted. In a typical case, the award may direct that a party accept delivery of the goods and pay for them; or it may order the buyer to return defective goods to the seller; or it may permit an offset for goods that did not measure up to contract specifications. The overall effect of the award will be to end the controversy.

In most instances, parties abide by the decision of the arbitrator. If they lose, they pay. But in the event that a party refuses to comply with the terms of an award, both GAC and AAA rules provide that judgment on the award may be entered in the state or federal court having jurisdiction over such matters. An agreement to that effect should be contained in the arbitration clause. When the award is confirmed into a judgment, it can be used as the basis for collection.

GAC EXPEDITED PROCEDURES

In addition to the regular arbitration procedures, the rules of the GAC provide for an expedited procedure for cases involving less than $25,000. This procedure enables parties with smaller claims to have their disputes resolved quickly and inexpensively.

For this expedited procedure, a single arbitrator is appointed by the GAC from among its official panel of arbitrators. Hearings are scheduled and announced by telephone, as are all other notices from the Council to the parties. All such notices and announcements are subsequently confirmed in writing.

The hearing is generally completed within one day, and the award is rendered within five business days of the closing of the hearing.

CONCLUSION

Textile and apparel industry members have greatly benefited from submitting their disagreements to arbitration. It has been an accepted principle that disputes between merchants should be resolved by arbitrators from within the same industry.

The textile industry has its own definitions:

> The standards of acceptability of particular shipments of fabric vary by the practice, usage, and custom of the trade, from (a) "mill standard" (what can be expected from particular sellers as their major and minor defect count to distinguish firsts from seconds), (b) "by sample" (whether the production delivery is a fair match to the sample which the seller furnished to the buyer) and (c) "end use standards" (standards established by buying trade practices, which may or may not have been incorporated in the "agreement" in the particular case). A similar peculiarity of the textile industry is the "perishability" of the merchandise, in the sense that "season," "style," and general economic conditions can make a fabric that was of substantial value when purchased of far less value at the time of the dispute or its resolution. Arbitrators, actively engaged in the textile industry, can more expeditiously and more accurately

understand and apply these principles than can judges and juries, who must, of necessity, rely solely on so-called "expert-witness" testimony.

Merchantability is particularly important in the textile industry. Price fluctuations are frequent. Manufacturers must be alert to opportunities in the market. Yarn may be knitted or woven to serve whatever purpose the knitter or weaver needs to meet the demand. The fabric may be dyed, printed, laminated, or converted for a different use. The layperson is incapable of understanding these complexities. An arbitrator from the trade can determine whether claimed defects justify the return of the goods or a price allowance, or whether they are so minimal as to warrant no adjustment at all.

Arbitration has made a substantial contribution to the operating efficiency of the textile industry. The combined backgrounds, expertise, and energetic support of industry arbitrators, together with the cooperation of the parties, have greatly contributed to the success of the process. The textile procedures have served as a model for other highly technical industries that have decided to use arbitration.

ARBITRATION RULES OF THE GENERAL ARBITRATION COUNCIL OF THE TEXTILE AND APPAREL INDUSTRIES

As Amended and Effective on July 1, 1993

1. The General Arbitration Council—The General Arbitration Council of the Textile and Apparel Industries as presently constituted is composed of one representative from each of the organizations listed below. The membership may be expanded at the GAC's discretion, upon application by a trade association serving the textile or apparel industries. The GAC shall have general charge of all matters referred for resolution under these rules and shall be authorized to amend these rules or adopt special rules as hereafter provided.

The member organizations of the GAC follow. American Apparel Manufacturers Association; American Association of Textile Chemists & Colorists; American Textile Manufacturers Institute, Inc.; American Yarn Spinners Association, Inc.; Carpet and Rug Institute; Knitted Textile Association; Menswear Retailers of America; National Association of Textile and Apparel Wholesalers; National Knitwear and Sportswear Association; National Knitwear Manufacturers Association; Textile Distributors Association, Inc.

2. Agreement of Parties—Any party to an agreement for arbitration pursuant to these rules, unless the parties thereto have otherwise agreed in writing, consents that such arbitration shall be held in the City of New York and in accordance with the laws of the State of New York and the United States District Court for the Southern District of New York and agrees that any process, notice of motion, or other application to the court or a judge thereof may be served within or outside the State of New York by registered or certified mail or by personal service, providing that a reasonable time for appearance is allowed.

3. The Tribunal—Wherever the word "party" or "parties" is used in these rules, it shall refer to the parties to the Submission or the parties to a controversy; wherever the word "arbitrator" or "arbitrators" is used, it shall refer to the arbitrator or arbitrators, as the case might be, whether there is one or more. Wherever the word "GAC" is used, it shall refer to the General Arbitration Council of the Textile and Apparel Industries. Wherever the word "AAA" is used, it shall refer to the American Arbitration Association, of which the GAC is a division. Wherever the word "Chairperson" or "Secretary" is used, it shall refer to the Chairperson or the Secretary of the GAC. Wherever the phrases "Major Division of the Textile and Apparel Industries" and "Industry Division" are used, they shall refer to any of the following. Apparel Manufacturers; Brokers; Coated-Fabric Suppliers; Converters; Credit Persons; Factors; Finishers; Importers/Exporters; Jobbers/Wholesalers; Knit-Goods Manufacturers; Knitted-Outerwear Manufacturers; Narrow-Fabric Manufacturers; Retailers; Textile-Mill Selling Agents; Thread Manufacturers; Throwsters; Yarn Manufacturers, Selling Agents, and Distributors.

4. Delegation of Duties—The duties of the GAC under these rules may be carried out through the Secretary or such other administrators, officers, or committees as the GAC may direct.

5. The Panel of Arbitrators—The GAC shall appoint and maintain an official Panel of Arbitrators, which shall include, but not be limited to, members of the various divisions of the textile/apparel industries represented in the GAC.

6. Initiation under an Arbitration Provision in a Contract—Arbitration under an arbitration provision in a contract may be initiated in the following manner.

(a) The initiating party (Claimant) shall give notice to the other party (Respondent) of its intention to arbitrate (Demand), which notice shall contain a statement setting forth the nature of the dispute, a sufficient description of the merchandise or service, the amount involved, and the remedy sought. A copy of each of the document(s) containing the arbitration clause(s) shall accompany the Demand filed with the other party.

(b) The Claimant shall also file with the GAC three copies of the said notice, together with one copy of the document or documents containing the arbitration clause(s), together with the filing fee as provided in the schedule.

The GAC shall give notice of the filing to the Respondent(s). The party upon whom the Demand for arbitration is made, within ten days of mailing of notification by the Secretary, shall file with the Claimant and with the Secretary an answer and/or counterclaim in writing, setting forth in concise form the claims and contentions of the Respondent with respect to the document(s) submitted by the Claimant for arbitration. If a monetary claim is made in the answer, the appropriate fee provided in the schedule shall be forwarded to the GAC with the answer. If no answer is filed within the stated time, it will be assumed that the claim is denied. Failure to file an answer shall not operate to delay the arbitration.

7. Initiation under a Submission—Parties to an existing dispute may commence an arbitration under these rules by filing with the GAC three copies of a written agreement to arbitrate under these rules (Submission), signed by the parties. It shall contain a statement of the matter in dispute, a detailed description of the merchandise or service, the amount involved, the remedy sought, and the appropriate filing fee as provided in the schedule.

8. Changes of Claim—After filing of the claim, if either party desires to make any new or different claim or counterclaim, the same shall be made in writing and filed with the Secretary, and a copy shall be mailed to the other party, who shall have a period of ten days from the date of the mailing within which to file an answer with the Secretary. After the arbitrator is appointed, however, no new or different claim may be submitted except with the arbitrator's consent.

9. Applicable Procedures—Unless the GAC in its discretion determines otherwise, the Expedited Procedures shall be applied in any case where no disclosed claim or counterclaim exceeds $25,000, exclusive of interest and arbitration costs. Parties may also agree to the Expedited Procedures in cases involving claims in excess of $25,000. The Expedited Procedures shall be applied as described in Sections 50 through 54 of these rules, in addition to any other portion of these rules that is not in conflict with the Expedited Procedures.

All other cases shall be administered in accordance with Sections 1 through 49 of these rules.

10. Administrative Conference, Preliminary Hearing, and Mediation Conference—At the request of any party or at the discretion of the Secretary, an administrative conference with the Secretary and the parties and/or their representatives will be scheduled in appropriate cases to expedite the arbitration proceedings.

In large or complex cases, at the request of any party or at the discretion of the arbitrator or the Secretary, a preliminary hearing with the parties and/or their representatives and the arbitrator may be scheduled by the arbitrator to specify the issues to be resolved, to stipulate uncontested facts, and to consider any other matters that will expedite the arbitration proceedings. Consistent with the expedited nature of arbitration, the arbitrator may, at the preliminary hearing, establish (i) the extent of and schedule for the production of relevant documents and other information, (ii) the identification of any witnesses to be called, and (iii) a schedule for further hearings to resolve the dispute.

With the consent of the parties, the Secretary at any stage of the proceeding may arrange a mediation conference under the Commercial Mediation Rules, in order to facilitate settlement. The mediator shall not be an arbitrator appointed to the case. Where the parties to a pending arbitration agree to mediate under the AAA's rules, no additional administrative fee is required to initiate the mediation.

11. Number of Arbitrators—In any case where the claim of a party does not exceed $200,000, exclusive of interest and arbitration costs, the dispute shall be heard and determined by one arbitrator, unless the Secretary directs that a greater number of arbitrators be appointed.

In all other cases, the dispute shall be heard and determined by three arbitrators, unless the parties agree that a single arbitrator serve or unless the Secretary determines that a greater number of arbitrators be appointed.

12. Qualifications of Arbitrator(s)—Any arbitrator appointed pursuant to Section 13 shall be neutral, subject to disqualification for the reasons specified in Section 15.

13. Appointment of Arbitrator(s)—(a) Where a case is to be heard by a sole arbitrator, the Secretary shall submit simultaneously to each party an identical list of proposed arbitrators selected from the official Panel of Arbitrators. All such proposed arbitrators must be active or have been active, within the ten-year period prior to appointment, in the textile/apparel industries but should not be or have been, during that ten-year period, actively engaged in the Industry Division of any party to the dispute. Each party shall have ten days from the mailing date to return the list to the Secretary, striking the names of persons to whom it objects and consecutively numbering the remaining names in the order of preference. The Secretary shall invite those persons from the respective lists returned by the parties, in accordance with their order of preference, to serve as arbitrator. If a party fails to return the list within the time specified, all persons named therein shall be deemed acceptable to that party. If the parties fail to agree on any of the persons named or if, for any other reason, the appointment cannot be made from the submitted list, the Secretary shall have the power to make the appointment from other members of the panel without submitting an additional list.

(b) Where a case is to be heard by three arbitrators, the Secretary shall submit simultaneously to each party an identical list of proposed arbitrators selected from the official Panel of Arbitrators. The list shall contain only proposed arbitrators selected, in equal number, from an Industry Division in which each party is engaged. If the official panel does not contain names of available arbitrators engaged in, allied with, or formerly active in the Industry Division in which a party is engaged, the Secretary may submit to the parties names of qualified persons who are not on the official panel.

Each party shall have ten days from the mailing date to return the list to the Secretary, crossing off the names of persons to whom it objects and consecutively numbering the remaining names on the list submitted from each Industry Division in the order of preference. The Secretary shall invite one person on each list from each Industry Division to serve as arbitrator in accordance with the order of preference of the parties, provided that the names acceptable to a party have not been crossed off by another party. If a party does not return the list within the time specified, all persons named therein shall be deemed acceptable to that party. If the parties fail to agree on any of the persons named, if acceptable arbitrators are unable to act, or if for any other reason the appointment cannot be made from the submitted lists, the Secretary will have the power to make the appointment from other members of the panel without submitting additional lists.

After two arbitrators have been appointed, the Secretary shall submit simultaneously to each such arbitrator a list of names of arbitrators selected from panel groups other than those from which the appointed arbitrators shall be chosen. All such proposed arbitrators must be active or have been active in the textile/apparel industries. Each such arbitrator shall have ten days from the mailing of the list to the Secretary, crossing off any objectionable names and numbering the remaining names in order of preference. If an arbitrator fails to return the list within the time specified, all names thereon shall be deemed acceptable to that arbitrator. From the names so approved, and in accordance with the order of mutual preference, if any, the Secretary shall invite an arbitrator to serve. The arbitrator so selected shall serve as chairperson of the panel. If the arbitrators fail to agree on any of the persons named, if acceptable arbitrators are unable to act, or if for any other reason the appointment cannot be made from the submitted list, the Secretary shall have the power to make the appointment from other members of the panel without submitting additional lists.

14. Notice to Arbitrator(s) of Appointment—Notice of the appointment of the neutral arbitrator, whether appointed mutually by the parties or by the AAA, shall be mailed to the arbitrator by the Secretary, together with a copy of these rules, and the signed acceptance of the arbitrator shall be filed prior to the opening of the first hearing.

15. Disclosure and Challenge Procedure—Any person appointed as neutral arbitrator shall disclose to the Secretary any circumstance likely to affect impartiality, including any bias or any financial or personal interest in the result of the arbitration or any past or present relationship with the parties or their representatives. The Secretary shall also request, and each party and their representatives shall disclose to the Secretary, any such circumstance known to them. Upon receipt of such information from the arbitrator or another source, the Secretary shall communicate the information to the parties and, if deemed appropriate, to the arbitrator and others. Upon objection of a party to the continued service of a neutral arbitrator, the Secretary shall determine whether the arbitrator should be disqualified and shall inform the parties of the decision, which shall be conclusive.

16. Vacancies—If for any reason an arbitrator is unable to perform the duties of the office, the Secretary may, on proof satisfactory to it, declare the office vacant. Vacancies shall be filled in accordance with the applicable provisions of these rules.

In the event of a vacancy in a panel of neutral arbitrators after the hearings have commenced, the remaining arbitrator or arbitrators may continue with the hearing and determination of the controversy, unless the parties agree otherwise.

17. Date, Time, and Place of Hearing—The arbitrator shall set the date, time, and place for each hearing. The Secretary shall send a notice of hearing to the parties at least ten days in advance, unless the parties by mutual agreement waive such notice or modify the terms thereof.

18. Representation—Any party may be represented by counsel or another authorized representative. A party intending to be so represented shall notify the other party and the Secretary of the name and address of the representative at least three days prior to the date set for the hearing at which that person is first to appear. When such a representative initiates an arbitration or responds for a party, notice is deemed to have been given.

19. Stenographic Records—Any party desiring a stenographic record shall make arrangements directly with a stenographer and shall notify the other party of these arrangements in advance of the hearing. The requesting party or parties shall pay the cost of the record. If the transcript is agreed by the parties to be, or determined by the arbitrator to be, the official record of the proceeding, it must be made available to the arbitrator and to the other parties for inspection, at a date, time, and place determined by the arbitrator.

20. Interpreters—Any party wishing an interpreter shall make all arrangements directly with the interpreter and shall assume the costs of the service.

21. Oaths—Before proceeding with the first hearing each arbitrator may take an oath of office and, if required by law, shall do so. The arbitrator may require witnesses to testify under an oath administered by any duly qualified person and, if it is required by law or requested by any party, shall do so.

22. Attendance at Hearings—The arbitrator shall maintain the privacy of the hearings unless the law provides to the contrary. Any person having a direct interest in the arbitration is entitled to attend hearings. The arbitrator shall otherwise have the power to require the exclusion of any witness, other than a party or other essential person, during the testimony of any other witness. It shall be discretionary with the arbitrator to determine the propriety of the attendance of any other person.

23. Postponements—The arbitrator for good cause shown may postpone any hearing upon the request of a party or upon the arbitrator's own initiative and shall also grant a postponement when all of the parties agree thereto.

24. Majority Decision—All decisions of the arbitrators must be by a majority. The award must also be made by a majority unless the concurrence of all is expressly required by the arbitration agreement or by law.

25. Order of Proceedings and Communication with Arbitrator(s)—A hearing shall be opened by the filing of the oath of the arbitrator, where required; by the recording of the date, time, and place of the hearing and the presence of the arbitrator, the parties, and their representatives, if any; and by the receipt by the arbitrator of the statement of the claim and the answering statement, if any.

The arbitrator may, at the beginning of the hearing, ask for statements clarifying the issues involved. In some cases, part or all of the above will have been accomplished at the preliminary hearing conducted by the arbitrator pursuant to Section 10.

The complaining party shall then present evidence to support its claim. The defending party shall then present evidence supporting its defense. Witnesses for each party shall submit to questions or other examination. The arbitrator has the discretion to vary this procedure but shall afford a full and equal opportunity to all parties for the presentation of any material and relevant evidence.

Exhibits, when offered by either party, may be received in evidence by the arbitrator.

The names and addresses of all witnesses and a description of the exhibits in the order received shall be made a part of the record.

There shall be no direct communication between the parties and a neutral arbitrator other than at oral hearing, unless the parties and the arbitrator agree otherwise. Any other oral or written communication from the parties to the neutral arbitrator shall be directed to the Secretary for transmittal to the arbitrator.

26. Arbitration in the Absence of a Party or Representative—Unless the law provides to the contrary, the arbitration may proceed in the absence of any party or representative who, after due notice, fails to be present or fails to obtain a postponement. An award shall not be made solely on the default of a party. The arbitrator shall require the party who is present to submit such additional evidence as the arbitrator requires for the making of an award.

27. Evidence—The parties may offer such evidence as is relevant and material to the dispute and shall produce such additional evidence as the arbitrator deems necessary to an understanding and determination of the dispute. An arbitrator or other person authorized by law to subpoena witnesses or documents may do so upon the request of any party or independently.

The arbitrator shall be the judge of the relevance and materiality of the evidence offered, and conformity to legal rules of evidence shall not be necessary. All evidence shall be taken in the presence of all of the arbitrators and all of the parties, except where any of the parties is absent in default or has waived the right to be present.

28. Evidence by Affidavits and Posthearing Filing of Documents or Other Evidence—The arbitrator may receive and consider the evidence of witnesses by affidavit, but shall give it only such weight as the arbitrator deems it entitled to after consideration of any objection made to its admission.

If the parties agree or the arbitrator directs that documents or other evidence be submitted to the arbitrator after the hearing, the documents or other evidence shall be filed with the Secretary for transmission to the arbitrator. All parties shall be afforded an opportunity to examine such documents or other evidence.

29. Inspection or Investigation—An arbitrator finding it necessary to make an inspection or investigation in connection with the arbitration shall direct the Secretary to so advise the parties. The arbitrator shall set the date and time and the Secretary shall notify the parties. Any party who so desires may be present at such an inspection or investigation. In the event that one or all parties are not present at the inspection or investigation, the arbitrator shall make a verbal or written report to the parties and afford them an opportunity to comment.

30. Interim Measures—The arbitrator may issue such orders for interim relief as are deemed necessary to safeguard the property that is the subject matter of the arbitration without prejudice to the rights of the parties or to the final determination of the dispute.

31. Closing of Hearing—The arbitrator shall specifically inquire of all parties whether they have any further proofs to offer or witnesses to be heard. Upon receiving negative replies or if satisfied that the record is complete, the arbitrator shall declare the hearing closed and a minute thereof shall be recorded. If briefs are to be filed, the hearing shall be declared closed as of the final date set by the arbitrator for the receipt of briefs. If documents are to be filed as provided in Section 28 and the date set for their receipt is later than that set for the receipt of briefs, the later date shall be the date of closing the hearing. The time limit within which the arbitrator is required to make the award shall commence to run, in the absence of other agreements by the parties, upon the closing of the hearing.

32. Reopening of Hearing—The hearing may be reopened on the arbitrator's initiative, or upon application of a party, at any time before the award is made. If reopening the hearing would prevent the making of the award within the specific time agreed on by the parties in the contract(s) out of which the controversy has arisen, the matter may not be reopened unless the parties agree on an extension of time. When no specific date is fixed in the contract, the arbitrator may reopen the hearing and shall have ten business days from the closing of the reopened hearing within which to make an award.

33. Waiver of Oral Hearing—The parties may provide, by written agreement, for the waiver of oral hearing in any case. If the parties are unable to agree as to the procedure, the Secretary shall specify a fair and equitable procedure.

34. Waiver of Rules—Any party who proceeds with the arbitration after knowledge that any provision or requirement of these rules has not been complied with and who fails to state an objection thereto in writing shall be deemed to have waived the right to object.

35. Extensions of Time—The parties may modify any period of time by mutual agreement. The Secretary or the arbitrator may for good cause extend any period of time established by these rules, except the time for making the award. The Secretary shall notify the parties of any extension.

36. Serving of Notice—Each party shall be deemed to have consented that any paper, notice, or process necessary or proper for the initiation or continuation of an arbitration under these rules; for any court action in connection therewith; or for the entry of judgment on any award made under these rules may be served on a party by mail addressed to the party or its representative at the last known address or by personal service, in or outside the state where the arbitration is to be held, provided that reasonable opportunity to be heard with regard thereto has been granted to the party.

The Secretary and the parties may also use facsimile transmission, telex, telegram, or other written forms of electronic communication to give the notice required by these rules.

37. Time of Award—The award shall be made promptly by the arbitrator and, unless otherwise agreed by the parties or specified by law, no later than ten business days from the date of closing the hearing or, if oral hearing has been waived, from the date of the Secretary's transmittal of the final statements and proofs to the arbitrator.

38. Form of Award—The award shall be in writing and shall be signed by a majority of the arbitrators. It shall be executed in the manner required by law.

39. Scope of Award—The arbitrator may grant any remedy or relief that the arbitrator deems just and equitable and within the scope of the agreement of the parties, including, but not limited to, specific performance of a contract; require the acceptance or replacement of merchandise; fix allowances for defective merchandise; declare a contract breached in whole or in part; award money damages in the alternative or otherwise; and/or assess arbitration fees, expenses, and compensation as provided in Sections 45, 46, 47, and 48 in favor of any party and, in the event that administrative fees or expenses are due the AAA, in favor of the AAA.

If, in the opinion of the arbitrator, an award that is not for money only has not been complied with fully within a reasonable time, the arbitrator may make a supplemental award for money only, and the powers of the arbitrator shall continue for this purpose.

40. Award upon Settlement—If the parties settle their dispute during the course of the arbitration, the arbitrator may set forth the terms of the agreed settlement in an award.

Such an award is referred to as a consent award.

41. Delivery of Award to Parties—Parties shall accept as legal delivery of the award the placing of the award or a true copy thereof in the mail addressed to a party or its representative at the last known address, personal service of the award, or the filing of the award in any other manner that is permitted by law.

42. Release of Documents for Judicial Proceedings—The GAC/AAA shall, upon the written request of a party, furnish to the party, at its expense, certified copies of any papers in the GAC's possession that are required in judicial proceedings relating to the arbitration.

43. Applications to Court and Exclusion of Liability—(a) No judicial proceeding by a party relating to the subject matter of the arbitration shall be deemed a waiver of the party's right to arbitrate.

(b) Neither the GAC/AAA nor any arbitrator in a proceeding under these rules is a necessary party in judicial proceedings relating to the arbitration.

(c) Parties to these rules shall be deemed to have consented that judgment upon the arbitration award may be entered in any federal or state court having jurisdiction thereof.

(d) Neither the GAC/AAA nor any arbitrator shall be liable to any party for any act or omission in connection with any arbitration conducted under these rules.

44. The Standing Committee—The Chairperson of the GAC shall appoint a Standing Committee of five member representatives of whom not less than three shall constitute a quorum. The Standing Committee is empowered to hear and make decisions in matters involving interpretations of these rules. Whenever, in the opinion of the GAC or a majority of the arbitrators, the foregoing rules are not fully applicable or whenever an unusual or unforeseen situation arises, the GAC, in its judgment, may adopt special rules and, in case of conflict between the foregoing rules and the special rules, the special rules shall prevail.

The Standing Committee, in its absolute discretion, may refuse to extend the arbitration services of the GAC in any case that it deems appropriate, or may discontinue such services during the pendency of any proceedings, and in such an event shall notify the parties in writing of its action.

Actions taken by the Standing Committee hereunder shall be reported to the other members of the GAC at the Annual Meeting thereof or in such other manner as the GAC from time to time may direct. In all other matters, the GAC may delegate all of its power under these rules to the Chairperson or to the Standing Committee or any three members thereof.

45. Administrative Fees—As a not-for-profit organization, the AAA shall prescribe filing and other administrative fees to compensate it for the cost of providing administrative services. The fees in effect when the Demand for arbitration or Submission agreement is received shall be applicable.

The filing fee shall be advanced by the initiating party or parties, subject to final apportionment by the arbitrator in the award.

The AAA may, in the event of extreme hardship on the part of any party, defer or reduce the administrative fee.

46. Expenses—The expenses of witnesses for either side shall be paid by the party producing such witnesses. All other expenses of the arbitration, including required travel and other expenses of the arbitrator, GAC/AAA representatives, and any witness and the cost of any proof produced at the direct request of the arbitrator, shall be borne equally by the parties, unless they agree otherwise or unless the arbitrator in the award assesses such expenses or any part thereof against any specified party or parties.

47. Neutral Arbitrator's Fee—Unless the parties agree otherwise, members of the Textile/ Apparel Panel of Arbitrators (National Panel of Commercial Arbitrators) appointed as neutrals will serve without compensation except in protracted cases and, in that event, the Secretary will arrange with the parties for reasonable compensation.

Compensation shall be based on the amount of service involved and the number of hearings. If the parties fail to agree to the terms of compensation, an appropriate rate shall be established by the Secretary and communicated in writing to the parties.

Any arrangement for the compensation of a neutral arbitrator shall be made through the Secretary and not directly between the parties and the arbitrator. The terms of compensation of neutral arbitrators on a panel shall be identical.

48. Deposits—The GAC/AAA may require the parties to deposit in advance of any hearings such sums of money as it deems necessary to defray the expense of the arbitration, including the arbitrator's fee, if any, and shall render an accounting to the parties and return any unexpended balance at the conclusion of the case.

49. Interpretation and Application of Rules—The arbitrator shall interpret and apply these rules insofar as they relate to the arbitrator's powers and duties. When there is more than one arbitrator and a difference arises among them concerning the meaning or application of these rules, it shall be decided by a majority vote. If that is unobtainable, either an arbitrator or a party may refer the question to the GAC for final decision. All other rules shall be interpreted and applied by the GAC.

Expedited Procedures

50. Notice by Telephone—The parties shall accept all notice from the GAC by telephone. Such notice by the GAC shall subsequently be confirmed in writing to the parties. Should there be a failure to confirm in writing any notice hereunder, the proceeding shall nonetheless be valid if notice has, in fact, been given by telephone.

51. Appointment and Qualifications of Arbitrator—Upon the GAC's receipt of the Demand for arbitration or Submission to arbitration, in accordance with Section 6, 7, or 9 of these rules, the GAC shall, without the submission to the parties of a list of proposed arbitrators, appoint one arbitrator from its official Panel of Arbitrators, as provided in Section 5. The arbitrator appointed must be active, or have been active within the ten-year period prior to appointment, in the textile/apparel industries but should not be, or have been during the said five-year period, actively engaged in the Industry Division of any party to the dispute. Such an appointment shall be subject to disqualification for the reasons specified in Section 15.

The parties shall be given notice, by telephone, from the GAC, of the appointment of the arbitrator. The parties shall notify the GAC, by telephone, within fifteen days, of any objection by a party to the arbitrator appointed. Any objection by a party to the arbitrator shall be confirmed in writing to the GAC, with a copy to the other party(ies).

52. Date, Time, and Place of Hearing—The arbitrator appointed shall set the date, time, and place of the hearing. The GAC will notify the parties, by telephone, within ten days in advance of the hearing date. A formal Notice of Hearing will be sent by the GAC to the parties.

53. The Hearing—Generally, the hearing shall be completed within one day. The arbitrator, for good cause shown, may schedule an additional hearing to be held within ten days.

54. Time of Award—Unless otherwise agreed by the parties, the award shall be rendered not later than five business days from the date of the closing of the hearing.

BIBLIOGRAPHY

American Arbitration Association, *Arbitration Rules of the General Arbitration Council of the Textile and Apparel Industries As Amended and Effective July 1, 1993* (New York: American Arbitration Association)

_____, *A Guide to Arbitration/Mediation for the Textile and Apparel Industries* (New York: American Arbitration Association; August, 1993)

American Textile Manufacturers Institute, Knitted Textile Association, and Textile Distributors Association, *Worth Street Textile Market Rules Effective July 1, 1986* (New York: American Textile Manufacturers Institute)

Friedman, George H., "Textile Arbitration—Recent Cases" in *The New York Law Journal* (March 9, 1988): 1

_____, "Textile Arbitration—Recent Developments" in *The New York Law Journal* (November 23, 1984): 1

Houston, Frederic P., "A Barrier to Arbitration" (New York: New York Board of Trade, 1983)

Marx, Gary S., "Arbitration: An Affordable Dispute Resolution" in *Bobbin Magazine*, Volume 29, Number 9 (May, 1988): 36-40

"Textile Arbitration: Rules and Issues" in *Lawyers' Arbitration Letter*, Volume 13, Number 2 (June, 1989): 1-12

CHAPTER 4

INSURANCE CLAIMS

The insurance industry in the United States should be the most concerned about the cost and inefficiency of litigation. The industry has been eager to move its disputes into more modern channels. For intercompany disagreements, it has established a broad range of internal arbitration procedures.

Bernard L. Hines' book, *Arbitration: A Guide to Insurance Industry Forums*, contains a comprehensive description of programs under which companies settle intercompany claims through a network of arbitration committees. This industrywide system has been a boon to the courts, relieving them of the burden of many thousands of subrogation and other claims between insurance companies.

In addition, the casualty industry has participated in the creation of major uninsured-motorist and no-fault arbitration systems, under which the claims of individuals against their own automobile insurance companies are settled by impartial arbitrators.

UNINSURED-MOTORIST CLAIMS

Uninsured-motorist coverage has become well accepted in the United States. It helps to protect insured motorists by providing damages when they suffer personal injuries because of the negligence of an uninsured or hit-and-run driver. This coverage is required by law in most states. A typical uninsured-motorist endorsement promises

> to pay all sums which the insured shall be legally entitled to recover as damages from the owner or operator of an uninsured automobile because of bodily injury sustained by the insured, caused by an accident arising out of the ownership, maintenance, or use of such uninsured automobile, provided determination as to whether the insured is legally entitled to recover such damages, and if so, the amount therefor, shall be made by agreement between the insured and the company, or, if they fail to agree, by arbitration.

This endorsement usually describes an arbitration procedure. A typical insurance policy endorsement contains the following language

> If any person making claim hereunder and the company do not agree that such person is legally entitled to recover damages from the owner or operator of such uninsured automobile because of the amount of payment which may be owing under this endorsement, then, upon written demand of either, the matter or matters upon which such person and the company do not agree shall be settled by arbitration in accordance with the rules of the American Arbitration Association, and judgment upon the award rendered by the arbitrators may be entered in any court having jurisdiction thereof. Such person and the company each agree to consider itself bound and to be bound by any award made by the arbitrators pursuant to this endorsement.

The AAA's accident-claim arbitration system was established in 1956 at the request of the insurance industry. It relies upon a panel of lawyers with negligence experience who have been nominated by bar associations or by other attorneys and have volunteered to serve as arbitrators in uninsured motorist cases. The AAA helps the parties to select an arbitrator and provides administrative assistance in accordance with the Accident Claims Arbitration Rules (Including Mediation). The AAA rules also give parties the chance to mediate, which has proven to be a prompt, fair, and economical method of settling insurance claims. These services are supported by fees paid by the filing party and the insurance carrier. Each year, thousands of cases are resolved under such procedures.

The Arbitration Procedure

The injured person may initiate a claim by serving a demand for arbitration on the insurance company, with copies to the nearest AAA office. The demand should describe the nature of the injury, the amount of the claim, other information required by the rules, and a copy of the arbitration provision of the policy.

Arbitrators are appointed by the AAA, in most cases from a list of names submitted to the parties. Cases involving claims exceeding the minimum uninsured-motorist coverage available in a jurisdiction, either because of multiple policies ("stacking") or because of optional additional coverage, are upon request of any party heard by a panel of three neutral arbitrators unless local law provides otherwise. Other cases are heard by a single arbitrator unless the AAA determines that more arbitrators would be appropriate.

The insured individual may designate the place of hearing (either the insured's county or residence or the county where the accident took place). If no objection is raised by the insurance carrier, the case will be heard at that location. The date and place of the hearing are set after considering the mutual convenience of the parties. A notice of at least twenty days must be given. The parties may be represented at the hearing by counsel.

Uninsured motorist arbitration hearings tend to be brief and informal. Each side is given an opportunity to convince the arbitrator through the testimony of witnesses and the presentation of exhibits. Cross examination of opposing witnesses is available, and the lawyers present and argue cases in their own way. The arbitrator is required to determine the issues submitted. A written award must be signed by the arbitrator within thirty days after the hearing is declared closed. Prompt decisions are encouraged. It is not customary for the arbitrator to explain the reasoning behind the award. The award is prepared by the AAA and, when signed by the arbitrator, is mailed simultaneously to the parties.

Arbitration provides an expedited method of dispute settlement. This is advantageous to everyone. Claimants need not face court delays. Insurers do not have to maintain files for long periods of time. The arbitration of uninsured-motorist claims has demonstrated how private voluntary arbitration can work in the public interest. The lawyers who serve as arbitrators are providing an important service.

Mediation

Mediators appointed in accident claims cases are experienced attorneys. They have mediation training or experience and are required to inform the AAA of any circumstance that might prevent a prompt hearing or create a presumption of bias. Upon the objection of either party, the AAA will replace the mediator.

Because mediation is voluntary, all parties to the dispute must consent to participate. Upon request, a mediation submission form will be provided by the AAA.

If there is no agreement or mediation proves unsuccessful, the parties can continue with the arbitration.

NO-FAULT INSURANCE CLAIMS

Prior to the enactment of no-fault laws, anyone injured in an auto accident had to show that the other driver's negligence caused the accident in order to collect from an insurer for losses due to the injury. For example, if a car ran off the road into a tree, an injured passenger might have a negligence claim against the driver or the owner; if another vehicle was involved in the accident, an injured person might have the right to recover against the driver or the owner of either vehicle. Ordinarily, the driver or owner would be insured. Where the other vehicle was not covered by insurance, injured claimants could obtain relief under the uninsured-motorist provision of their policy. In all of these examples, however, injured persons must establish another party's negligence and their own freedom from contributory negligence. If such negligence can be established, the claimant can collect for actual damages and for pain and suffering.

No fault operates on a different principle. Its theory is that it is important for victims of automobile accidents to be reimbursed for their economic loss and that it might be unnecessary to determine negligence. The no-fault statutes provide protection for anyone—driver, passenger, or pedestrian—who sustains injuries arising out of use or operation of an insured vehicle, without regard to fault or whether another vehicle was involved.

Coverage varies from state to state. The federal government has not required a uniform approach. In general, no-fault laws provide compensation for medical expenses, lost wages, and other reasonable and necessary expenses arising out of the personal injuries sustained in an accident. Disputes still arise between insurers and claimants as to whether coverage exists and as to the extent of coverage but the issues tend to be less complicated than they were under the prior law. On the other hand, no-fault claimants no longer have a right to collect for pain and suffering.

Unlike arbitration of uninsured-motorist claims, which is based solely upon the agreement of the insurer and policyholder, no-fault arbitration arises out of provisions in the law. Five states—Hawaii, Minnesota, New Jersey, New York, and Oregon—have no-fault automobile-insurance laws that provide for arbitration of disputes between claimants and carriers.

NO-FAULT ARBITRATION IN NEW YORK

New York's no-fault law provides that:

> Each insurer shall provide a claimant with the option of submitting any dispute involving the insurers' liability to pay first-party benefits . . . to arbitration pursuant to simplified procedures to be promulgated or approved by the superintendent.

New York's law became effective February 1, 1974. The arbitration procedures provided for arbitration by the AAA of all legal and medical claims. The procedures were applicable to injuries sustained prior to December 1, 1977. Amendments of the law in 1977 established medical- and attorney-fee schedules and provided appeals to master arbitrators.

Under new regulations applicable to requests received at the insurance department on or after July 1, 1988, requests must be mailed in duplicate (the original and a copy) directly to the insurance department, together with a filing fee of $40. The filing may be made by completing the form on the reverse side of the form (NYS Form NF-10) sent by insurers to claimants to deny them benefits or, if thirty days have already elapsed without a response from the insurer, by mailing a separate arbitration-request form (AR-1) to the insurance department and a copy to the insurer against which arbitration is requested. If the department cannot conciliate the matter, the case is referred to the American Arbitration Association, except where

(1) the remaining issues involve correct computation of fees of health-service providers, whether or not the fees are specifically covered by the schedules promulgated in the regulations;

(2) the amount in dispute is less than $400 and the dispute neither involves a coverage question nor affects the outcome of any other portion of the applicant's claim; or

(3) the remaining issues involve whether the claim was overdue when it was paid, how long the claim was overdue, or whether the correct amount of interest or attorney fees on an overdue claim was paid.

Such issues are decided by Insurance Department Arbitration (IDA).

The AAA Forum

Questions of basic economic loss, such as amounts of wage loss or incurred expense, or health services are submitted to AAA arbitration. Under the regulations, parties are provided with the name of an arbitrator selected by the AAA and the right to challenge the selection for financial or personal interest in the outcome or for bias. Upon receiving specific grounds for a challenge by a party in writing, the AAA will determine within fifteen days whether the arbitrator is to be disqualified and its determination will be final.

Issues regarding necessity or accident relatedness of health services are determined by independent health-service consultants. Arbitrators can request consultants from specific fields to review records or examine applicants. The insurance department maintains the pool from which consultants are selected. A consultant's report, due within fifteen days of the review, is submitted via the AAA to the arbitrator for consideration.

The hearing must be held within thirty days of the arbitrator's appointment, unless the parties agree otherwise. The award must be mailed within fifteen days.

The IDA Forum

IDA arbitrators are examiners or attorneys appointed by the state's superintendent of insurance. Hearing is on written submissions from the parties only, with no oral argument permitted. Parties have 21 days within which to forward their submissions to the arbitrator and the award is rendered within 21 days thereafter.

AAA Awards

No-fault arbitration awards are required to contain reasoned opinions. The AAA publishes a monthly reporter, *New York No-Fault Arbitration Reports*, that summarizes interesting lower awards, master awards, and court decisions and provides information on other no-fault developments.

Qualifications of AAA Arbitrators

AAA no-fault arbitrators are attorneys heavily experienced in negligence and insurance practice in the State of New York and serve as full-time or part-time members of a permanent panel of professional arbitrators.

Attorney and Witness Fees

Arbitrators may award attorney fees to successful claimants. A fee schedule contained in the regulations governs the amount that may be awarded. Arbitrators are also empowered to award witness fees.

Appellate Procedure: Master Arbitration

Although it is not typical in arbitration, the New York no-fault arbitration system has its own review procedure. Awards can be appealed to a master arbitrator. The grounds for review go far beyond those applicable to traditional arbitration awards. They include:

(1) the statutory grounds for vacating an award contained in the New York arbitration law, except failure to follow procedures contained therein;
(2) that the award required an insurer to pay amounts in excess of policy limitations;
(3) that the award was incorrect as a matter of law;
(4) that attorney fees awarded by the hearing arbitrator were not in accordance with the fee schedule; or
(5) that an award was "inconsistent and irreconcilable" with an earlier award involving the same injuries.

The regulations require that an insurer pay all amounts not in dispute before submitting an issue for review by a master arbitrator. The master arbitrators, who serve at the superintendent's pleasure, are required to have been licensed to practice law in New York for at least 15 years. Reviews by master arbitrators are based solely on submitted documents unless a master arbitrator requests oral argument. Only issues that were raised in the lower arbitration may be considered. Where a master award exceeds $5,000, exclusive of interest and attorney fees, the law permits a trial *de novo* in court.

MINNESOTA NO-FAULT ARBITRATION

A claimant in Minnesota can request arbitration of a no-fault dispute when a claim for benefits is denied by the insurer. The arbitration is heard by a single arbitrator mutually selected by the parties from a list supplied by the AAA. Arbitrators receive a fee of $150 for each half day of hearing and $50 if a case is settled prior to a hearing. The arbitrator's fee is paid by the insurer but may be assessed as a cost by the arbitrator.

Under the Minnesota no-fault law, the arbitrator is encouraged to conciliate the claim prior to the arbitration hearing. Ten days prior to the scheduled date of hearings, the parties are asked by the arbitrator to stipulate facts that are not in dispute. If conciliation is unsuccessful, a hearing is held, usually at the arbitrator's office. The rules provide the arbitrator with subpoena power and authorize him or her to permit any discovery allowable under court rules.

The hearing itself proceeds along the familiar lines of opening statements, presentation of witnesses and exhibits, cross examinations, and summations. Consistent with other types of arbitration, strict conformity to rules of evidence is not required. The arbitrator is sole judge of the relevance and materiality of evidence. The award is due no later than thirty days after the closing of the hearings, unless the parties agree otherwise.

NEW JERSEY NO-FAULT ARBITRATION

Effective in 1984, New Jersey's automobile insurance law was amended to require that all automobile insurers provide any claimant with the option of submitting a dispute concerning personal injury protection benefits to binding arbitration under the auspices of the AAA. Personal-injury protection (PIP) benefits comprise compensation for direct economic loss (medical expenses, wage loss, funeral expenses). The benefits are the heart of the "no-fault" concept, in which the right to sue for pain and suffering is traded off for immediate compensation of out-of-pocket expenses. The system established incorporates several innovative features in an effort to make the process pliable to the needs of the parties.

Evidence may be presented by submission of documents only or at an oral hearing. Either side may request an oral hearing but, where there is no such request, arrangements are made for document submission. The party requesting oral hearing pays a surcharge. Additionally, either party, for the purpose of attempting settlement, may request a prehearing conference with AAA administrative staff or a mediation conference.

A single arbitrator is administratively appointed from a rotating list of arbitrators selected by a balanced advisory committee of practitioners active in the field. Either side may object to the appointment of a specific arbitrator for cause. If the amount claimed exceeds $50,000, three arbitrators will be appointed upon a request of either party.

Parties make their own arrangements for stenographers, if desired, and pay the stenographer directly. Arbitrators are compensated at the rate of $350 per case, split evenly by the parties.

In accordance with the law, where the claimant prevails, the arbitrator must direct the insurer to pay all the costs of the proceedings, including reasonable attorney fees.

THE ADR PROGRAM

Responding to a need for a simple, inexpensive, and expeditious way to resolve liability claims, the American Arbitration Association prepared Dispute Resolution Procedures for Insurance Claims. Initiated in 1983 on a pilot basis, the alternative dispute resolution (ADR) program speeds claim resolution and helps to control litigation costs.

The ADR program is entirely voluntary. Both insurers and claiming parties are invited to submit cases. Cases are filed by submission to arbitration or to nonbinding mediation, at the parties' option; there need not be a previous contractual arrangement between the parties to use the program. Insurers or claimants list with the AAA cases that they would be willing to submit under the ADR procedures. The AAA then serves as intermediary, explaining the program to the other party with an invitation to submit the case to either mediation or arbitration. If there is agreement, the AAA appoints a neutral and proceeds to schedule the matter.

Arbitrators and mediators selected by the AAA for this program are experienced, neutral individuals with an understanding of personal-injury litigation practices. Arbitrators must be attorneys or retired judges. Mediators are not necessarily attorneys, yet all have many years' experience in mediation techniques. They are required to inform the AAA of any circumstance that might prevent a prompt hearing or create a presumption of bias. The AAA is authorized to replace neutrals when necessary.

The costs of the ADR program are reasonable. There is an administrative fee of $150 per party, plus a compensation fee for the neutral to be paid equally by the parties. The exact compensation rate for the neutral is arranged by the AAA with the parties before the hearings.

There is no limit on the amount of claims that may be submitted to the program. The average claim in the pilot program has been $10,000 but many claims are recently substantially greater.

Case Selection

Parties are urged to exhaust their own direct-negotiation efforts prior to submitting a case to the program. When there are multiple parties, all parties must agree to the submission. Generally, cases concern matters where the insurer acknowledges some liability. Although there is no limit on the amount of claim, the parties may wish to limit the dollar amount an arbitrator can award.

Examples of the types of issues that may be submitted include

- a rear-end collision with a truck;
- a "slip and fall" case that had been in suit for 10 years;
- a passenger on a bus injured when the bus made a sudden stop;
- a guest at a hotel who was injured when a heavy steel fire door closed quickly, crushing her finger between the door and its jamb;
- a claimant struck by clothes rack blown over during sidewalk sale;
- a false arrest of shopper at a department store;
- an uninsured motorist who ran a stop light, hitting another car; and
- a patient unhappy with medical treatment.

Resolution of Disputes

The results of the pilot program show that mediation, the more informal process, is selected more often as the means of settlement than arbitration.

The mediator works with both sides toward establishing realistic, acceptable claims and offers. When the parties reach agreement, they reduce the terms to writing and exchange releases. They may also request the agreement be put in the form of a consent award, for which the AAA will make the arrangements.

If there are any issues not resolved in mediation, the parties may submit them to arbitration for a final, binding determination.

If arbitration is the settlement technique selected under the ADR procedures, hearings will be held to provide the arbitrator with the information necessary to decide the dispute. After listening to the evidence and arguments, the arbitrator declares the hearing closed. Under the ADR procedures, the arbitrator has thirty days from that time within which to render a binding award.

The award is usually a brief statement directing one or both parties to provide specific relief. It is not accompanied by a written opinion unless the parties and the arbitrator agree that an opinion is desirable.

CONCLUSION

Arbitration of insurance claims has proven to be an attractive alternative to litigation. Claimants can be compensated sooner and the time and expense of processing claims can be reduced. Finally, the public's perception of justice is enhanced when the system works efficiently.

Uninsured-motorist arbitration has been in operation for more than twenty years and no-fault arbitration has become an established part of the claim system in many jurisdictions. As other states begin to modernize their systems for compensating injured persons, they should take advantage of the impartial services of the AAA.

In addition, as exemplified by the ADR program, new procedures are being continuously tested to provide claimants with the best possible systems for resolving their insurance disputes.

ACCIDENT CLAIMS ARBITRATION RULES
(INCLUDING MEDIATION)

As Amended and in Effect on January 1, 1990

1. Agreement of Parties—The parties make these rules a part of their arbitration agreement whenever a policy of insurance or applicable insurance-department regulation provides for arbitration by the American Arbitration Association (AAA) in connection with a dispute involving a motor-vehicle liability claim. These rules and any amendment of them shall apply in the form obtaining at the time the arbitration is initiated, except for any such provision that may be inconsistent with the arbitration agreement or with applicable law.

2. Administrator and Delegation of Duties—When parties agree to arbitrate under these rules, or when they provide for arbitration by the AAA and an arbitration is initiated under these rules, they thereby authorize the AAA to administer the arbitration. The duties of the AAA under these rules may be carried out through such representatives as the AAA may direct.

3. Panel of Arbitrators—The AAA shall establish and maintain an Accident Claims Panel of arbitrators made up of attorneys with negligence experience. Each of the AAA's regional offices will maintain an Advisory Committee, made up of equal numbers of at least three members of the defense bar and/or the insurance industry and three members of the plaintiff's bar, which will approve the qualifications of the members of that panel. Each committee shall meet at least once a year.

4. Initiation under an Arbitration Provision in a Policy—When the conditions precedent contained in the insurance policy or state insurance-department regulations have been complied with, arbitration shall be initiated by filing a written Demand for Arbitration. The demand shall be served by US certified mail–return receipt requested. When filed by an insured, it shall be directed to the claims office of the insurer under whose policy arbitration is sought, at the office where the claim has been discussed, or at the office of the insurer closest to the residence of the insured. The demand shall set forth the following information: (1) the name, address, and telephone number of the insured person(s) and the filing attorney; (2) the name, address, and policy number of the policyholder; (3) the identity and location of the claims office of the insurer, if known; the claim's file number, if known; and the name of the individual with whom the claim was discussed; (4) the date and location of the accident; (5) nature of dispute and injuries alleged; (6) amount of uninsured-motorist policy limits and the amount claimed thereunder; and (7) address of the AAA regional office at which copies of the demand are being filed.

Three copies of the demand must be filed with an AAA regional office at the same time, with a copy of the parts of the policy or regulations relating to the dispute, including the arbitration provisions, together with the administrative filing fee.

The AAA will acknowledge receipt of the demand to all parties. If, within thirty calendar days after acknowledgment of the demand by the AAA, the insurer moves in court to contest coverage, applicable policy limits, or the stacking of policy coverage, administration will be suspended until such issues are decided.

Issues as to coverage, applicable policy limits, or stacking of policy coverage may be referred to voluntary coverage arbitration with the agreement of all parties before an arbitrator appointed by the AAA from a panel designated to hear such issues. These issues will be submitted to the arbitrator on documents only, unless the parties agree otherwise or the arbitrator determines that an oral hearing is necessary. In the absence of an agreement to submit such issues to arbitration, accident claims arbitrators may only decide contested issues of coverage, applicable policy limits, or stacking of policy coverage where ordered to do so by a court or where so authorized by law.

Unless there is (1) an agreement to submit such issues to voluntary coverage arbitration, (2) a motion to contest coverage, applicable policy limits, or the stacking of policy coverage made within thirty calendar days after acknowledgment of the demand by the AAA, or (3) a court order staying arbitration, the AAA will proceed with the administration of the case.

5. Change of Claim—If any party desires to make any new or different claim, same shall be made in writing and filed with the AAA and a copy thereof mailed to the other party. After the arbitrator is appointed, no new or different claim may be submitted except with the arbitrator's consent.

6. Initiation under a Submission—Parties to any existing dispute may commence an arbitration under these rules by filing at any regional office of the AAA three copies of a written submission to arbitrate under these rules, setting forth the information specified in Section 4.

7. Fixing of Locale—Either the county of residence of the insured or the county where the accident occurred may be designated by the insured as the locale in which the hearing is to be held. Only if all parties agree shall the hearing be held in some other locale.

8. Designation of Arbitrator—Unless applicable law or the agreement of the parties provides otherwise, the dispute shall be determined by one arbitrator, except as otherwise provided in this section. The AAA will submit a list of nine members of the Accident Claims Panel from which each party shall have the right to strike up to two names on a peremptory basis, within twenty days of the AAA's submission of the list. The AAA will appoint the arbitrator from among the remaining names.

Where the amount claimed and available coverage limits exceed minimum statutory financial-responsibility limits, upon the request of a party made within thirty calendar days after acknowledgment of the demand by the AAA, the dispute shall be determined by three arbitrators. The AAA will submit a list of thirteen names from the Accident Claims Panel, allowing each party to strike up to three names on a peremptory basis, within twenty days of the AAA's submission of the list. The AAA will appoint three arbitrators from among the remaining names.

9. Qualifications of Arbitrator—No person shall serve as an arbitrator in any arbitration in which that person has any financial or personal interest. An arbitrator shall disclose any circumstances likely to create a presumption of bias which might disqualify that arbitrator as an impartial arbitrator. Any party shall have the right to challenge the appointment of an arbitrator for reasonable cause. The AAA shall determine whether the arbitrator should be disqualified, and shall inform the parties of its decision, which shall be conclusive.

If for any reason an appointed arbitrator should be unable to perform the duties of the office, the AAA shall appoint a replacement from among those names remaining on the list(s) submitted to the parties. If an appointment cannot be made from the list(s), the AAA shall appoint a replacement in accordance with the provisions of Section 8.

10. Time and Place—The arbitrator shall fix the time and place for each hearing. The AAA shall mail to each party notice thereof at least twenty calendar days in advance, unless the parties by mutual agreement waive such notice or modify the terms thereof.

11. Representation—Any party may be represented by counsel or other authorized representative. A party intending to be so represented shall notify the other party and the AAA of the name and address of such representative at least three days prior to the date set for the hearing at which the representative is first to appear. When an arbitration is initiated by counsel or when an attorney replies for the other party, such notice is deemed to have been given.

12. Stenographic Record—Any party wishing a stenographic record shall make arrangements directly with a stenographer and shall notify the other party of such arrangements in advance of the hearing. The requesting party or parties shall pay the cost of the record. If such transcript is agreed by the parties to be, or determined by the arbitrator to be, the official record of the proceeding, it must be made available to the arbitrator and to the other party for inspection, at a time and place determined by the arbitrator.

13. Interpreters—Any party wishing an interpreter shall make all arrangements directly with the interpreter and shall assume the costs of such service.

14. Attendance at Hearings—The arbitrator shall maintain the privacy of the hearings unless the law provides to the contrary. Any person having a direct interest in the arbitration is entitled to attend hearings. The arbitrator shall otherwise have the power to require the exclusion of any witness, other than a party or other essential person, during the testimony of any other witness. It shall be discretionary with the arbitrator to determine the propriety of the attendance of any other person.

15. Postponements—The arbitrator may, for good cause, postpone the hearing upon the request of a party or upon the arbitrator's own initiative, and shall grant such postponement when all of the parties agree thereto.

16. Oaths—Before proceeding with the first hearing, each arbitrator may take an oath of office and, if required by law, shall do so. The arbitrator may require witnesses to testify under oath administered by any duly qualified person and, if required by law or requested by either party, shall do so.

17. Arbitration in the Absence of a Party or Counsel—Unless the law provides to the contrary, the arbitration may proceed in the absence of any party or counsel who, after due notice, fails to be present or fails to obtain an adjournment. An award shall not be made solely on the default of a party. The arbitrator shall require the party who is present to submit such evidence as is deemed necessary for the making of an award.

18. Order of Proceedings—A hearing shall be opened by the filing of the oath of the arbitrator, where required; by the recording of the place, time, and date of the hearing and the presence of the arbitrator, the parties, and counsel, if any; and by the receipt by the arbitrator of the statement of the claim and answer, if any. The arbitrator may, at the beginning of the hearing, ask for statements clarifying the issues involved. The claimant shall then present its claims, proofs, and witnesses, who shall submit to questions or other examination. The respondent shall then present its defenses, proofs, and witnesses, who shall submit to questions or other examination. The arbitrator has discretion to vary this procedure but shall afford full and equal opportunity to the parties for the presentation of any material or relevant proofs.

Exhibits, when offered by either party, may be received in evidence by the arbitrator.

The names and addresses of all witnesses and exhibits in the order received shall be made a part of the record.

The parties may, by written agreement, provide for the waiver of oral hearings. If the parties are unable to agree as to the procedure, the AAA shall specify a fair and equitable procedure.

19. Evidence—The parties may offer such evidence as is relevant and material to the dispute and shall produce such additional evidence as the arbitrator may deem necessary to an understanding and determination of the dispute. An arbitrator authorized by law to subpoena witnesses or documents may do so upon the request of any party or independently.

The arbitrator shall be the judge of the relevance and materiality of the evidence offered, and conformity to legal rules of evidence shall not be necessary. All evidence shall be taken in the presence of all of the arbitrators and all of the parties, except where any of the parties is absent in default or waives the right to be present.

Any party intending to offer any medical report or record at the hearing must provide the other party with a copy at least twenty days in advance thereof.

20. Evidence by Affidavit and Post-hearing Filing of Documents—The arbitrator may receive and consider the evidence of witnesses by affidavit, but shall give it only such weight as the arbitrator deems it entitled to after consideration of any objection made to its admission.

If the parties agree or the arbitrator directs that documents are to be submitted to the arbitrator after the hearing, they shall be filed with the AAA for transmission to the arbitrator. All parties shall be afforded an opportunity to examine such documents.

21. Majority Decision—Whenever there is more than one arbitrator, all decisions of the arbitrators must be by at least a majority. The award must also be made by at least a majority unless the concurrence of all is expressly required by the arbitration agreement or by law.

22. Closing of Hearing—The arbitrator shall specifically inquire of all parties whether they have any further proofs to offer or witnesses to be heard. Upon receiving negative replies, or if satisfied that the record is complete, the arbitrator shall declare the hearing closed and a minute thereof shall be recorded. If briefs are to be filed, the hearing shall be declared closed as of the final date set by the arbitrator for the receipt of briefs. If documents are to be filed as provided for in Section 20 and the date set for their receipt is later than that set for the receipt of briefs, the later date shall be the date of closing the hearing. The time limit within which the arbitrator is required to make the award shall commence to run, in the absence of other agreements by the parties, upon the closing of the hearing.

23. Reopening of Hearing—The hearing may be reopened by the arbitrator at will or upon application of a party at any time before the award is made. If reopening the hearing would prevent the making of the award within the specific time agreed upon by the parties in the contract out of which the controversy has arisen, the matter may not be reopened, unless the parties agree upon an extension of time. When no specific date is fixed in the contract, the arbitrator may reopen the hearing, and the arbitrator shall have thirty days from the closing of the reopened hearing within which to make an award.

24. Waiver of Rules—Any party who proceeds with the arbitration after knowledge that any provision or requirement of these rules has not been complied with and who fails to state objection thereto in writing shall be deemed to have waived the right to object.

25. Extensions of Time—The parties may modify any period of time by mutual agreement. The AAA may for good cause extend any period of time established by these rules except the time for making the award. The AAA shall notify the parties of any such extension and its reason therefor.

26. Serving of Notice—(a) With the exception of the demand, which shall be served by US certified mail–return receipt requested, each party shall be deemed to have consented that any papers, notices, or process necessary or proper for the initiation or continuation of an arbitration under these rules; for any court action in connection therewith; or for the entry of judgment on any award made under these rules may be served upon such party by mail addressed to such party or its attorney at the last known address or by personal service, in or outside the state where the arbitration is to be held, provided that reasonable opportunity to be heard with regard thereto has been granted to such party.

(b) To facilitate communication between the parties and the AAA, the parties agree that communications received from each other or the AAA via facsimile machine, telex, telegram, or other written forms of electronic communication are valid and proper notice under these rules.

27. Communication with Arbitrator—There shall be no direct communication between the parties and an arbitrator other than at oral hearings. Any other oral or written communication from the parties to an arbitrator shall be directed to the AAA for transmission to the arbitrator.

28. Time of Award—The arbitrator shall render the award promptly and, unless otherwise agreed by the parties or specified by law, no later than thirty days from the date of closing the hearing, or, if oral hearings have been waived, from the date of transmitting the final statements and proofs to the arbitrator.

29. Form of Award—The award shall be in writing and shall be signed either by the sole arbitrator or by at least a majority if there is more than one arbitrator. It shall be executed in the manner required by law.

30. Scope of Award—The arbitrator shall render a decision determining whether the insured person has a right to receive any damages under the policy and the amount thereof, not in excess of the applicable policy limits. The award shall not contain a determination as to issues of coverage except as provided in Section 4 above.

31. Award upon Settlement—If the parties settle their dispute during the course of the arbitration, the arbitrator may, upon their request, set forth the terms of the agreed settlement in an award.

32. Delivery of Award to Parties—Parties shall accept as legal delivery of the award the placing of the award or a true copy thereof in the mail addressed to such party or its attorney at the last known address, personal service of the award, or the filing of the award in any other manner that may be permitted by law.

33. Expenses—The expenses of witnesses for either side shall be paid by the party producing such witnesses. All other expenses of the arbitration, including required traveling and other expenses of the arbitrator and of AAA representatives, and the expenses of any witness and the cost of any proof produced at the direct request of the arbitrator, shall be borne equally by the parties, unless they agree otherwise or unless the arbitrator in the award assesses such expenses or any part thereof against any specified party or parties.

34. Applications to Court and Exclusion of Liability—(a) No judicial proceeding by a party relating to the subject matter of the arbitration or mediation shall be deemed a waiver of the party's right to arbitrate.

(b) Neither the AAA nor any arbitrator or mediator in a proceeding under these rules is a necessary party in judicial proceedings relating to the arbitration or mediation.

(c) Parties to these rules shall be deemed to have consented that judgment upon the arbitration award may be entered in any federal or state court having jurisdiction thereof.

(d) Neither the AAA nor any arbitrator or mediator shall be liable to any party for any act or omission in connection with any arbitration or mediation conducted under these rules.

35. Release of Documents for Judicial Proceedings—The AAA shall, upon the written request of a party, furnish to such party, at its expense, certified copies of any papers in the AAA's possession that may be required in judicial proceedings relating to the arbitration.

36. Interpretation and Application of Rules—The arbitrator shall interpret and apply these rules insofar as they relate to the arbitrator's powers and duties. When there is more than one arbitrator and a difference arises among them concerning the meaning or application of these rules, it shall be decided by a majority vote. If that is unobtainable, either an arbitrator or a party may refer the question to the AAA for final decision. All other rules shall be interpreted and applied by the AAA.

AMERICAN ARBITRATION ASSOCIATION RULES FOR NEW YORK STATE NO-FAULT ARBITRATION

Effective for Requests Filed with the New York State Insurance Department on and after July 1st, 1988, for Disputes Involving First-Party Benefits Arising out of Accidents Occurring on and after December 1st, 1977, and Disputes Involving Additional First-Party Benefits Arising out of Accidents Occurring on and after January 1st, 1982. Adopted Pursuant to Regulations Promulgated by the New York State Superintendent of Insurance as Amended on November 12th, 1991

1. American Arbitration Association Arbitrations—All disputes involving issues other than those to be resolved by Insurance Department Arbitration (IDA) or conciliation shall be forwarded to the American Arbitration Association (AAA), which shall be the forum for their resolution. Where a request for arbitration involves issues which fall within the jurisdiction of both of the fora, the dispute shall be resolved by an AAA arbitration except those disputes involving the correct computation of health service provider fees, whether or not such fees are specifically covered by the fee schedules promulgated in 11 NYCRR 68 (Regulation 83).

2. Notice—Upon receipt of the request for arbitration from the Insurance Department, the AAA shall send to the insurer written notice that arbitration has been requested.

3. Consolidation—The AAA shall, except where impracticable, consolidate disputes for which a request for arbitration has been received, if the claims involved arose out of the same accident and involve common issues of fact.

4. Qualifications of Arbitrators for a Hearing Held in New York State—(a) *The No-Fault Arbitrator Screening Committee* The superintendent shall appoint an advisory committee composed of six members who will review the qualifications of applicants for the position of no-fault arbitrator for hearings to be held in New York State and review the performance of the appointed arbitrators. The screening committee shall make recommendations to the superintendent pertaining to the appointment and dismissal of no-fault arbitrators. The committee shall consist of one representative of the New York State Bar Association, one representative of the New York State Trial Lawyer's Association, two representatives of the insurance industry selected by the No-Fault Optional Arbitration Advisory Committee, a nonvoting AAA representative, and a nonvoting representative of the Insurance Department. Tie votes shall be reported as such to the superintendent.

(b) An arbitrator shall be an attorney, licensed to practice law in New York State, who has at least ten years' experience which the No-Fault Arbitrator Screening Committee has determined qualifies such attorney to review and resolve the issues involved in no-fault insurance disputes. Documentation of such experience shall be submitted to and reviewed by the superintendent prior to the appointment of an arbitrator.

(c) All arbitrators shall be appointed by and serve at the pleasure of the superintendent. An arbitrator candidate shall disclose to the superintendent any circumstance which is likely to create an appearance of bias or which might disqualify such person as an arbitrator and the superintendent shall determine whether the candidate should be disqualified. The superintendent shall forward the names of all arbitrators to the AAA and promptly inform the AAA of all additions to and deletions from the panel.

(d) No person shall during the period of appointment as an arbitrator have any practice or professional connection with any firm or insurer involved in any degree with automobile insurance or negligence law. The No-Fault Arbitrator Screening Committee, subject to the approval of the superintendent, shall establish any additional qualifications for appointment as a no-fault arbitrator.

(e) Arbitrators shall contract on an annual basis with the AAA. The rate of annual compensation shall be determined by the AAA after consultation with the No-Fault Arbitrator Screening Committee. Arbitrators shall be independent contractors and shall not be employees or agents of the AAA.

5. Qualifications of Arbitrators for a Hearing Held outside New York—For a hearing which will be held outside New York State, the arbitrator shall be a licensed attorney in the state or Canadian province where the hearing is held.

6. Appointment of the Arbitrator—The AAA shall select an arbitrator who will hear the case, and shall submit the name of the arbitrator to each party to the arbitration. The AAA shall maintain a file containing the professional background of each of its no-fault arbitrators and the information contained therein shall be available to any party to the arbitration upon written or oral request.

No person shall serve as an arbitrator in any arbitration in which such person has any financial or personal interest or bias. If a party challenges an arbitrator, the specific grounds for the challenge shall be submitted in writing to the AAA, which shall determine within fifteen calendar days after receipt of the challenge whether the arbitrator shall be disqualified. Such determination shall be final and binding. If an arbitrator should resign, be disqualified, or be otherwise unable to perform the duties of the office, the AAA shall appoint another arbitrator to the case.

7. **Oaths**—Arbitrators shall take an annual oath of office. Arbitrators shall require all witnesses to testify under oath or affirm that their statements are true under the penalties of perjury.

8. **Time and Place of Arbitration**—The arbitration hearing shall be held in the arbitrator's office or any other appropriate place selected by the AAA and, to the extent practicable, within the general locale of the applicant's residence but, in no event, more than a hundred miles from such residence. The arbitrator shall fix the time and place for such hearing. At least fifteen calendar days prior to the hearing, the AAA shall mail a Notice of Hearing to each party. Unless otherwise agreed by the parties, the hearing shall be scheduled to be held within thirty calendar days of the date of the appointment of the arbitrator. The parties to the arbitration shall not directly contact the arbitrator at any time prior to or subsequent to the hearing, but may submit to the AAA material intended for the arbitrator.

9. **Postponements and Adjournments**—The AAA or the arbitrator may for good cause postpone or adjourn the hearing upon request of a party or upon the arbitrator's own initiative. Each party may cause one adjournment without the payment of an adjournment fee if the adjournment request is received by the AAA at least two business days prior to the scheduled arbitration. There shall be an adjournment fee of $50 payable to the AAA by the party requesting any subsequent adjournment. An adjournment fee of $100 shall be payable to the AAA by the party causing any adjournment within two business days prior to the scheduled hearing. Such fees shall be used to defray the cost of administration of the AAA forum.

10. **Representation at Arbitration**—Any party may be represented by an attorney.

11. **Records of Proceedings**—A stenographic record of the arbitration proceedings shall not be required. However, a party requesting such a record shall inform the other party or parties of such intent, make the necessary arrangements, and pay the cost thereof directly to the person or agency making such record. Any other party to the arbitration shall be entitled to a copy of such record upon agreeing to share the cost of the total stenographic expense. Whether or not a stenographic record of the proceeding is made, the arbitrator shall, at a minimum, record the names and addresses of all parties and witnesses and the exhibits offered by each party.

12. **Interpreters**—Any party wishing an interpreter shall make all arrangements directly with the interpreter and shall assume the costs of such services.

13. **Attendance at Hearings**—Persons having a direct interest in the arbitration are entitled to attend hearings. It shall be discretionary with the arbitrator to determine the propriety of the attendance of any other person.

14. **Evidence**—(a) The arbitrator shall be the judge of the relevance and materiality of the evidence offered and strict conformity to legal rules of evidence shall not be necessary.

(b) The arbitrator or an attorney of record in the arbitration may subpoena witnesses or documents upon the arbitrator's own initiative or upon the request of any party, when the issues to be resolved require such witnesses or documents.

(c) All documents to be submitted to the arbitrator shall be simultaneously transmitted to the other parties at least seven calendar days prior to the hearing. The arbitrator shall determine whether all parties received such documents prior to the commencement of the hearing.

(d) If a party to the arbitration intends to introduce an expert witness at the hearing, the identity of the expert witness must be given to all parties at least seven calendar days prior to the hearing.

15. Arbitration in the Absence of a Party—The arbitration may proceed in the absence of any party, who, after due notice, fails to be present or fails to obtain a postponement or adjournment. An award shall not be made in favor of an appearing party solely on the default of another party. The arbitrator shall require the appearing party to submit such evidence as may be required for the making of an award. The arbitrator may require the appearance of a party at the hearing if the arbitrator determines that the party's appearance is necessary to realize a fair and just resolution of the dispute and to afford all parties due process.

16. Independent Health Consultants—(a) The AAA shall maintain a list of independent health consultants who will review medical evidence or examine the injured person upon the request of an IDA arbitrator or an AAA arbitrator.

(b) The independent health consultant shall be selected by the AAA from its list and, to the extent practicable, shall be a specialist in the field requested by the arbitrator. If a medical examination is requested by the arbitrator, it shall be conducted at the health consultant's office, which shall be located in the general locale of the applicant's residence, or at a place agreed by the parties and the consultant.

(c) Within fifteen calendar days after the review of medical evidence or examination of the eligible injured person, the health consultant shall submit to the AAA a written report which shall contain the consultant's advisory opinion for consideration by the arbitrator. The AAA shall submit such report to the arbitrator and the parties.(d) The independent health consultant's fee shall include the written report and be paid by the AAA, with the cost thereof charged as an administrative expense of the AAA forum.

(e) No person shall serve as an independent health consultant in any arbitration in which such person has any financial or personal interest or bias. An independent health consultant shall disclose to the AAA any circumstance likely to create an appearance of bias or which might serve to disqualify the consultant. Upon receipt of such information, the AAA shall immediately disclose it to the parties. If a party challenges a health consultant, the specific grounds for the challenge shall be submitted in writing. The AAA shall determine whether the health consultant should be disqualified and shall inform the parties of its decision, which shall be final and binding. If a health consultant should resign, be disqualified, or be otherwise unable to perform necessary duties, the AAA shall appoint another health consultant to the case.

17. Reopening of Hearing—The hearing may be reopened by the arbitrator, for good cause, at any time before the award is made.

18. Time of the Award—The award shall be made and delivered no later than thirty calendar days from the date the hearing is completed. Failure to adhere to this time limit shall not nullify the award.

19. Form and Scope of the Award—The award shall be in writing in a format approved by the superintendent. It shall state the issues in dispute and contain the arbitrator's findings and conclusions based on the Insurance Law and Insurance Department regulations. It shall be signed by the arbitrator and shall be transmitted to the parties by the AAA with a copy to the Insurance Department. The award shall contain a decision on all issues submitted to the arbitrator by the parties. In the event that the applicant prevails in whole or in part on the claim, the arbitrator shall also direct the insurer to

(a) reimburse the applicant for the amount of the filing fee paid, unless the filing fee had already been returned to the applicant;

(b) if due under section 5106 of the Insurance Law, pay a reasonable attorney fee in accordance with the limitations set forth in Section 25 of these rules; and

(c) in an award of interest, compute the amount due for each element of first-party benefits in dispute, commencing thirty days after proof of claim therefor was received by the insurer and ending with the date of payment of the award, subject to the provisions of 11 NYCRR 65.15(h)(3) (stay of interest).

20. Awards upon Settlement—(a) If the parties settle their dispute during the course of arbitration, the arbitrator shall set forth the terms of the agreed settlement in an award that shall provide that the parties agree that the settlement is final and binding and shall not be subject to review by a master arbitrator or by a court. If an attorney fee is due under section 5106 of the Insurance Law, the fee shall be awarded in accordance with the limitations set forth in Section 25 of these rules. The award shall be signed by the arbitrator and shall be transmitted to the parties by the AAA, with a copy to the Insurance Department.

(b) The insurer shall provide the arbitrator with the terms of settlement no later than thirty calendar days following the scheduled date of the hearing.

21. Delivery of the Award to the Parties—The parties shall accept as delivery of the award the placing of the award or a true copy thereof in the mail, addressed to the parties or their designated representatives at their last known addresses or by any other form of service permitted by law. The AAA shall note on such award or transmittal letter thereof the date of mailing and keep a record.

22. Interpretation and Application of Rules—The arbitrator shall interpret and apply these rules insofar as they relate to the arbitrator's powers and duties. All other rules shall be interpreted by the AAA, subject to consultation with and approval by the superintendent.

23. Alternative Legal Remedies—The AAA shall not be made a party to a court proceeding relating to an arbitration award unless the AAA's presence as a party is pertinent to the issues raised in the litigation. The participation of a party in an arbitration proceeding shall be a waiver of any claim against an arbitrator or the AAA for any act or omission in connection with any arbitration conducted under these rules. The AAA shall transmit to the superintendent copies of any legal papers served upon the AAA or an arbitrator relating to any stay or appeal of an arbitration.

24. Payment of the Award—Insurers shall, within thirty calendar days of the date of mailing of the award, either pay the amounts set forth in the award or, where grounds exist, appeal to a master arbitrator as provided for in 11 NYCRR 65.18, which appeal shall stay payment of the award. The award need not be confirmed into judgment.

25. Limitations on Attorney Fees Pursuant to Section 5106 of the Insurance Law—The following limitations shall apply to the payment by insurers of applicants' attorney fees for services necessarily performed in the resolution of no-fault disputes.

(a) If an arbitration was initiated or a court action was commenced by an attorney on behalf of an applicant and the claim or portion thereof was not denied or overdue when the arbitration proceeding was initiated or the action was commenced, no attorney fee shall be granted.

(b) If the claim is resolved by the Insurance Department at any time prior to transmittal to an arbitration forum and it was initially denied by the insurer or overdue, the payment of the applicant's attorney fee by the insurer shall be limited as follows.

 (i) If the resolved claim was initially denied, the attorney fee shall be $60.

 (ii) If the resolved claim was overdue but not denied, the attorney fee shall not exceed the amount of first-party benefits and any additional first-party benefits, plus interest thereon, which the insurer agreed to pay and the applicant agreed to accept in full settlement of the dispute submitted, subject to a maximum fee of $60 dollars.

 (iii) In disputes solely involving interest, the attorney fee shall be equal to the amount of interest that the insurer agreed to pay and the applicant agreed to accept in full settlement of the dispute submitted, subject to a maximum fee of $60.

(c) Except as provided in paragraphs (a) and (b) of this section, the minimum attorney fee payable pursuant to these rules shall be $60.

(d) For disputes subject to AAA arbitration where one of the issues involves a policy issue as enumerated on the prescribed denial of claim form (NYS Form N-F 10), subject to the provisions of paragraphs (a) and (c) of this section, the attorney fee for the arbitration of all issues shall be limited as follows—

 (i) for preparatory services relating to the arbitration forum or a court, an attorney shall be entitled to receive a fee of up to $70 per hour, subject to a maximum fee of $1,400, and

 (ii) in addition, an attorney shall be entitled to receive a fee of up to $80 per hour for each personal appearance before the arbitration forum or a court.

(e) For all other disputes subject to AAA and IDA arbitrations, subject to the provisions of paragraphs (a) and (c) of this section, the attorney fee shall be limited as follows— twenty percent of the amount of first-party benefits, plus interest thereon, awarded by the arbitrator or a court, subject to a maximum fee of $850. If the nature of the dispute results in an attorney fee which could be computed in accordance with the limitations prescribed in both paragraphs (d) and (e) of this section, above, the higher fee shall be payable.

(f) Notwithstanding the limitations listed in this section, if the arbitrator or a court determines that the issues in dispute were of such a novel or unique nature as to require extraordinary skills or services, the arbitrator or court may award an attorney fee in excess of the limitations set forth in this section. An excess-fee award shall detail the specific novel or unique nature of the dispute that justifies the award. An excess award of an attorney fee by an arbitrator shall be appealable to a master arbitrator.

(g) If a dispute involving an overdue or denied claim is resolved by the parties after it has been forwarded by the Insurance Department to the appropriate arbitration forum or after a court action has been commenced, the claimant's attorney shall be entitled to a fee which shall be computed in accordance with the limitations set forth in this section.

(h) No attorney shall demand, request, or receive from the insurer any payment of fees not permitted by this section.*

26. Witness Fees—(a) No witness fee shall be payable to a person who is a party to the arbitration.

(b) The arbitrator shall not approve the payment of a fee to a witness appearing on behalf of an applicant or an assignee, unless the witness was subpoenaed by the arbitrator or, prior to appearance, the witness' presence was determined by the arbitrator to be necessary for the resolution of the dispute.

(c) Whenever a witness fee is determined by the arbitrator to be payable, the cost thereof shall be charged as an administrative expense of the AAA forum.

(d) Any witness fee awarded pursuant to paragraphs (b) and (c) of this section shall be determined as follows.

  (i) If the witness is testifying as an expert, the fee shall be calculated on the basis of such witness' documented usual and customary hourly charge for an appearance, plus necessary verified disbursements.

  (ii) Any other witness shall only be entitled to reimbursement for verified expenses and economic losses necessarily incurred in connection with an appearance before the arbitrator.

27. Financing—The cost of administering the AAA arbitration forum shall be paid annually by insurers to the AAA upon receipt of a statement therefrom. This cost shall be distributed among insurers in an equitable manner approved by the Superintendent of Insurance. This distribution shall, to the extent practicable, be a function of the degree to which an insurer is named as a respondent in AAA arbitration proceedings.

28. The No-Fault Optional Arbitration Advisory Committee—The superintendent shall select an advisory committee composed of twelve members to review the operations and the actual costs of all arbitration forums set forth in the regulations implementing the no-fault law. Not more than four of the members of the advisory committee shall be representatives of self insurers.

---

* Attorneys should be aware of the appellate-division rules prohibiting contingent fees in connection with the collection of first-party no-fault benefits. See 22 NYCRR 603.7(e)(7), 691.20(e)(7), and 806.12(f).

AMERICAN ARBITRATION ASSOCIATION PROCEDURES FOR NEW YORK STATE MASTER ARBITRATION

Effective for Requests Filed with the New York State Insurance Department on and after July 1, 1988, for Disputes Involving First-Party Benefits Arising out of Accidents Occurring on and after December 1, 1977, and Disputes Involving Additional First-Party Benefits Arising out of Accidents Occurring on and after January 1, 1982. Adopted Pursuant to Regulations Promulgated by the New York State Superintendent of Insurance As Amended on August 14, 1991.

(a) Grounds for Review—An award by an arbitrator rendered pursuant to section 5106(b) of the Insurance Law and 11 NYCRR 65.16 and 65.17 (Regulation No. 68) may be vacated or modified solely by appeal to a master arbitrator and only upon one or more of the following grounds:

(1) any ground for vacating or modifying an award enumerated in Article 75 of the Civil Practice Law and Rules (an Article 75 proceeding), except the ground enumerated in CPLR section 7511(b)(1)(iv) (failure to follow Article 75 procedure);

(2) that the award required the insurer to pay amounts in excess of the policy limitations for any element of first-party benefits; provided that, as a condition precedent to review by a master arbitrator, the insurer shall pay all other amounts set forth in the award which will not be subjects of the appeal, as provided for in sections 65.16 or 65.17;

(3) that the award required the insurer to pay amounts in excess of the policy limitations for any element of additional first-party benefits (when the parties had agreed to arbitrate the dispute under the additional personal injury protection endorsement for an accident which occurred prior to January 1, 1982), provided that, as a condition precedent to review by a master arbitrator, the insurer shall pay all other amounts set forth in the award which will not be subjects of the appeal, as provided for in 11 NYCRR 65.16 or 65.17;

(4) that an award rendered in an AAA expedited arbitration under 11 NYCRR 65.16(c)(3)(i), a regular AAA arbitration under 11 NYCRR 65.16(c)(3)(iv), or an arbitration under 11 NYCRR 65.17 was incorrect as a matter of law (procedural or factual errors committed in the arbitration below are not encompassed within this ground);

(5) that the attorney fee awarded by an arbitrator below was not rendered in accordance with the limitations prescribed in 11 NYCRR 65.16(c)(8) or 65.17(b)(6), provided that, as a condition precedent to review by a master arbitrator, the insurer shall pay all other amounts set forth in the award which will not be subjects of the appeal, as provided for in 11 NYCRR 65.16 or 65.17;

(6) that the award rendered in the AAA arbitration is inconsistent and irreconcilable with the award rendered in the HSA arbitration involving the same personal injury.

(b) Qualifications of Master Arbitrators—(1) A master arbitrator shall be an attorney licensed to practice law in New York State who has at least fifteen years' experience which the superintendent has determined qualifies such attorney to review and resolve the issues involved in no-fault insurance disputes. Documentation of such experience shall be submitted to and reviewed by the superintendent prior to appointment of a master arbitrator.

(2) All master arbitrators shall be appointed by and serve at the pleasure of the superintendent. A master arbitrator candidate shall disclose to the superintendent any circumstance which is likely to create an appearance of bias or which might disqualify such per-

son as a master arbitrator, and the superintendent shall determine whether the candidate should be disqualified. The superintendent shall forward the names of all master arbitrators to the American Arbitration Association and promptly inform it of all additions to and deletions from the panel.

(3) No person shall, during the period of appointment as a master arbitrator, also serve as an arbitrator under the optional arbitration systems prescribed in section 5106(b) of the Insurance Law and 11 NYCRR 65.7, 65.16, and 65.17 or serve as an attorney to a party to any such arbitration.

(4) All master arbitrators shall take an oath of office.

(5) No person shall serve as a master arbitrator in any master arbitration in which such person has any financial or personal interest or bias. If a party challenges a master arbitrator, the specific grounds for the challenge shall be submitted in writing to the AAA, which, in consultation with the superintendent, shall determine within fifteen calendar days after receipt of the challenge whether the master arbitrator should be disqualified. Such determination shall be final and binding. If a master arbitrator should resign, be disqualified, or be otherwise unable to perform necessary duties of the office, the AAA shall assign another master arbitrator to the case within seven calendar days after receipt of notice thereof.

(c) **Scope of Master Arbitration Review**—(1) Review by a master arbitrator shall be based solely on submitted documents, including any record made of the arbitration below, unless a master arbitrator requires oral argument on specified issues.

(2) Legal briefs shall not be submitted unless requested by the master arbitrator.

(3) The master arbitrator shall initially consider and determine whether the facts alleged in the submitted documents set forth a ground for review pursuant to subdivision (a) of this section, and whether the request for arbitration was made in accordance with subdivision (d)(1) and (2) of this section.

(4) If the master arbitrator determines that either subdivision (a) or subdivision (d)(1) or (2) of this section has not been complied with, the master arbitrator shall, in lieu of rendering an award, deny the request for review. The procedural requirements contained in this section applicable to a master award shall also be applicable to a denial of request for review but such denial shall not form the basis of an action *de novo*, within the meaning of section 5106(b) of the Insurance Law.

(5) If the master arbitrator determines that subdivisions (a) and (d)(1) and (2) of this section have been complied with, the master arbitrator shall proceed to review the matter and render an award accordingly.

(6) The master arbitrator shall only consider those matters which were the subject of the arbitration below or which were included in the arbitration award appealed from.

(d) **Procedure for Review**—(1) If grounds exist, pursuant to subdivision (a) of this section, any party to an arbitration may request that the arbitration award be vacated or modified by a master arbitrator.

(2) The request for review by a master arbitrator shall be in writing and shall be mailed or delivered to the American Arbitration Association office which processed the lower arbitration or, in other cases, the AAA office covering the region in which the applicant resides:

    (i) within fifteen calendar days of the mailing of an award rendered in an AAA expedited arbitration, or

(ii)   within 21 calendar days of the mailing of any other appealable award.

The request shall include a copy of the award in issue and shall state the nature of the dispute and the grounds for review. A request by an applicant for benefits shall be accompanied by a filing fee of $75, payable by check or money order to the American Arbitration Association. Upon the filing of a demand for arbitration by an applicant, the AAA shall bill the respondent insurer the sum of $250, which shall be payable by the insurer within thirty days after billing. A request by an insurer shall be accompanied by a filing fee of $325, payable by check or money order to the American Arbitration Association.

(3) The applicant for master arbitration shall send, by certified mail, a copy of the filing papers to the opposing party at the same time that it submits the request for review to the AAA.

(4) Within seven calendar days of receipt of the request, the AAA shall assign a master arbitrator, selected in sequence from a panel of master arbitrators appointed by the superintendent and shall forward to the master arbitrator a copy of the request for review.

(5) The master arbitrator shall render an award no later than ninety calendar days after assignment.

(i)   *Submission of Materials*   Within fifteen calendar days after assignment, the master arbitrator shall set a date (which date shall not be more than 45 calendar days after assignment) by which all evidence, documents and briefs, if any, must be submitted to the master arbitrator by the parties. The master arbitrator shall give the parties thirty calendar days' written notice of this date.

(ii)   *Oral Argument*   If, after receipt of these materials, the master arbitrator determines that oral argument on specific issues is necessary, the master arbitrator shall give the parties ten calendar days' notice of the place, time, and date for oral argument and the issues to be argued. Oral argument shall be conducted at the office of the master arbitrator, at the office of the American Arbitration Association, or at a location agreeable to the parties and the master arbitrator.

(iii) The master arbitrator may postpone or adjourn the date for submission of materials or of oral argument to a date within the ninety-day period for good cause shown. A postponement or adjournment shall also be granted when all the parties agree thereto. The postponement or adjournment shall not extend the ninety-day period for rendering of an award.

(6) The failure of a master arbitrator to adhere to the procedural time frames, contained in paragraph (5) of this subdivision, shall not affect the validity of an award.

(7) Any party may be represented in a master arbitration by an attorney.

(8) A master arbitration shall proceed if any party, after due notice of the date to submit materials or the date of oral argument, fails to appear, to submit materials, or to obtain a postponement or adjournment. However, an award shall not be made in favor of an appearing party solely on the default of another party. A master arbitrator shall direct the appearing party to submit such materials as may be required in order to render a decision in the matter.

(e) Awards by Master Arbitrators—(1) *Form and Scope of Awards*

(i)   The award shall be in writing in a format approved by the superintendent. It shall state the issues in dispute and contain the master arbitrator's findings and conclusions based on the materials submitted. It shall be signed by the master and shall be transmitted to the parties by the AAA with a copy to the Insurance Department. The award shall be determinative of all issues submitted to the master arbitrator by the parties.

(ii) If the applicant for benefits prevails in whole or in part on the claim, the award shall also direct the insurer to:

(a) if the applicant requested review by a master arbitrator, pay to the applicant reimbursement of the amount of the master arbitration filing fee paid;

(b) reimburse the applicant for the filing fee originally paid to the Insurance Department for the arbitration below, unless the filing fee had already been returned to the applicant pursuant to an earlier award;

(c) if due under section 5106 of the Insurance Law, pay a reasonable attorney fee in accordance with the limitations set forth in subdivision (k) of this section;

(d) if due, compute and pay the amount of interest for each element of first-party benefits in dispute, commencing thirty days after proof of claim therefor was received by the insurer and ending with the date of payment of the award, subject to the provisions of 11 NYCRR 65.15(h)(3) (stay of interest).

(2) *Awards upon Settlement*   If the parties settle their dispute during the course of the master arbitration, the master arbitrator shall set forth the terms of the agreed settlement in an award which shall provide that the parties agree that the settlement is final and binding and shall not be subject to review by a court or the subject of a *de novo* court action. The award shall be signed by the master arbitrator and shall be transmitted to the parties by the AAA with a copy to the Insurance Department.

(3) *Delivery of Awards to Parties*   The parties shall accept as delivery of the award the placing of the award or a true copy thereof in the mail, addressed to the parties or their designated representatives at their last known addresses, or by any other form of service permitted by law. The AAA shall note on such award or transmittal letter thereof the date of mailing and keep a record of same.

(4) *Payment of Awards*   Subject to subdivision (i) below, the insurer shall, within 21 calendar days of the date of mailing of the award, pay the amounts set forth in the award. The award need not be confirmed into judgment.

(f) Adjustment of Fees—(1) If the master arbitrator's award reverses in whole an AAA arbitration or AAA expedited arbitration award which was adverse to an insurer, the AAA shall reimburse the insurer its filing fee paid by the applicant insurer in the arbitration below. The reimbursement shall, in accordance with 1 NYCRR 65.16(c)(7)(xxiii)(a) and (b), be charged to the cost of administering the AAA arbitration fora below.

(2) If the master arbitrator's award reverses in whole an AAA arbitration or AAA expedited arbitration award which was adverse to the applicant, the AAA shall bill the insurer the filing fee refunded below pursuant to 11 NYCRR 65.16(c)(7)(xxiii)(a) and (b). Such payments shall reduce the cost of administering the AAA arbitration fora below.

(g) Interpretation and Application of Procedures—The master arbitrator shall interpret and apply the procedures of this section insofar as they relate to the master arbitrator's powers and duties. All other procedures shall be administered by the AAA, subject to consultation with and approval by the superintendent.

(h) Alternative Legal Remedies—The AAA or the master arbitrator shall transmit to the superintendent copies of any legal papers served upon the AAA or the master arbitrator relating to any stay or appeal of a master arbitration.

(i) Appeals from Master Arbitrators' Awards—(1) A decision of a master arbitrator is final and binding except for:

(i)   court review pursuant to an Article 75 proceeding; or

(ii) if the award of the master arbitrator is $5,000 or greater, exclusive of interest and attorney fees, either party may, in lieu of an Article 75 proceeding, institute a court action to adjudicate the dispute *de novo.*

(2) A party who intends to commence an Article 75 proceeding or an action to adjudicate a dispute *de novo* shall follow the applicable procedures as set forth in CPLR Article 75. If the party initiating such action is an insurer, payment of all amounts set forth in the master arbitration award which will not be subjects of judicial action or review shall be made prior to the commencement of such action.

(j) Master Arbitrators' Fees—The master arbitrator shall be compensated in the amount of $250 for each case. Such fee will be paid by the AAA. The master arbitrator's fee shall be charged to the cost of administering the master arbitration system.

(k) Limitations on Attorney Fees Pursuant to Section 5106 of the Insurance Law—The following limitations shall apply to the payment by insurers of applicants' attorney fees for services rendered in a master arbitration to resolve a no-fault dispute.

(1) The minimum attorney fee payable pursuant to this section shall be $60.

(2) (i)   For preparatory services necessarily rendered, the attorney shall be entitled to receive a fee of up to $65 per hour, subject to a maximum fee of $650.

(ii) An attorney shall be entitled to receive a fee of up to $80 per hour for oral argument before the master arbitrator, made pursuant to subdivision (c)(1).

(iii) If an applicant is successful in obtaining a reversal of the arbitration(s) below, wherein no attorney fee was awarded, the attorney in the arbitration below shall also be entitled to receive a fee, computed in accordance with the provisions of 11 NYCRR 65.16(c)(8) or 65.17(b)(6), which shall be payable in the manner provided in 11 NYCRR 65.16 or 65.17.

(3) Notwithstanding the above limitations, if the master arbitrator determines that the issues in dispute were of such a novel or unique nature as to require extraordinary skills or services, the master arbitrator may award an attorney fee in excess of the limitations set forth above. An excess fee award shall detail the specific novel or unique nature of the dispute which justifies the award.

(4) The attorney fee for services rendered in connection with a court adjudication of a dispute *de novo*, as provided in section 5106(c) of the Insurance Law, or in a court appeal from a master arbitration award and any further appeals shall be fixed by the court adjudicating the matter.

(5) No attorney shall demand, request, or receive from the insurer any payment or fee in excess of the fees permitted by this subdivision for services rendered with respect to a no-fault master arbitration dispute.

DISPUTE RESOLUTION PROCEDURES FOR INSURANCE CLAIMS

As Amended and in Effect on January 1, 1989

1. Agreement of Parties—These dispute resolution procedures shall apply whenever the parties have agreed to use them. By mutual agreement, in writing, the parties may modify any provision.

2. Initiation of Dispute Resolution Procedures—Where there is no submission or contract providing for dispute resolution, a party may request the AAA to invite other parties to join in a submission to dispute resolution. Upon receipt of such a request, the AAA will contact the other parties involved in the dispute and attempt to obtain a submission. There will be no charge to the filing party if the other parties do not agree to submit the claim to dispute resolution. If, however, the case settles after AAA involvement but prior to submission to the dispute resolution process, the filing party will pay a $150 filing fee.

Cases may be initiated by a joint submission in writing, containing a brief description of the dispute and the names and addresses of the parties, together with the $150 per party filing fee as provided in the Administrative Fee Schedule.

3. Appointment of Arbitrator or Mediator—The AAA shall appoint a neutral knowledgeable in the area of the dispute, and provide the parties with biographical information about the neutral. Arbitrators shall be attorneys or retired judges. Mediators are not necessarily attorneys. The parties shall agree in advance as to whether the neutral is to issue a binding decision as an arbitrator.

4. Qualifications of Neutral—No person shall serve as a neutral in any matter in which that person has any financial or personal interest in the result of the proceeding. Prior to accepting appointment, a person being considered for such appointment shall disclose any circumstance likely to prevent a prompt hearing or to create a presumption of bias. Upon receipt of such information, the AAA will either replace that person or communicate the information to the parties for comments. After reviewing any comments received from the parties, the AAA may disqualify that person. Vacancies shall be filled in accordance with Section 3 of these procedures.

5. Date, Time, and Place of Mediation Conference or Arbitration Hearing—The neutral shall set the date, time, and place of the mediation conference or arbitration hearing. The AAA shall mail to each party notice thereof at least ten days in advance, unless the parties by mutual agreement waive such notice or modify the terms thereof. If the matter is to be mediated, the mediator will arrange an appropriate format with the parties.

6. Representation—Any party may be represented by counsel or other authorized representative.

7. Postponements—Conferences or hearings may be postponed by the neutral for good cause.

8. Stenographic Record—There shall be no stenographic record of any mediation conferences. In an arbitration, any party desiring a stenographic record shall make arrangements directly with a stenographer and shall notify the other parties of such arrangements in advance of the hearing. The requesting party or parties shall pay the cost of the record.

If the transcript is agreed by the parties to be, or determined by the arbitrator to be, the official record of the proceeding, it must be made available to the arbitrator and to the other parties for inspection, at a date, time, and place determined by the arbitrator.

9. Interpreters—Any party wishing an interpreter shall make all arrangements directly with the interpreter and shall assume the costs of the service.

10. Attendance at Mediation Conference or Arbitration Hearing—The neutral shall maintain the privacy of the proceedings unless the law provides to the contrary. Any person having a direct interest in the mediation or arbitration is entitled to attend conferences or hearings. The neutral shall otherwise have the power to require the exclusion of any witness, other than a party or other essential person, during the testimony of any other witness. It shall be discretionary with the neutral to determine the propriety of the attendance of any other person.

11. Arbitration Hearing—A hearing may be conducted by the arbitrator in any manner which permits a fair presentation of the case by the parties. Normally, the hearing shall be completed within one day. Only for good cause shown may the arbitrator schedule additional hearings.

12. Evidence in Arbitration—The arbitrator shall be the judge of the relevance and materiality of the evidence offered.

13. Closing of Arbitration Hearing—The arbitrator shall ask whether the parties have any further proofs or testimony to offer. Upon determining that the presentations are concluded, the arbitrator shall declare the hearing closed.

14. Arbitration Award—The award shall be in writing and shall be signed by the arbitrator. It shall be rendered promptly and, unless otherwise stipulated, no later than thirty days following the closing of the hearing.

15. Arbitration Award upon Settlement—If the parties settle their dispute during the course of the mediation or arbitration, the neutral, upon their request, may set forth the terms of the agreed settlement in an award. Such an award is referred to as a consent award.

16. Delivery of Arbitration Award to Parties—The parties shall accept as legal delivery of the award the placing of the award or a true copy thereof in the mail addressed to the party or its representative at the last known address, personal service of the award, or the filing of the award in any other manner that is permitted by law.

17. Confidentiality in Mediation—Confidential information disclosed to a mediator by the parties or by witnesses in the course of the mediation shall not be divulged by the mediator. All records, reports, or other documents received by a mediator while serving in that capacity shall be confidential. The mediator shall not be compelled to divulge such records or to testify in regard to the mediation in any adversary proceeding or judicial forum.

The parties shall maintain the confidentiality of the mediation and shall not rely on, or introduce as evidence in any arbitral, judicial, or other proceeding:

(a) views expressed or suggestions made by another party with respect to a possible settlement of the dispute;

(b) admissions made by another party in the course of the mediation proceedings;

(c) proposals made or views expressed by the mediator, or

(d) the fact that another party had or had not indicated willingness to accept a proposal for settlement made by the mediator.

18. Serving of Notice—Each party shall be deemed to have consented that any papers, notices, or process necessary or proper for the initiation or continuation of a proceeding under these procedures; for any court action in connection therewith; or for the entry of judgment on any award made under these rules may be served on a party by mail addressed to the party or its representative at the last known address or by personal service, in or outside the state where the mediation or arbitration is to be held, provided that reasonable opportunity to be heard with regard thereto has been granted to the party. The AAA and the parties may also use facsimile transmission, telex, telegram, or other written forms of electronic communication to give the notices required by these procedures.

19. Waiver of Procedures—Any party who proceeds with a mediation or arbitration after knowledge that any provision or requirement of these procedures has not been complied with, and who fails to state an objection thereto in writing, shall be deemed to have waived the right to object.

20. Extensions of Time—The parties may modify any period of time by mutual agreement. The AAA or the neutral may for good cause extend any period of time established by these procedures, except the time for making the arbitration award. The AAA shall notify the parties of any extension of time.

21. Expenses—The expenses of witnesses for any party shall be paid by the party producing such witnesses. All expenses of the arbitration, including required travel and other expenses of the arbitrator, AAA representatives, and any witness and the cost of any proof produced at the direct request of the arbitrator, shall be borne equally by the parties, unless they agree otherwise or unless the arbitrator in the award assesses such expenses or any part thereof against any specified party or parties.

22. Interpretation and Application of Procedures—The neutral shall interpret and apply these procedures insofar as they relate to the neutral's powers and duties. All other procedures shall be interpreted and applied by the AAA.

23. Applications to Court and Exclusion of Liability—(a) No judicial proceedings by a party relating to the subject matter of a proceeding under these procedures shall be deemed a waiver of the party's right to mediate or arbitrate.

  (b) Neither the AAA nor any neutral serving under these procedures is a necessary party in judicial proceedings relating to the arbitration or mediation.

  (c) Parties to these procedures shall be deemed to have consented that judgment upon an arbitration award rendered under these procedures may be entered in any federal or state court having jurisdiction thereof.

  (d) Neither the AAA nor any neutral shall be liable to any party for any act or omission in connection with any mediation or arbitration conducted under these procedures.

BIBLIOGRAPHY

AF Newsbriefs: A Quarterly Newsletter of AF's Services (Previously known as *Arbitration News Briefs* April, 1982–1988; *Insurance Arbitration Newsletter* February–March, 1982; and *The Arbitration Newsletter* 1969–1981; Tarrytown, NY: Arbitration Forums, Quarterly)

"Alternative Dispute Resolution in High Volume Third Party Insurance Disputes" in *Model ADR Procedures* (New York: Center for Public Resources, 1989): Section 11, 1–14

American Arbitration Association, *Accident Claim Arbitration Rules (Including Mediation) As Amended and Effective on January 1, 1990* (New York: American Arbitration Association)

———, *American Arbitration Association Procedures for New York State No-Fault Master Arbitration Effective for Requests Filed with the New York State Insurance Department on or after July 1, 1988 Adopted Pursuant to Regulations Promulgated by the New York State Superintendent of Insurance As Amended on August 14, 1991* (New York: American Arbitration Association)

———, *American Arbitration Association Rules for New York State No-Fault Arbitration Effective for Requests Filed with the New York State Insurance Department on or after July 1, 1988, Adopted Pursuant to Regulations Promulgated by the New York State Superintendent of Insurance As Amended on August 14, 1991* (New York: American Arbitration Association)

———, *Arbitration of Accident Claims* (New York: American Arbitration Association, 1988)

———, *The Claims Forum: An Insurance Dispute Resolution Quarterly* (New York: American Arbitration Association, Quarterly from 1987)

———, *Dispute Resolution Procedures for Insurance Claims As Amended and Effective on January 1, 1989* (New York: American Arbitration Association)

———, *Dispute Resolution Program for Insurance Claims* (New York: American Arbitration Association, 1989)

———, *A Guide for Accident Claim Arbitrators* (New York: American Arbitration Association, 1990)

———, *A Legal Course Outline on New York No-Fault Arbitration Supplement Cases* (New York: American Arbitration Association, 1991)

———, *Minnesota No-Fault Comprehensive or Collision Damage Automobile Insurance Arbitration Rules: Promulgated by the Minnesota Supreme Court Effective April 1, 1988* (Minneapolis: American Arbitration Association)

————, *Title Insurance Arbitration Rules Effective June 1, 1987* (New York: American Arbitration Association)

Arbitration & the Law: AAA General Counsel's Annual Report (New York: American Arbitration Association, since 1981)

"Auto Arbitration Program Expands to Washington" in *Best's Review: Property/ Casualty Insurance Edition* (February, 1987): 72

Barber, Edwin B., "A Look at the Alternatives" in Best's *Review: Property/Casualty Insurance Edition*, Volume 87, Number 6 (October, 1986): 48–52

Cullen, Kathleen M., "ADR: Shaking Hands Instead of Shackling Them" in *Risk Management*, Volume 34, Number 6 (June, 1987): 28–30 and 32

Cunningham, J. R., "Arbitration of Marine Insurance Disputes" in *Federation of Insurance & Corporate Counsel Quarterly* (Spring, 1988): 209

Dimond, Diane, "See You in ADR" in *Insurance Review*, Volume 50, Number 8 (August, 1989): 18–22

Elms, Roy A., "A Business Viewpoint in Support of Arbitration" in *Canadian Insurance/Agent & Broker*, Volume 93, Number 8 (July, 1988): 36–38

Geisel, Jerry, "Insurer Advocates Arbitration, Mediation" in *Business Insurance* (April 13, 1987): 35

Goldberg, Neil A., and Lawrence D. Behr, "Underinsured Motorist Coverage: the New York Experience" in *The Arbitration Journal*, Volume 42, Number 3 (September, 1987): 36–45

Healey, Thomas S., "Alternatives to Litigation" in *Insurance Review*, Volume 47, Number 3 (June, 1986): 46–50, 52

Henry, James F., "ADR and Personal Injury Litigation: An Early Settlement Technique for Injury Cases" in *Trial*, Volume 23, Number 4 (April, 1987): 73–76

Hines, Bernard L., Jr., "Arbitration Spells Relief" in *Best's Review: Property/Casualty Insurance Edition* (January, 1986): 47–48

————, *Insurance Arbitration: A Guide to Insurance Industry Forums* (New York: Board of Governors—Insurance Arbitration Forums, 1981)

Jericho, Eugene, "Insurance and Reinsurance Disputes" in *The Defense Counsel Journal*, Volume 55, Number 3 (July, 1988): 289–296

"Judge Suggests Remedy for Clogged Courts" in *National Underwriter: Property & Casualty/Employee Benefits*, Volume 93, Number 13 (March 27, 1989): 38

Lamson, Stephen, "The Impact of the Federal Arbitration Act and the McCarran-Ferguson Act on Uninsured Motorist Arbitration" in *Connecticut Law Review*, Volume 19, Number 2 (Winter, 1987): 241–285

Lerner, Richard E., "AAA's Arbitration Rules on Title Insurance" in *The New York Law Journal* (May 22, 1987): 1

McKeon, George A., "Keeping Cases out of Court" in *The Brief*, Volume 18, Number 4 (Summer, 1989): 10–13 and 35–36

McLaughlin, Joseph T., "Disputes Involving Products, Services, and Insurance" in *John E. Sands, Chairman, Alternative Dispute Resolution and Risk Management: Controlling Conflict and Its Costs* in the Litigation Course Handbook, Litigation and Administrative Practice Series, Number 338 (New York: Practising Law Institute, 1987): 109–154

"Minnesota's 1986 Tort Reform Act and Arbitrations: Can They Work Together? Notes" in *Hamline Law Review*, Volume 11, Number 1 (Spring, 1988): 105–122

Mooney, Roger F., "Recent Cases under the New York No-Fault Arbitration Law" in *The Arbitration Journal*, Volume 42, Number 4 (December, 1987): 38–46

New York No-Fault Arbitration Reports (New York: American Arbitration Association, Monthly from 1977)

Nonna, John M., and Jonathan E. Strassberg, "Reinsurance Arbitration: Boon or Bust?" in *Tort and Insurance Law Journal*, Volume 22, Number 4 (Summer, 1987): 586–611

Pellegrino, Frank J., "Thumbs up to Arbitration" in *Best's Review: Property/Casualty Insurance Edition* (December, 1987): 28

Penna, Carolyn M., "Rules Amended for Arbitration Accident Claims" in *The New York Law Journal* (August 11, 1987): 1

Reinsurance Association of America, *Suggested Guidelines for Resolving Reinsurance Disputes: Mediation and Arbitration* (Washington, DC: 1988)

Schermer, Irvin E., *Automobile Liability Insurance* (New York: Clark Boardman Callahan, 1988)

Smith, Michael R., "The 'Catch 22' of Underinsured Motorist Settlements" in *The Colorado Lawyer* (January, 1988): 49–52

Thueson, Erik B., "Fair Claims Practice for Self-Insureds: The Common Law Requires It" in *Trial*, Volume 23, Number 12 (December, 1987): 29–34

Widiss, Alan I., *Uninsured and Underinsured Motorist Insurance* (Cincinnati: Anderson Publishing Company, 1987)

Woodruff, M. G., III, John R. Fonseca, and Alphonse M. Squillante, *Automobile Insurance and No-Fault Law* (Rochester: Lawyers Cooperative Publishing, 1974 with a 1988 supplement)

Zinkewicz, Phil, "Arbitration, Alternative to Costly Litigation, Available to Insurers, Reinsurers, Insureds and Buyers" in *International Insurance Monitor*, Volume 41, Number 6 (October, 1987): 10–11

CHAPTER 5

AN INTRODUCTION TO ADR

Alternative Dispute Resolution (ADR) describes various techniques used to resolve legal claims otherwise than through traditional litigation. This chapter covers some of the primary ADR techniques, explaining how and why they are being used increasingly by business executives. They can be classified on a continuum, involving increasingly greater involvement by third parties, beginning with party-to-party negotiations and continuing to final and binding impartial arbitration. Most private ADR processes are voluntary, requiring little or no intervention by the courts. On the other hand, some courts have adopted ADR procedures in an effort to reduce their caseload.

Bilateral Negotiations

Most business disagreements are resolved through relatively informal negotiations on the telephone or through face-to-face discussions. It is relatively rare for attorneys to be involved, and exceptional for any other outside person to participate. Bargaining techniques are manipulated by the respective representatives of the parties, with people from various levels of each party organization drawn into the discussions. Many books and articles have been compiled on the bargaining process, with numerous continuing-education and academic training facilities offering instruction on negotiating techniques. A few recent books on the subject are listed in the bibliography at the end of this chapter.

In some cases, parties utilize the professional services of an attorney to negotiate on their behalf, perhaps thinking that a better understanding of the law or a higher degree of negotiating skill will prevail. In other situations, executives maintain control over the entire process, believing that they are better able to handle the transaction and to reach a practical solution.

Negotiating techniques are fairly well understood by most active executives and business lawyers. Skill in such matters can be acquired through both experience and training.

Mediation

When parties are unable to resolve their dispute through direct negotiations or have not established a viable bargaining format, they may find it helpful to call upon the services of a mediator, a neutral expert in negotiations.

Mediation is a totally voluntary process, with the parties free to participate, to utilize an acceptable neutral mediator, or to withdraw from the mediation at any time. The mediator is serving the interests of the parties, maintaining no personal interest in the dispute, committed only to helping the parties settle.

The American Arbitration Association maintains a list of trained mediators who are available for various kinds of business negotiations. In general, it is sensible for the parties to select a mediator who is familiar with the issues involved in their dispute. It is also important that the mediator be experienced in the negotiating process, able to persuade the parties to bargain in good faith in an effort to reach agreement, usually by making reasonable concessions.

The process itself is relatively simple, beginning with a joint session where the mediator explains that decisions must be made by the parties, not by the mediator. Discussions will be confidential. The mediator's role is merely to facilitate the bargaining.

Then, parties will be encouraged to share their views of the situation and disclose all of the relevant facts. Often, a mediator will discuss the case with each side in a separate caucus, attempting to identify points of compromise. When the parties negotiate in good faith, they usually reach agreement. Four out of five mediations result in settlement. Even where the discussions lead to an impasse, many of the issues may have been resolved or clarified to the point where a third-party determination can be easily obtained.

When parties are willing to make mutual concessions, mediation can be an efficient method for resolving their disagreement. Since it is entirely voluntary, neither party has much to lose from entering into such discussions. The mediator is not authorized to make decisions and can be dismissed at any time. Risk is minimal.

Typical questions about mediation concern whether confidential information may be disclosed in the discussions that would not otherwise come to the attention of the other side. That, of course, is possible and participants must rely somewhat upon the mediator's good judgment and discretion. Mediators agree not to disclose information to anyone who is not a party to the dispute.

Some parties are reluctant to suggest mediation to their adversary. In such a situation, a party willing to mediate can ask the AAA to invite both parties to participate in the mediation. It not only is an excellent source of trained professional mediators, but will work with parties in persuading them to mediate their disputes. Mediation rules appear at the end of this chapter.

Minitrials

When corporations become bogged down in extensive litigation over important matters, they can sometimes use a procedure known as the minitrial. In effect, they agree to construct a private tribunal, composed of respective senior executives and a neutral third person. The panel listens to presentations made by trial counsel as to the facts and issues involved in the dispute. These presentations are generally made on an expedited basis, without witnesses or extensive documentation. The attorneys explain the basis of their clients' claims or defenses.

Often, the minitrial is designed by the corporate legal departments of each company, perhaps with outside attorneys making the presentation of the case. The neutral member of the panel, who chairs the hearing, sometimes questions the attorneys and comments on the strengths or the weaknesses of their arguments.

After the presentation has concluded, the senior executives confer in an effort to negotiate a settlement. In these meetings, the neutral member of the panel may act as a mediator or a factfinder or simply give advice as to how such a dispute might be resolved in court. The executives are free to enter into any settlement that meets their mutual interests. That is a strength of the minitrial. The settlement can be based solely on the parties' business consideration, rather than on the legal issues, as would be the case in court. For example, an appropriate settlement might involve readjustment of prices in future years, rather than a direct settlement of the claim in question. Minitrials are private and confidential and don't create a public record available to outsiders.

The benefit of the minitrial is that disagreements over complex business matters in litigation can be privatized, freeing them from their legalistic setting and bringing them to the attention of senior executives who can resolve the underlying disputes in accordance with the best interests of their corporations. Minitrial Procedures appear at the end of this chapter.

Med–Arb

In some situations, parties are willing to authorize a neutral third person to first attempt to facilitate a negotiated settlement as a mediator and, if resolution seems impossible, to convert the process to arbitration. Med–arb combines two ADR procedures and is only appropriate when parties have enough confidence in the neutral person's ability to play both roles. In mediation, the neutral will be exposed to information that would not be acceptable in an arbitration. An example would be confidential information received in a caucus about the bargaining history of the parties as to the particular dispute. When an impasse is reached, the mediator, now an arbitrator, will be knowledgeable about those aspects of the dispute. Then, the neutral must be able to focus upon the information that would be relevant in an arbitration. Med–arb has been used in complex labor negotiations and in other situations where parties have a long-term project and are able to agree upon a neutral person in whom they have a high degree of trust.

Court-Administered ADR

In recent years, both state and federal trial courts have become over-burdened with criminal and civil litigation. In many jurisdictions, trial judges have turned to various kinds of ADR in an effort to relieve their congested calendars so that they can provide a forum to parties who are unable to resolve their disputes through negotiation.

One of the more common ADR procedures is court-annexed arbitration, a process that provides an impartial appraisal of the value of claims involved. In most such programs, created either by court rule or by legislation, certain categories of disputes, usually those involving relatively small sums of money, must be submitted to panels of arbitrators, usually lawyers provided by the local bar association. The attorneys for the parties present their case in summary fashion to the arbitration panel. The award will be issued by the panel and will contain its best judgment as to the value of the claim. Usually, parties are able to settle on the basis of such an award, so that the matter can be concluded. If one of the parties believes that the decision is not acceptable, a petition can be filed for a trial *de novo*, usually after the payment of certain additional fees.

At the present time, 20 federal district courts have such programs, as do many state jurisdictions, particularly in high-volume urban areas. These court-annexed arbitration programs usually result in a high percentage of settlements, either just before or right after the arbitration. The net effect of such a program is to settle cases earlier than they would have been settled if the program were not in effect.

Over 90% of civil lawsuits are settled by the attorneys, often shortly before the scheduled trial date. The main benefit of court-annexed arbitration is to provide a somewhat earlier point of settlement, and thereby to speed up the process.

These programs vary as to the scheduling of the arbitration, the makeup of the panel of arbitrators, the size of cases forced into the system, and the penalties imposed upon a party who is not willing to accept an arbitrator's decision.

In some jurisdictions, court-annexed arbitration is called mediation, but involves a hearing before one or more lawyers and results in a recommended settlement.

Some trial judges have encouraged the use of a process called the summary jury trial, where a panel of jurors is made available to hear a summarized presentation of the case by the attorneys. The jury is then asked to disclose the verdict they would have issued if they had been serving in a trial. Here, the jury is giving an evaluation of how they think the case would have been decided in litigation. Judges have been able to use such mock verdicts to settle cases, avoiding the need to try them in court.

Trial judges are using other methods to encourage settlements. They appoint masters and referees to hold hearings or provide a complete trial over the issues. The effect of such decisions varies, depending on court rules. In some cases, the award will be a recommendation to the trial judge. In others, it may be final, subject to a trial *de novo* or to an appeal.

Trial judges also use settlement conferences or neutral evaluations to encourage the parties to settle. In some cases, the intervention of the judge may resemble that of a mediator. In other situations, the judge may simply tell the parties what the claim appears to be worth, directing them to carry out further negotiations around that figure. In all such processes, where judges are personally involved, their effort is to resolve the issues so that they do not have to be tried.

Some judges are also encouraging parties to submit their disputes to private mediation or arbitration. Then, the trained panel members of the AAA can be an important resource.

CONCLUSION

The ADR procedures described above are only an introduction to an exciting effort by parties and their attorneys to channel legal disputes into more rational procedures. It is clear to most observers that the courts are no longer able to offer prompt and efficient justice in many typical business disputes. Neither juries nor judges have the necessary technical knowledge. Nor are the procedures in step with current business practices. Litigation is expensive, slow, and unreliable. The modern business executive is well advised to utilize one or more of the ADR systems that have been described in this book.

COMMERCIAL MEDIATION RULES

as Amended and in Effect January 1, 1992

1. Agreement of Parties—Whenever, by stipulation or in their contract, the parties have provided for mediation or conciliation of existing or future disputes under the auspices of the American Arbitration Association (AAA) or under these rules, they shall be deemed to have made these rules, as amended and in effect as of the date of the submission of the dispute, a part of their agreement.

2. Initiation of Mediation—Any party or parties to a dispute may initiate mediation by filing with the AAA a submission to mediation or a written request for mediation pursuant to these rules, together with the appropriate administrative fee contained in the Fee Schedule. Where there is no submission to mediation or contract providing for mediation, a party may request the AAA to invite another party to join in a submission to mediation. Upon receipt of such a request, the AAA will contact the other parties involved in the dispute and attempt to obtain a submission to mediation.

3. Request for Mediation—A request for mediation shall contain a brief statement of the nature of the dispute and the names, addresses, and telephone numbers of all parties to the dispute and those who will represent them, if any, in the mediation. The initiating party shall simultaneously file two copies of the request with the AAA and one copy with every other party to the dispute.

4. Appointment of Mediator—Upon receipt of a request for mediation, the AAA will appoint a qualified mediator to serve. Normally, a single mediator will be appointed unless the parties agree otherwise or the AAA determines otherwise. If the agreement of the parties names a mediator or specifies a method of appointing a mediator, that designation or method shall be followed.

5. Qualifications of Mediator—No person shall serve as a mediator in any dispute in which that person has any financial or personal interest in the result of the mediation, except by the written consent of all parties. Prior to accepting an appointment, the prospective mediator shall disclose any circumstance likely to create a presumption of bias or prevent a prompt meeting with the parties. Upon receipt of such information, the AAA shall either replace the mediator or immediately communicate the information to the parties for their comments. In the event that the parties disagree as to whether the mediator shall serve, the AAA will appoint another mediator. The AAA is authorized to appoint another mediator if the appointed mediator is unable to serve promptly.

6. Vacancies—If any mediator shall become unwilling or unable to serve, the AAA will appoint another mediator, unless the parties agree otherwise.

7. Representation—Any party may be represented by persons of the party's choice. The names and addresses of such persons shall be communicated in writing to all parties and to the AAA.

8. Date, Time, and Place of Mediation—The mediator shall fix the date and time of each mediation session. The mediation shall be held at the appropriate regional office of the AAA, or at any other convenient location agreeable to the mediator and the parties, as the mediator shall determine.

9. Identification of Matters in Dispute—At least ten days prior to the first scheduled mediation session, each party shall provide the mediator with a brief memorandum setting forth its position with regard to the issues that need to be resolved. At the discretion of the mediator, such memoranda may be mutually exchanged by the parties.

At the first session, the parties will be expected to produce all information reasonably required for the mediator to understand the issues presented.

The mediator may require any party to supplement such information.

10. Authority of Mediator—The mediator does not have the authority to impose a settlement on the parties but will attempt to help them reach a satisfactory resolution of their dispute. The mediator is authorized to conduct joint and separate meetings with the parties and to make oral and written recommendations for settlement. Whenever necessary, the mediator may also obtain expert advice concerning technical aspects of the dispute, provided that the parties agree and assume the expenses of obtaining such advice. Arrangements for obtaining such advice shall be made by the mediator or the parties, as the mediator shall determine.

The mediator is authorized to end the mediation whenever, in the judgment of the mediator, further efforts at mediation would not contribute to a resolution of the dispute between the parties.

11. Privacy—Mediation sessions are private. The parties and their representatives may attend mediation sessions. Other persons may attend only with the permission of the parties and with the consent of the mediator.

12. Confidentiality—Confidential information disclosed to a mediator by the parties or by witnesses in the course of the mediation shall not be divulged by the mediator. All records, reports, or other documents received by a mediator while serving in that capacity shall be confidential. The mediator shall not be compelled to divulge such records or to testify in regard to the mediation in any adversary proceeding or judicial forum.

The parties shall maintain the confidentiality of the mediation and shall not rely on, or introduce as evidence in any arbitral, judicial, or other proceeding:

(a) views expressed or suggestions made by another party with respect to a possible settlement of the dispute;

(b) admissions made by another party in the course of the mediation proceedings;

(c) proposals made or views expressed by the mediator; or

(d) the fact that another party had or had not indicated willingness to accept a proposal for settlement made by the mediator.

13. No Stenographic Record—There shall be no stenographic record of the mediation process.

14. Termination of Mediation—The mediation shall be terminated:

(a) by the execution of a settlement agreement by the parties;

(b) by a written declaration of the mediator to the effect that further efforts at mediation are no longer worthwhile; or

(c) by a written declaration of a party or parties to the effect that the mediation proceedings are terminated.

15. Exclusion of Liability—Neither the AAA nor any mediator is a necessary party in judicial proceedings relating to the mediation.

Neither the AAA nor any mediator shall be liable to any party for any act or omission in connection with any mediation conducted under these rules.

16. Interpretation and Application of Rules—The mediator shall interpret and apply these rules insofar as they relate to the mediator's duties and responsibilities. All other rules shall be interpreted and applied by the AAA.

17. Expenses—The expenses of witnesses for either side shall be paid by the party producing such witnesses. All other expenses of the mediation, including required traveling and other expenses of the mediator and representatives of the AAA, and the expenses of any witness and the cost of any proofs or expert advice produced at the direct request of the mediator, shall be borne equally by the parties unless they agree otherwise.

CONSTRUCTION INDUSTRY MEDIATION RULES

as Amended and in Effect January 1, 1992

1. Agreement of Parties—Whenever, by stipulation or in their contract, the parties have provided for mediation of existing or future disputes under the auspices of the American Arbitration Association (AAA) or under these rules, they shall be deemed to have made these rules, as amended and in effect as of the date of the submission of the dispute, a part of their agreement.

2. Initiation of Mediation—Any party or parties to a dispute may initiate mediation by filing with the AAA a submission to mediation or a written request for mediation pursuant to these rules, together with the appropriate administrative fee contained in the Fee Schedule. Where there is no submission to mediation or contract providing for mediation, a party may request the AAA to invite another party to join in a submission to mediation. Upon receipt of such a request, the AAA will contact the other parties involved in the dispute and attempt to obtain a submission to mediation.

3. Request for Mediation—A request for mediation shall contain a brief statement of the nature of the dispute and the names, addresses, and telephone numbers of all parties to the dispute and those who will represent them, if any, in the mediation. The initiating party shall simultaneously file two copies of the request with the AAA and one copy with every other party to the dispute.

4. Appointment of Mediator—Upon receipt of a request for mediation, the AAA will appoint a qualified mediator to serve. Normally, a single mediator will be appointed unless the parties agree otherwise or the AAA determines otherwise. If the agreement of the parties names a mediator or specifies a method of appointing a mediator, that designation or method shall be followed.

5. Qualifications of Mediator—Any mediator appointed shall be a member of the AAA's Construction Mediation Panel, with expertise in the area of the dispute and knowledgeable in the mediation process.

No person shall serve as a mediator in any dispute in which that person has any financial or personal interest in the result of the mediation, except by the written consent of all parties. Prior to accepting an appointment, the prospective mediator shall disclose any circumstance likely to create a presumption of bias or prevent a prompt meeting with the parties. Upon receipt of such information, the AAA shall either replace the mediator or immediately communicate the information to the parties for their comments. In the event that the parties disagree as to whether the mediator shall serve, the AAA will appoint another mediator. The AAA is authorized to appoint another mediator if the appointed mediator is unable to serve promptly.

6. Vacancies—If any mediator shall become unwilling or unable to serve, the AAA will appoint another mediator, unless the parties agree otherwise.

7. Representation—Any party may be represented by persons of the party's choice. The names and addresses of such persons shall be communicated in writing to all parties and to the AAA.

8. Date, Time, and Place of Mediation—The mediator shall fix the date and time of each mediation session. The mediation shall be held at the appropriate regional office of the AAA, or at any other convenient location agreeable to the mediator and the parties, as the mediator shall determine.

9. Identification of Matters in Dispute—At least ten days prior to the first scheduled mediation session, each party shall provide the mediator with a brief memorandum setting forth its position with regard to the issues that need to be resolved. At the discretion of the mediator, such memoranda may be mutually exchanged by the parties.

At the first session, the parties will be expected to produce all information reasonably required for the mediator to understand the issues presented. The mediator may require any party to supplement such information.

10. Authority of Mediator—The mediator does not have the authority to impose a settlement on the parties but will attempt to help them reach a satisfactory resolution of their dispute. The mediator is authorized to conduct joint and separate meetings with the parties and to make oral and written recommendations for settlement. Whenever necessary, the mediator may also obtain expert advice concerning technical aspects of the dispute, provided that the parties agree and assume the expenses of obtaining such advice. Arrangements for obtaining such advice shall be made by the mediator or the parties, as the mediator shall determine.

The mediator is authorized to end the mediation whenever, in the judgment of the mediator, further efforts at mediation would not contribute to a resolution of the dispute between the parties.

11. Privacy—Mediation sessions are private. The parties and their representatives may attend mediation sessions. Other persons may attend only with the permission of the parties and with the consent of the mediator.

12. Confidentiality—Confidential information disclosed to a mediator by the parties or by witnesses in the course of the mediation shall not be divulged by the mediator. All records, reports, or other documents received by a mediator while serving in such capacity shall be confidential. The mediator shall not be compelled to divulge such records or to testify in regard to the mediation in any adversary proceeding or judicial forum.

The parties shall maintain the confidentiality of the mediation and shall not rely on, or introduce as evidence in any arbitral, judicial, or other proceeding:

(a) views expressed or suggestions made by another party with respect to a possible settlement of the dispute;

(b) admissions made by another party in the course of the mediation proceedings;

(c) proposals made or views expressed by the mediator; or

(d) the fact that another party had or had not indicated willingness to accept a proposal for settlement made by the mediator.

13. No Stenographic Record—There shall be no stenographic record of the mediation process.

14. Termination of Mediation—The mediation shall be terminated:

(a) by the execution of a settlement agreement by the parties;

(b) by a written declaration of the mediator to the effect that further efforts at mediation are no longer worthwhile; or

(c) by a written declaration of a party or parties to the effect that the mediation proceedings are terminated.

15. Exclusion of Liability—Neither the AAA nor any mediator is a necessary party in judicial proceedings relating to the mediation.

Neither the AAA nor any mediator shall be liable to any party for any act or omission in connection with any mediation conducted under these rules.

16. Interpretation and Application of Rules—The mediator shall interpret and apply these rules insofar as they relate to the mediator's duties and responsibilities. All other rules shall be interpreted and applied by the AAA.

17. Expenses—The expenses of witnesses for either side shall be paid by the party producing such witnesses. All other expenses of the mediation, including required traveling and other expenses of the mediator and representatives of the AAA, and the expenses of any witness and the cost of any proofs or expert advice produced at the direct request of the mediator, shall be borne equally by the parties unless they agree otherwise.

MINITRIAL PROCEDURES

1. The minitrial process may be initiated by the written or oral request of either party, made to any regional office of the AAA, but will not be pursued unless both parties agree to resolve their dispute by means of a minitrial.

2. The course of the minitrial process shall be governed by a written agreement between the parties.

3. The minitrial shall consist of an information exchange and settlement negotiation.

4. Each party is represented throughout the minitrial process by legal counsel whose role is to prepare and present the party's "best case" at the information exchange.

5. Each party shall have in attendance throughout the information exchange and settlement negotiation a senior executive with settlement authority.

6. A neutral advisor shall be present at the information exchange to decide questions of procedure and to render advice to the party representatives when requested by them.

7. The neutral advisor shall be selected by mutual agreement of the parties, who may consult with the AAA for recommendations. To facilitate the selection process, the AAA will make available to the parties a list of individuals to serve as neutral advisors. If the parties fail to agree upon the selection of a neutral advisor, they shall ask that the AAA appoint an advisor from the panel it has compiled for this purpose.

8. Discovery between the parties may take place prior to the information exchange, in accordance with the agreement between the parties.

9. Prior to the information exchange, the parties shall exchange written statements summarizing the issues in the case, and copies of all documents they intend to present at the information exchange.

10. Federal or state rules of evidence do not apply to presentations made at the information exchange. Any limitation on the scope of the evidence offered at the information exchange shall be determined by mutual agreement of the parties prior to the exchange and shall be enforced by the neutral advisor.

11. After the information exchange, the senior executives shall meet and attempt, in good faith, to formulate a voluntary settlement of the dispute.

12. If the senior executives are unable to settle the dispute, the neutral advisor shall render an advisory opinion as to the likely outcome of the case if it were litigated in a court of law. The neutral advisor's opinion shall identify the issues of law and fact which are critical to the disposition of the case and give the reasons for the opinion that is offered.

13. After the neutral advisor has rendered an advisory opinion, the senior executives shall meet for a second time in an attempt to resolve the dispute. If they are unable to reach a settlement at this time, they may either abandon the proceeding or submit to the neutral advisor written offers of settlement. If the parties elect to make such written offers, the neutral advisor shall make a recommendation for settlement based on those offers. If the parties reject the recommendation of the neutral advisor, either party may declare the minitrial terminated and resolve the dispute by other means.

14. Minitrial proceedings are confidential; no written or oral statement made by any participant in the proceeding may be used as evidence or in admission in any other proceeding.

15. The fees and expenses of the neutral advisor shall be borne equally by the parties, and each party is responsible for its own costs, including legal fees, incurred in connection with the minitrial. The parties may, however, in their written agreement alter the allocation of fees and expenses.

16. Neither the AAA nor any neutral advisor serving in a minitrial proceeding governed by these procedures shall be liable to any party for any act or omission in connection with the minitrial. The parties shall indemnify the AAA and the neutral advisor for any liability to third parties arising out of the minitrial process.

JUDICIAL REFERENCE PROCEDURES

Effective January 1, 1990

1. Judicial Reference—The parties shall be deemed to have made these procedures a part of their agreement whenever they have provided for Judicial Reference by the American Arbitration Association, or when a Court orders, directs, or refers a matter for reference to the American Arbitration Association (hereinafter "AAA").

2. Panel of Referees—The AAA shall establish and maintain a panel of referees. All referees or special masters shall be attorneys or retired judges.

3. Initiation Pursuant to Judicial Reference—By agreement of the parties or when a Court orders, directs, or refers a dispute to the AAA, the reference procedure shall be initiated in the following manner:

(a) The initiating party (hereinafter "Claimant") shall, within the time period, if any, specified by the court order or reference, give written notice to the other party(ies) (hereinafter "Respondent(s)") of its intention to initiate reference proceedings. This notice shall contain a statement setting forth: the nature of the dispute; any orders or remedies sought; the names and addresses of the parties and their representatives, if any; and the hearing locale requested; and

(b) shall file at any California regional office of the AAA three (3) copies of the notice and three (3) copies of the court order or reference directing or referring the parties to submit their dispute to the AAA, together with the appropriate administrative fee, as provided in the Administrative Fee Schedule, and

(c) the AAA shall give notice of such filing to the Respondent(s).

4. Appointment from Panel—The AAA shall appoint a referee from its panel.

5. Disclosure and Challenge Procedure—Any person appointed as a referee shall disclose to the AAA any circumstance likely to affect impartiality, including any bias or any financial or personal interest in the result of the reference or any past or present relationship with the parties or their representative(s). Upon receipt of such information from the referee or another source, the AAA shall communicate the information to the parties and, if it deems it appropriate to do so, to the referee and others. Upon objection of a party to the continued service of a neutral referee, the AAA shall determine whether the referee should be disqualified and shall inform the parties of its decision, which shall be conclusive.

6. Telephone Conference/Preliminary Hearing—At the referee's discretion, a telephone conference call or a preliminary hearing shall be arranged by the AAA for the purpose of determining the appropriate procedures, as determined by the referee, for briefing of the issues involved in the dispute, exchanging documents, scheduling an oral hearing, if necessary, and any other procedures that the referee deems appropriate to render a decision.

7. Date, Time, and Place of Hearing—The referee shall set the date, time, and place for each oral hearing, if such a hearing is deemed necessary by the referee. The AAA shall mail to each party notice thereof at least seven (7) days in advance, unless the parties by mutual agreement waive such notice or modify the terms thereof.

8. Representation—Any party may be represented by counsel or other authorized representative. A party intending to be so represented shall notify the other party and the AAA of the name and address of the representative at least three (3) days prior to the date set for the hearing at which that person is first to appear. When such a representative initiates a reference or responds for a party, notice is deemed to have been given.

9. Stenographic Record—Any party desiring a stenographic record shall make arrangements directly with a stenographer and shall notify the other party of these arrangements in advance of the hearing. The requesting party or parties shall pay the cost of the record. If the transcript is agreed by the parties to be, or determined by the referee to be, the official record of the proceeding, it must be made available to the referee and to the other parties for inspection, at a date, time, and place determined by the referee.

10. Attendance at Hearings—The referee shall maintain the privacy of the hearings unless the law provides to the contrary. Any person having a direct interest in the reference is entitled to attend hearings. The referee shall otherwise have the power to require the exclusion of any witness, other than a party or other essential person, during the testimony of any other witness. It shall be discretionary with the referee to determine the propriety of the attendance of any other person.

11. Postponements—The referee for good cause shown may postpone any hearing upon the request of a party or upon the referee's own initiative, and shall also grant such postponement when all of the parties agree thereto.

12. Oaths—Before proceeding with the first hearing, each referee may take an oath of office and, if required by law, shall do so. The referee may require witnesses to testify under oath administered by any duly qualified person and, if it is required by law or requested by any party, shall do so.

13. Reference Proceedings in the Absence of a Party or Representative—Unless the law provides to the contrary, the reference may proceed in the absence of any party or representative who, after due notice, fails to be present or fails to obtain a postponement. A decision shall not be made solely on the default of a party. The referee shall require the party who is present to submit such evidence as the referee may require for the making of the Findings or Statement of Decision.

14. Serving of Notice—Each party shall be deemed to have consented that any papers, notices or process necessary or proper for the initiation or continuation of a reference under these rules; for any court action in connection therewith; or for the entry of the Findings or Decision made under these procedures may be served on a party by mail addressed to the party or its representative at the last know address or by personal service, in or outside the state where the reference is to be held, provided that reasonable opportunity to be heard with regard thereto has been granted to the party. The AAA and the parties may also use facsimile transmission, telex, telegrams or other written forms of electronic communication to give notices required by these procedures.

15. Waiver of Rules—Any party who proceeds with the reference after knowledge that any provision or requirement of these procedures has not been complied with and who fails to state an objection thereto in writing shall be deemed to have waived the right to object.

16. Closing of Hearing—The referee shall specifically inquire of all parties whether they have any further proofs to offer or witnesses to be heard. Upon receiving negative replies or if satisfied that the record is complete, the referee shall declare the hearing closed and a minute thereof shall be recorded. If briefs are to be filed, the hearing shall be declared closed as of the final date set by the referee for the receipt of briefs. If documents are to be filed and the date set for their receipt is later than that set for the receipt of briefs, the later date shall be the date of closing the hearing. The time limit within which the referee is require to make their Findings or Statement of Decision shall commence to run, in the absence of other agreements by the parties, upon the closing of the hearing.

17. Time of Findings or Statement of Decision—The Findings or Statement of Decision by the referee shall be rendered within twenty days from the close of the hearing, or as otherwise directed by the court.

18. Form of Decision—The referee shall report the Findings or Statement of Decision in writing to the AAA for transmittal to the referring court and the parties. The Findings or Statement of Decision shall be signed by the Referee and executed in the manner required by law.

19. Applications to Court and Exclusion of Liability—(a) Neither the AAA nor any referee in a proceeding under these procedures is a necessary party in judicial proceedings relating to the reference or collateral court proceedings.

(b) Neither the AAA nor any referee shall be liable to any party for any act or omission in connection with any reference conducted under these procedures.

20. Administrative Fee—As a not-for-profit organization, the AAA shall prescribe an Administrative Fee Schedule and a Refund Schedule to compensate it for the cost of providing administrative services. The schedule in effect at the time the reference is received by the AAA shall be applicable.

21. Expenses—The expenses of witnesses for either side shall be paid by the party producing such witnesses. All other expenses of the reference, including required travel and other expenses of the referee, AAA representatives, and any witness and the cost of any proof produced at the direct request of the referee, shall be borne equally by the parties, unless they agree otherwise or unless the referee in the Findings or Decision assesses such expenses or any part thereof against any specified party or parties.

22. Deposits—The AAA may require the parties to deposit in advance of any hearings such sums of money as it deems necessary to defray the expense of the reference, including the referee's fee, if any, and shall render an accounting to the parties and return any unexpended balance at the conclusion of the case.

23. Interpretation and Application of Procedures—The referee shall interpret and apply these procedures insofar as they relate to the referee's powers and duties. If that is unobtainable, either a referee or a party may refer the question to the AAA for final decision. All other procedures shall be interpreted and applied by the AAA.

BIBLIOGRAPHY

American Arbitration Association *Commercial Mediation Rules as Amended and in Effect January 1, 1992* (New York: American Arbitration Association)

_____, *A Guide to Mediation for Business People* (New York: American Arbitration Association, 1992)

_____, *Judicial Reference Procedures Effective January 1, 1990* (New York: American Arbitration Association)

_____, *Minitrial Procedures* (New York: American Arbitration Association, 1985)

Cooley, John W., "Arbitration vs. Mediation—It's Time to Settle the Differences" in *The Chicago Bar Record*, Volume 66, Number 4 (January/February, 1985): 204–221

Coulson, Robert, *Business Mediation—What You Need to Know* (New York: American Arbitration Association, 1987)

_____, *How to Stay out of Court* (New York: American Arbitration Association, 1984)

_____, *Professional Mediation of Civil Disputes* (New York: American Arbitration Association, 1984)

Feinberg, Kenneth R., "Mediation: A Preferred Method of Dispute Resolution" in *Pepperdine Law Review*, Volume 16, Number S5 (1989): S5–S42

Fine, Erica S., Editor, *ADR and the Courts: A Manual for Judges and Lawyers,* Stoneham, MA: Butterworth Legal Publishers, 1987)

_____, and Elizabeth S. Plapinger, *Containing Legal Costs: ADR Strategies for Corporations, Law Firms, and Government* (Stoneham, MA: Butterworth Legal Publishers, 1988)

Fisher, Roger, and Scott Brown, *Getting Together: Building a Relationship that Gets to Yes* (Boston: Houghton Mifflin, 1988)

_____, and William Ury, *Getting to Yes: Negotiating Agreement without Giving in* (Boston: Houghton Mifflin, 1981)

Goldberg, Stephen B., Eric D. Green, and Frank E. A. Sander, *Dispute Resolution* (Boston: Little, Brown, 1985)

Hancock, William A., and M. J. Gillan, *Corporate Counsel's Guide to Alternative Dispute Resolution Techniques* (Chesterland, OH: Business Laws, 1989)

Hart, B. C., "Alternative Dispute Resolution: Negotiation, Mediation, and Minitrial" in *The Federation of Insurance and Corporate Counsel Quarterly*, Volume 37, Number 2 (Winter, 1987): 113–131

Harter, Philip J., Lawrence R. Freedman, and Prudence B. Kestner, Editors, *Alternative Dispute Resolution: A Handbook for Judges* American Bar Association Monograph Number 3 (Washington, DC: American Bar Association, Standing Committee on Dispute Resolution, 1987)

Henry, James F., and Jethro K. Lieberman, *The Manager's Guide to Resolving Legal Disputes: Better Results without Litigation* (New York: Harper and Row, 1985)

Izbiky, Julian, and Cynthia Savage, "ADR: Explanations, Examples and Effective Use" in *The Colorado Lawyer*, Volume 18, Number 5 (May, 1989): 843–857

Kagel, Sam, and Kathy Kelly, *The Anatomy of Mediation: What Makes It Work* (Washington, DC: Bureau of National Affairs, 1989)

Kanowitz, Leo, *Cases and Materials on Alternative Dispute Resolution* (St. Paul: West Publishing, 1986)

Lovenheim, Peter, *Mediate, Don't Litigate: How to Resolve Disputes Quickly, Privately, and Inexpensively—without Going to Court* (New York: McGraw–Hill Publishers, 1989)

Murray, John S., Alan Scott Rau, and Edward F. Sherman, *Processes of Dispute Resolution: The Role of Lawyers* (Westbury, NY: Foundation Press, 1989)

Resolving Disputes without Litigation: A BNA Special Report. (Rockville, MD: Bureau of National Affairs, 1985)

Riskin, Leonard L., "The Special Place of Mediation in Alternative Dispute Resolution" in *University of Florida Law Review*, Volume 37, Number 1 (Winter, 1985): 19–27

Riskin, Leonard L., and James E. Westbrook, *Dispute Resolution and Lawyers* (St. Paul: West Publishing, 1987)

Rogers, Nancy H., and Craig A. McEwen, *Mediation: Law, Policy, Practice* (Rochester: Lawyers Cooperative Publishing, 1989)

_____, and Richard A. Salem, *A Student's Guide to Mediation and the Law* (New York: Matthew Bender, 1987)

_____, *Teacher's Guide to a Student's Guide to Mediation and the Law* (New York: Matthew Bender, 1987)

Sbarboro, Gerald L., "Guide for a Successful Settlement Conference" in *The CBA Record*, Volume 2, Number 4 (April, 1988): 12-17

Schwartz, Allen D., "A Primer on Alternative Dispute Resolution" in *The CBA Record*, Volume 2, Number 8 (September, 1988): 19-23

Tannon, Elizabeth M., "Implementing a Successful Minitrial" in *Kentucky Bench and Bar*, Volume 52, Number 1 (Winter, 1988): 12

Wilkinson, John H., *Donovan Leisure Newton & Irvine ADR Practice Book* (New York: Wiley Law Publications, 1990)

CHAPTER 6

INTERNATIONAL ARBITRATION–A SMORGASBORD OF SYSTEMS

.

Anyone doing business abroad or with foreign interests operating in the United States should be familiar with arbitration. Arbitration clauses are frequently included in contracts in international trade because both American and foreign parties show a strong preference for submitting their disputes to arbitration. They use arbitration because they can avoid the formalities, complexities, and uncertainties of foreign court proceedings.

In international trade, parties prefer to use clauses that provide for administration by a recognized, impartial institution under a definite set of rules. Such a procedure helps to eliminate potential conflicts. The agency will enforce such a clause by moving ahead with the arbitration even if the other party is reluctant. The agency also arranges for the filing of papers, the appointment of arbitrators, the filling of any vacancies caused by the death or disability of an arbitrator, and the details of the hearing.

When an American business person does work abroad, the foreign party may suggest using an arbitration system available in that country. It is important that a U.S. lawyer be knowledgeable about such systems. Foreign practices may be less attractive to an American party.

Some of the leading international systems in Europe are the London Court of International Arbitration, the Court of Arbitration of the International Chamber of Commerce in Paris, and the arbitration facilities in the Chamber of Commerce in Stockholm and Vienna. The need for such services is expanding. Competition among arbitration agencies will lead to better service and enhance the use of arbitration in the worldwide business community. A partial list of international arbitration institutions is printed at the end of this chapter.

When parties decide to use arbitration, an important choice will be *where* and *how* to arbitrate. The nature of the contract, the kind of project involved, and the preferences of the parties will determine that choice. The realities of the industry, the expectations of the interests involved, and their respective standards must also be considered. The contract specifications and the political and social setting within which the performance of the contract may take place are important considerations.

The arbitration clause is often the last item to be discussed. The selection of an arbitration mechanism may not even be talked about before the deal is closed. The prime negotiators may agree on principle but leave the procedure to the lawyers.

An arbitration clause can be a two-edged sword. If your client is a claimant, you may want to be able to enforce the obligations of the contract. If your party is the respondent, you may rejoice in interminable delays. Not every party wants a prompt award.

The location of the arbitration may determine the procedural law of the case, shaping the process. Specifying the locale and the applicable law will lend certainty to the process. For example, in the United States, contracts usually specify that the arbitrator's award is subject to confirmation in court. In the absence of such a clause, courts may refuse to enforce an award. If an international contract provides for arbitration in the United States, this kind of provision may be advisable. If the arbitration is in a country without such a rule, the provision may not be necessary, because, under the U.N. Convention on the Recognition and Enforcement of Foreign Arbitral Awards, confirmation in the courts of the forum is not required. A foreign arbitration award may be easier to enforce in some countries than a court judgment.

Arbitration is so frequently used to resolve international trade disputes that most international traders are familiar with the process and expect an arbitration clause to appear in their contracts. Disagreement will not arise over whether to use arbitration, but business people are likely to have fixed opinions as to the situs of the arbitration, the method of choosing arbitrators, and the procedural rules to be applied.

An arbitration clause in international contracts should select a tribunal that best suits the mutual needs of the parties. Some questions can be anticipated. The following checklist can help you decide what arbitration provisions should be inserted in an international contract.

DESIGNATION OF ARBITRAL INSTITUTION

Many kinds of international arbitration systems exist. Some are set within a particular national legal structure and are shaped by its traditions. Others are international in scope. Potential problems resulting from this diversity of systems can be minimized by designating an experienced arbitration agency to administer your case.

Parties are not required to use arbitration agencies, but they provide the benefit of orderly rules and an established panel of arbitrators. When the contracting parties choose such an institution, they designate that institution's rules of procedure. If they provide that their arbitration will be in accordance with the rules of an institution, it is understood that the case will be administered by that agency.

The rules of most arbitral institutions contain certain basic provisions: (1) a method of initiating arbitration through the filing of a notice; (2) the appointment of arbitrators, with procedures for substitution and challenge; (3) rules covering such matters as the submission of documents, representation by counsel, witnesses, fees, and security for costs; (4) ordering a transcript, if desired; and (5) the award, including its communication to the parties and its possible modification.

The international caseload of the American Arbitration Association has been increasing. The AAA handles hundreds of international cases annually, many of them involving substantial sums. Other international cases are administered by agencies in other countries.

International arbitration provides many options. Among the relevant considerations are the arbitration preferences of the client, the authority to be delegated to the arbitrator, the amount of institutional involvement desired, the hearing procedure, what criteria the arbitrator should consider, and the costs of the process. It is recommended that arbitrators be experienced in the particular industry.

Arbitration agencies will play an ever-greater role. They will need to be more responsive to the procedural preferences of lawyers and business people. The AAA recommends that parties discuss the arbitration clause in advance with their legal departments to take advantage of the Association's extensive experience.

ARBITRATION CONVENTIONS

The 1958 Convention on the Recognition and Enforcement of Foreign Arbitral Awards, adopted by the United Nations, is a multilateral treaty that encourages the use of arbitration for resolving international commercial disputes. Parties may be governments, private citizens, or corporations. The Convention is applicable to all systems of arbitration. The Convention provides for the enforcement of arbitration clauses in contracts, as well as for enforcement of awards.

There are no rules or permanent panels of arbitrators specified by the Convention. An award, if not voluntarily honored, may be enforced by means of a judgment obtained in the court of the contracting state. It is not subject to review by that court on the merits but, rather, as described in the Convention, on grounds of fairness, public policy, and due process.

The United Nations Commission on International Trade Law (UNCITRAL) published arbitration rules for international arbitrations. The AAA is prepared to serve as appointing agency under these rules and to provide its traditional administrative services. It also maintains international procedures for arbitration under which the administrative services of its various offices are available. In the Asia/Pacific area, cooperative relationships have been established with most of the arbitration institutions and both conciliation and arbitration are available.

PREARBITRATION PROCEDURES

Some international arbitration procedures include provisions for discovery, factfinding, or conciliation to help resolve the dispute early in the process.

American lawyers have a high regard for discovery procedures, but foreign parties worry about the cost in terms of both money and time.

In some Far Eastern cultures, business people believe that disagreements should be resolved through friendly discussions or conciliation. Arbitration is used only as a last resort and is regarded with the same disapproval as taking a case to court. People try very hard to settle their disagreements. Conciliation can be particularly helpful when a cultural gap exists between the parties or when each side hopes to resolve the dispute without disrupting future business opportunities. The AAA is a ready source of experienced business mediators, available when both parties are willing to engage in conciliation.

APPOINTMENT OF ARBITRATORS

Parties should specify whether their case is to be heard before a single arbitrator or before three arbitrators. In some systems, international parties utilize "party-appointed" arbitrators, who may participate in the selection of the third, neutral arbitrator. In international arbitration, party-appointed arbitrators are sometimes said to be neutral, rather than advocates for the parties that appointed them. Parties should determine in advance whether the other party's arbitrator will be impartial. Multiple-arbitrator panels should be used only where the amount of claims is large or where the parties prefer to include arbitrators from different disciplines or industries.

Nationality is frequently taken into account in international arbitration, both to avoid national bias and to obtain arbitrators who are familiar with the cultural, legal, or commercial traditions that may be involved in the case.

THE PLACE OF HEARING

Often, an arbitration clause will designate where the hearing will take place. This may prove difficult—for example, when the parties are located in distant parts of the globe. Traveling to the country of the other party for an arbitration case can be expensive. Sometimes, parties have dealt with this problem by specifying an arrangement under which the party initiating the arbitration must go to the other's country. Parties may also agree upon a neutral third-country location.

It may be desirable to designate a major city in the United States because of the availability of experienced arbitrators. The AAA administers international cases between parties from all over the world. Its reputation and impartiality are internationally recognized, so that foreign parties often agree upon a site in the United States.

If the parties desire, they can exchange documents in advance. They can appoint arbitrators of their choice, perhaps from a neutral country. They also have broad discretion as to the procedural rules. The AAA is prepared to provide administrative services under any fair arrangement requested by the parties.

LANGUAGE

A party might prefer that the hearing be held in a language other than English. This should be specified in the arbitration agreement to avoid any subsequent dispute. The parties should also select arbitrators who are comfortable in that language. If the language of the arbitration is not one that both parties share, translation facilities may be required.

APPLICABLE LAW

The arbitration laws of most jurisdictions permit parties to create their own arbitration procedure by inserting special provisions in the contract or by selecting preestablished institutional rules. Where the arbitration clause has gaps, the local law may provide backup provisions. For example, the Federal Arbitration Act states that, where no method is provided for naming an arbitrator, the federal court will designate the arbitrator. Such a provision is not always available in other jurisdictions.

The local arbitration law may also determine whether attachments, preliminary injunctions, or other remedies are available. In some jurisdictions, neither the arbitrators nor the courts can provide such assistance. This aspect of the local procedure should be investigated in advance.

The selected procedures may conflict with the local law. For example, an arbitration clause may specify that the arbitrators shall be nationals of a third country, but local law may not permit foreign arbitrators. Counsel should be aware of such problems in advance; otherwise, such a dispute may have to be resolved in court, exactly the predicament parties try to avoid by selecting arbitration.

International contracts often specify which law shall be applicable. The reference may be to the applicable substantive law or the arbitration clause may tell the arbitrators which law to consider. In other situations, the parties may wish to have the dispute determined on the basis of trade practice and custom.

The selection of applicable law by the arbitrators will be determined based on their reading of the contract. If the parties want arbitrators to consider trade usages, they should include a statement to that effect. In some European countries, arbitrators are given the power to decide as *amiables compositeurs*; that is, without obligation to observe the rules of law but subject to the rules of "natural justice" or the fundamental principles of commercial law. Some contracts direct the arbitrator to decide the matter according to what is just and equitable in the circumstances. Then, the strict rules of law need not be observed.

The choice of locale for the arbitration may affect the applicable law. If no law is specified in the arbitration agreement, the law of the forum, procedural and substantive, may be applied.

COSTS AND EXPENSES

Parties to commercial arbitration pay their own legal fees and other costs of preparation. In international arbitration, arbitrators often charge a perdiem fee, negotiated with the parties in advance. This may be shared equally by the parties. Where an administrative agency is involved, fee discussions are carried out by that agency. Parties should settle the terms of the arbitrator's compensation at an early stage. In addition, an administrative charge, which will vary in accordance with the rules, is made by the agency.

ENTRY OF JUDGMENT

In the United States, parties usually include language in the arbitration clause authorizing the courts to enter judgment on the award. Without such a clause, some federal courts have refused to enforce arbitration awards. The clause recommended by the AAA includes a provision that "judgment upon the award may be entered in any court having jurisdiction thereof." Some parties have been unable to obtain judgments on awards in the absence of such a provision.

In 1970, the United States became a party to the 1958 Convention on the Recognition and Enforcement of Foreign Arbitral Awards. Congress added a new part to the Federal Arbitration Act to effectuate this treaty and to provide easy access to U.S. courts. Under the Convention, the winning party may take an award directly to the participating country where the respondent has property, procure a judgment confirming it, and obtain enforcement of the judgment therein. In addition, the United States has bilateral commercial treaties with some countries that are not members of the New York Convention. These treaties enable either party to seek enforcement of an arbitration award in the other party's country.

In general, there is no right to appeal an arbitration award. It is possible for parties to provide for an appeal.

ENFORCEMENT OF AN AWARD

Most developed countries have accepted the New York Convention. When both parties are nationals of countries that are signatories to the Convention, the following paragraph can be included in the arbitration provision: "The parties acknowledge that this agreement and any award rendered pursuant to it shall be governed by the 1958 Convention on the Recognition and Enforcement of Foreign Arbitral Awards."

DEFAULT

If one of the parties fails to appear at a hearing, arbitrators under AAA rules have the power to proceed on the basis of the evidence taken from one party. This is a major reason why parties refer to administrative rules. If it were possible for a party to block an arbitration by failing to appear at a hearing, the arbitration clause would be ineffectual. Most agency rules authorize the agency and the arbitrator to proceed in such a case. Under the New York Convention, the award may be enforced despite a party's failure to appear. Courts are authorized to enforce such ex parte awards.

THE AAA: AN INTERNATIONAL ARBITRATION RESOURCE

Lawyers and business people should know how to arbitrate. The AAA has emerged as an important resource for the American business community. The AAA's Eastman Arbitration Library contains a comprehensive collection of arbitration laws, rules, and regulations, as well as a collection of international arbitration cases. The AAA represents US interests at many international conferences where other national arbitration agencies are present. The Association maintains up-to-date information on foreign arbitration rules and institutions. The AAA has entered into cooperative relationships with arbitration agencies in many countries.

THE WORLD ARBITRATION INSTITUTE

The World Arbitration Institute, established in 1983, is a program of the American Arbitration Association, located at the New York headquarters of the AAA. The purpose of the World Arbitration Institute is to study international commercial arbitration. It acts as a clearinghouse for information, as well as acting as an administrator of international arbitration cases at the request of parties.

CONCLUSION

Arbitration has become increasingly useful for companies engaged in international business activities. The United States not only recognizes and enforces arbitration agreements and awards, but it is part of an international network of countries that have similar policies. The New York Convention encourages the use of contractual arbitration agencies.

There is growing cooperation among arbitration agencies. The AAA helps the business community to use arbitration effectively by maintaining relationships with agencies in other countries.

Arbitration in international trade can provide an efficient dispute settlement process if care is taken in selecting an administrative agency, a convenient locale, and a legal system that meets the expectations of the parties. Arbitration gives parties the right to place their international business disputes in trustworthy hands for an appropriate, impartial determination. When properly designed, arbitration can significantly reduce the risk of unanticipated determinations. It is important that American and foreign business firms be informed about this subject.

MAJOR ARBITRAL INSTITUTIONS *

AUSTRALIA
The Australian Centre for International Commercial Arbitration
Building B, Floor Six
World Trade Centre
Melbourne, Victoria 3005

Australian Commercial Disputes' Centre
Level 21, Remington Centre
175 Liverpool Street
Sydney, NSW 2000

AUSTRIA
The Arbitral Centre of the Federal Economic Chamber, Vienna
Wiedner Hauptstraße 63
PO Box 190
A–1045 Vienna

BELGIUM
The Belgian Center for the Study and the Practice of National and International Arbitration (CEPANI)
8, Rue des Sols
1000 Brussels

BULGARIA
The Bulgarian Chamber of Commerce and Industry
Court of Arbitration
11–A Stamboliisky Blvd.
Sofia

CANADA
Arbitrators' Institute of Canada
234 Eglinton Avenue East
Suite 411
Toronto, ON M4P 1K5

The British Columbia International Commercial Arbitration Centre
670–999 Canada Place
Vancouver, BC V6C 2E2

The Canadian Arbitration, Conciliation and Amicable Composition Centre
University of Ottawa
Ottawa, ON K1N 6N5

The Québec National and International Commercial Arbitration Centre
Edifice la Laurentienne
500 Grande-Allée Est
Rez de Chaussée
Québec, PQ G1R 2J7

CHINA
The China International Economic and Trade Arbitration Commission
1 Fu Xing Men Wai Street
Beijing

---

* The Library and Information Center on the Resolution of Disputes of the American Arbitration Association maintains an extensive worldwide listing of arbitral institutions. Contact the Library's Reference Desk for additional countries and institutions.

The China Maritime Arbitration
  Commission
1 Fu Xing Men Wai Street
Beijing

CZECHOSLOVAKIA
The Chamber of Commerce and
  Industry of Czechoslovakia
Arbitration Court
Argentinska 38
170 05 Prague   7

DENMARK
The Danish Institute of Arbitra-
  tion (Copenhagen Arbitration)
Frederiksborggade 1,3
DK–1360 Copenhagen K

EGYPT
The Regional Centre for Com-
  mercial Arbitration at Cairo
3 Abu-el-Feda Street
Zamalek
Cairo

FINLAND
The Central Chamber of Com-
  merce of Finland
Board of Arbitration
Fabianinkatu 14B
PO Box 1000
00101 Helsinki

FRANCE
The French Arbitration
  Association
2, Rue de Harley
75001 Paris

THE GERMAN DEMOCRATIC
  REPUBLIC
The Berlin Court of Arbitration
  Chamber of Foreign Trade of
  the German Democratic
  Republic
Am Kupfergraben 7
PO Box 70
1080 Berlin

THE GERMAN FEDERAL
  REPUBLIC
The German Arbitration Institute
PO Box 100 447
Kolumbastraße 5
D-5000 Köln 1

GREECE
The Greek Arbitration
  Association
102 ́Solonos Street
Athens   10680

HONG KONG
The Hong Kong International
  Arbitration Centre
1 Arbuthnot Road
Central

HUNGARY
The Hungarian Chamber
of Commerce
Arbitration Court
Kossuth Lajos ter 6–8
1389 Budapest V

INDIA
The Indian Council of
  Arbitration
Federation House, Tansen Marg
New Delhi   110001

INDONESIA
The Indonesian National Arbitration Board
Jalan Merdeka Timur 11
Jakarta

INTER-AMERICA
The Inter-American Commercial Arbitration Commission
Nineteenth Street and Constitution Avenue, NW, Room 211
Washington, DC   20006

INTERNATIONAL
The International Centre for Settlement of Investment Disputes
1818 H Street, NW
Washington, DC   20433

The ICC International Court of Arbitration
38, Cours Albert 1er
75008 Paris

The International Federation of Commercial Arbitration Institutions
c/o American Arbitration Association
140 West 51st Street
New York, NY   10020–1203

ITALY
The Italian Arbitration Association
5, Via XX Settembre
00187 Roma

JAPAN
The Japan Commercial Arbitration Association
Izumi Shibakoen Building
6–8, Shibakoen 1–chome
Minato-ku
Tokyo

KOREA
The Korean Commercial Arbitration Board
43rd Floor, Trade Tower (Korea World Trade Center)
159, Samsung-Dong, Kangnam-ku
CPO Box 50
Seoul   135–729

MALAYSIA
The Regional Centre for Arbitration at Kuala Lumpur
576, Jalan Sultan Salahuddin
50480, Kuala Lumpur

THE NETHERLANDS
Netherlands' Arbitration Institute
Schouwburgplein 30–34
PO Box 22105
3003 DC Rotterdam

NEW ZEALAND
Arbitrators' Institute of New Zealand
16 Palmer Street
PO Box 1477
Wellington

PAKISTAN
The Federation of Pakistan Chambers of Commerce and Industry
Commercial Arbitration Tribunal
Share a Firdousi
Main Clifton
Karachi-6

POLAND
The International Court of Arbitration for Marine and Inland Navigation, Gdynia
Ul. Pulaskiego 6
81-368 Gdynia

The Polish Chamber of Foreign Trade Arbitration Court
Trebacka 4
PO Box 361
00-074 Warsaw

ROMANIA
The Chamber of Commerce and Industry of the Socialist Republic of Romania Arbitration Commission
Boulevard N. Balcescu 22
Bucharest

SCOTLAND
The Scottish Council for Arbitration
55 Queen Street
Edinburgh   EH2 3PA

SINGAPORE
The Singapore Institute of Arbitrators
c/o Singapore Professional Centre
129-B Blk. 23
Outram Park   0316

SPAIN
The Spanish Arbitration Association
Plaza San Amaro 1
Madrid   20

SWEDEN
The Stockholm Chamber of Commerce Arbitration Institute
PO Box 16050
S-103 22 Stockholm   16

SWITZERLAND
The Chamber of Commerce of Basel
St. Alban-Graben   8
4001 Basel

The Berne Chamber of Commerce
Gutenbergstraße 1, PO Box 5464
3011 Berne

The Chamber of Commerce of Zürich
Bleicherweg 5
PO Box 4031
8022 Zürich

The Geneva Chamber of Commerce and Industry
4, Boulevard du Théâtre
1211 Geneva   11

TAIWAN
The Commercial Arbitration Association of the Republic of China
390 Fuhsing South Road, Sec. 1
6th Floor
Taipei

UNION OF SOVIET
  SOCIALIST REPUBLICS
The USSR Chamber of Com-
  merce and Industry
Foreign Trade Arbitration
  Commission
6 Kuibyshev Street
101000 Moscow

The USSR Chamber of Com-
  merce and Industry
Maritime Arbitration Commission
6 Kuibyshev Street
101000 Moscow

UNITED KINGDOM
The London Court of International Arbitration
30–32 St. Mary Axe
London   EC3A 8ET

UNITED STATES
The American Arbitration
  Association
140 West 51st Street
New York, NY   10020–1203

YUGOSLAVIA
The Economic Chamber of
  Yugoslavia
Foreign Trade Arbitration Court
Knez Mihajilova Street 10
11000 Belgrade

INTERNATIONAL ARBITRATION RULES

As Amended and Effective on May 1, 1992

Article 1—1. Where parties have agreed in writing to arbitrate disputes under these International Arbitration Rules, the arbitration shall take place in accordance with their provisions, as in effect at the date of commencement of the arbitration, subject to whatever modifications the parties may adopt in writing.

2. These rules govern the arbitration, except that, where any such rule is in conflict with any provision of the law applicable to the arbitration from which the parties cannot derogate, that provision shall prevail.

3. These rules specify the duties and responsibilities of the administrator, the American Arbitration Association. The administrator may provide services through its own facilities or through the facilities of arbitral institutions with whom it has agreements of cooperation.

I. Commencing the Arbitration

Notice of Arbitration and Statement of Claim
Article 2—1. The party initiating arbitration (''claimant'') shall give written notice of arbitration to the administrator and to the party or parties against whom a claim is being made (''respondent(s)'').

2. Arbitral proceedings shall be deemed to commence on the date on which the notice of arbitration is received by the administrator.

3. The notice of arbitration shall include the following: (a) a demand that the dispute be referred to arbitration; (b) the names and addresses of the parties; (c) a reference to the arbitration clause or agreement that is invoked; (d) a reference to any contract out of or in relation to which the dispute arises; (e) a description of the claim and an indication of the facts supporting it; (f) the relief or remedy sought and the amount claimed; and (g) may include proposals as to the number of arbitrators, the place of arbitration and the language(s) of the arbitration.

Upon receipt of such notice, the administrator will communicate with all parties with respect to the arbitration, including the matters set forth in (g) above, if the parties have not already agreed on these matters, and will acknowledge the commencement of the arbitration.

Statement of Defense and Counterclaim
Article 3—1. Within forty-five days after the date of the commencement of the arbitration, a respondent shall file a statement of defense in writing with the claimant and any other parties, and with the administrator for transmittal to the tribunal when appointed.

2. At the time a respondent submits its statement of defense, a respondent may make counterclaims or assert set-offs as to any claim covered by the agreement to arbitrate, as to which the claimant shall within forty-five days file a statement of defense.

3. A respondent shall respond to the administrator, the claimant and other parties within forty-five days as to any proposals the claimant may have made as to the number of arbitrators, the place of the arbitration or the language(s) of the arbitration, except to the extent that the parties have previously agreed as to these matters.

Amendments to Claims

Article 4—During the arbitral proceedings, any party may amend or supplement its claim, counterclaim or defense, unless the tribunal considers it inappropriate to allow such amendment because of the party's delay in making it or of prejudice to the other parties or any other circumstances. A claim or counterclaim may not be amended if the amendment would fall outside the scope of the agreement to arbitrate.

II. The Tribunal

Number of Arbitrators

Article 5—If the parties have not agreed on the number of arbitrators, one arbitrator shall be appointed unless the administrator determines in its discretion that three arbitrators are appropriate because of the large size, complexity or other circumstances of the case.

Appointment of Arbitrators

Article 6—1. The parties may mutually agree upon any procedure for appointing arbitrators and shall inform the administrator as to such procedure.

2. The parties may mutually designate arbitrators, with or without the assistance of the administrator. When such designations are made, the parties shall notify the administrator so that notice of the appointment can be communicated to the arbitrators, together with a copy of these rules.

3. If within sixty days after the commencement of the arbitration, all of the parties have not mutually agreed on a procedure for appointing the arbitrator(s) or have not mutually agreed on the designation of the arbitrator(s), the administrator shall, at the written request of any party, appoint the arbitrator(s) and designate the presiding arbitrator. If all of the parties have mutually agreed upon a procedure for appointing the arbitrator(s), but all appointments have not been made within the time limits provided in that procedure, the administrator shall, at the written request of any party, perform all functions provided for in that procedure.

4. In making such appointments, the administrator, after inviting consultation with the parties, shall endeavor to select suitable arbitrators. At the request of any party or on its own initiative, the administrator may appoint nationals of a country other than that of any of the parties.

Challenge of Arbitrators

Article 7—Unless the parties agree otherwise, arbitrators acting under these rules shall be impartial and independent. Prior to accepting appointment, a prospective arbitrator shall disclose to the administrator any circumstance likely to give rise to justifiable doubts as to the arbitrator's impartiality or independence. Once appointed, an arbitrator shall disclose any additional such information to the parties and to the administrator. Upon receipt of such information from an arbitrator or a party, the administrator shall communicate it to the parties and to the arbitrator.

Article 8—1. A party may challenge any arbitrator whenever circumstances exist that give rise to justifiable doubts as to the arbitrator's impartiality or independence. A party wishing to challenge an arbitrator shall send notice of the challenge to the administrator within fifteen days after being notified of the appointment of the arbitrator, or within fifteen days after the circumstances giving rise to the challenge became known to that party.

2. The challenge shall state in writing the reasons for the challenge.

3. Upon receipt of such a challenge, the administrator shall notify the other parties of the challenge. When an arbitrator has been challenged by one party, the other parties may agree to the acceptance of the challenge and, if there is agreement, the arbitrator shall withdraw. The challenged arbitrator may also withdraw from office in the absence of such agreement. In neither case does this imply acceptance of the validity of the grounds for the challenge.

Article 9—If the other party or parties do not agree to the challenge or the challenged arbitrator does not withdraw, the decision on the challenge shall be made by the administrator in its sole discretion.

Replacement of an Arbitrator

Article 10—If an arbitrator withdraws after a challenge, or the administrator sustains the challenge, or the administrator determines that there are sufficient reasons to accept the resignation of an arbitrator, or an arbitrator dies, a substitute arbitrator shall be appointed pursuant to the provisions of Article 6, unless the parties otherwise agree.

Article 11—1. If an arbitrator on a three-person tribunal fails to participate in the arbitration, the two other arbitrators shall have the power in their sole discretion to continue the arbitration and to make any decision, ruling or award, notwithstanding the failure of the third arbitrator to participate. In determining whether to continue the arbitration or to render any decision, ruling or award without the participation of an arbitrator, the two other arbitrators shall take into account the stage of the arbitration, the reason, if any, expressed by the third arbitrator for such nonparticipation, and such other matters as they consider appropriate in the circumstances of the case. In the event that the two other arbitrators determine not to continue the arbitration without the participation of the third arbitrator, the administrator on proof satisfactory to it shall declare the office vacant, and a substitute arbitrator shall be appointed pursuant to the provisions of Article 6, unless the parties otherwise agree.

2. If a substitute arbitrator is appointed, the tribunal shall determine at its sole discretion whether all or part of any prior hearings shall be repeated.

III. General Conditions

Representation

Article 12—Any party may be represented in the arbitration. The names, addresses and telephone numbers of representatives shall be communicated in writing to the other parties and to the administrator. Once the tribunal has been established, the parties or their representatives may communicate in writing directly with the tribunal.

Place of Arbitration

Article 13—1. If the parties disagree as to the place of arbitration, the place of arbitration may initially be determined by the administrator, subject to the power of the tribunal to determine finally the place of arbitration within sixty days after its constitution. All such determinations shall be made having regard for the contentions of the parties and the circumstances of the arbitration.

2. The tribunal may hold conferences or hear witnesses or inspect property or documents at any place it deems appropriate. The parties shall be given sufficient written notice to enable them to be present at any such proceedings.

Language

Article 14—If the parties have not agreed otherwise, the language(s) of the arbitration shall be that of the documents containing the arbitration agreement, subject to the power of the tribunal to determine otherwise based upon the contentions of the parties and the circumstances of the arbitration. The tribunal may order that any documents delivered in another language shall be accompanied by a translation into such language or languages.

Pleas as to Jurisdiction

Article 15—1. The tribunal shall have the power to rule on its own jurisdiction, including any objections with respect to the existence or validity of the arbitration agreement.

2. The tribunal shall have the power to determine the existence or validity of a contract of which an arbitration clause forms a part. Such an arbitration clause shall be treated as an agreement independent of the other terms of the contract.

3. Objections to the arbitrability of a claim must be raised no later than forty-five days after the commencement of the arbitration and, in respect to a counterclaim, no later than forty-five days after filing the counterclaim.

Conduct of the Arbitration

Article 16—1. Subject to these rules, the tribunal may conduct the arbitration in whatever manner it considers appropriate, provided that the parties are treated with equality and that each party has the right to be heard and is given a fair opportunity to present its case.

2. Documents or information supplied to the tribunal by one party shall at the same time be communicated by that party to the other party or parties.

Further Written Statements

Article 17—The tribunal may decide whether any written statements, in addition to statements of claims and counterclaims and statements of defense, shall be required from the parties or may be presented by them, and shall fix the periods of time for submitting such statements.

Periods of Time

Article 18—The periods of time fixed by the tribunal for the communication of written statements should not exceed forty-five days. However, the tribunal may extend such time limits if it considers such an extension justified.

Notices

Article 19—1. Unless otherwise agreed by the parties or ordered by the tribunal, all notices, statements and written communications may be served on a party by air mail or air courier addressed to the party or its representative at the last known address or by personal service. Facsimile transmission, telex, telegram, or other written forms of electronic communication may be used to give any such notices, statements or written communications.

2. For the purpose of calculating a period of time under these rules, such period shall begin to run on the day following the day when a notice, statement or written communication is received. If the last day of such period is an official holiday at the place received, the period is extended until the first business day which follows. Official holidays occurring during the running of the period of time are included in calculating the period.

Evidence

Article 20—1. Each party shall have the burden of proving the facts relied on to support its claim or defense.

2. The tribunal may order a party to deliver to the tribunal and to the other parties a summary of the documents and other evidence which that party intends to present in support of its claim, counterclaim or defense.

3. At any time during the proceedings, the tribunal may order parties to produce other documents, exhibits or other evidence it deems necessary or appropriate.

Hearings

Article 21—1. The tribunal shall give the parties at least thirty days' advance notice of the date, time and place of the initial oral hearing. The tribunal shall give reasonable notice of subsequent hearings.

2. At least fifteen days before the hearings, each party shall give the tribunal and the other parties the names and addresses of any witnesses it intends to present, the subject of their testimony and the languages in which such witnesses will give their testimony.

3. At the request of the tribunal or pursuant to mutual agreement of the parties, the administrator shall make arrangements for the interpretation of oral testimony or for a record of the hearing.

4. Hearings are private unless the parties agree otherwise or the law provides to the contrary. The tribunal may require any witness or witnesses to retire during the testimony of other witnesses. The tribunal may determine the manner in which witnesses are examined.

5. Evidence of witnesses may also be presented in the form of written statements signed by them.

6. The admissibility, relevance, materiality and weight of the evidence offered by any party shall be determined by the tribunal.

Interim Measures of Protection

Article 22—1. At the request of any party, the tribunal may take whatever interim measures it deems necessary in respect of the subject-matter of the dispute, including measures for the conservation of the goods which are the subject-matter in dispute, such as ordering their deposit with a third person or the sale of perishable goods.

2. Such interim measures may be taken in the form of an interim award and the tribunal may require security for the costs of such measures.

3. A request for interim measures addressed by a party to a judicial authority shall not be deemed incompatible with the agreement to arbitrate or a waiver of the right to arbitrate.

Experts

Article 23—1. The tribunal may appoint one or more independent experts to report to it, in writing, on specific issues designated by the tribunal and communicated to the parties.

2. The parties shall provide such an expert with any relevant information or produce for inspection any relevant documents or goods that the expert may require. Any dispute between a party and the expert as to the relevance of the requested information or goods shall be referred to the tribunal for decision.

3. Upon receipt of an expert's report, the tribunal shall send a copy of the report to all parties, who shall be given an opportunity to express, in writing, their opinion on the report. A party may examine any document on which the expert has relied in such a report.

4. At the request of any party, the parties shall be given an opportunity to question the expert at a hearing. At this hearing, parties may present expert witnesses to testify on the points at issue.

Default

Article 24—1. If a party fails to file a statement of defense within the time established by the tribunal without showing sufficient cause for such failure, as determined by the tribunal, the tribunal may proceed with the arbitration.

2. If a party, duly notified under these rules, fails to appear at a hearing without showing sufficient cause for such failure, as determined by the tribunal, the tribunal may proceed with the arbitration.

3. If a party, duly invited to produce evidence, fails to do so within the time established by the tribunal without showing sufficient cause for such failure, as determined by the tribunal, the tribunal may make the award on the evidence before it.

Closure of Hearing

Article 25—1. After asking the parties if they have any further testimony or evidentiary submissions and upon receiving negative replies or if satisfied that the record is complete, the tribunal may declare the hearings closed.

2. If it considers it appropriate, on its own motion or upon application of a party, the tribunal may reopen the hearings at any time before the award is made.

Waiver of Rules

Article 26—A party who knows that any provision of the rules or requirement under the rules has not been complied with, but proceeds with the arbitration without promptly stating an objection in writing thereto, shall be deemed to have waived the right to object.

Awards, Decisions and Rulings

Article 27—1. When there is more than one arbitrator, any award, decision or ruling of the arbitral tribunal shall be made by a majority of the arbitrators.

2. When the parties or the tribunal so authorize, decisions or rulings on questions of procedure may be made by the presiding arbitrator, subject to revision by the tribunal.

Form and Effect of the Award

Article 28—1. Awards shall be made in writing, promptly by the tribunal, and shall be final and binding on the parties. The parties undertake to carry out any such award without delay.

2. The tribunal shall state the reasons upon which the award is based, unless the parties have agreed that no reasons need be given.

3. An award signed by a majority of the arbitrators shall be sufficient. Where there are three arbitrators and one of them fails to sign, the award shall be accompanied by a statement of whether the third arbitrator was given the opportunity to sign. The award shall contain the date and the place where the award was made, which shall be the place designated pursuant to Article 13.

4. An award may be made public only with the consent of all parties or as required by law.

5. Copies of the award shall be communicated to the parties by the administrator.

6. If the arbitration law of the country where the award is made requires the award to be filed or registered, the tribunal shall comply with such requirement.

7. In addition to making a final award, the tribunal may make interim, interlocutory, or partial orders and awards.

Applicable Laws

Article 29—1. The tribunal shall apply the substantive law or laws designated by the parties as applicable to the dispute. Failing such a designation by the parties, the tribunal shall apply such law or laws as it determines to be appropriate.

2. In arbitrations involving the application of contracts, the tribunal shall decide in accordance with the terms of the contract and shall take into account usages of the trade applicable to the contract.

3. The tribunal shall not decide as *amiable compositeur* or *ex aequo et bono* unless the parties have expressly authorized it to do so.

Settlement or Other Reasons for Termination

Article 30—1. If the parties settle the dispute before an award is made, the tribunal shall terminate the arbitration and, if requested by all parties, may record the settlement in the form of an award on agreed terms. The tribunal is not obliged to give reasons for such an award.

2. If the continuation of the proceedings becomes unnecessary or impossible for any other reason, the tribunal shall inform the parties of its intention to terminate the proceedings. The tribunal shall thereafter issue an order terminating the arbitration, unless a party raises justifiable grounds for objection.

Interpretation or Correction of the Award

Article 31—1. Within thirty days after the receipt of an award, any party, with notice to the other parties, may request the tribunal to interpret the award or correct any clerical, typographical or computation errors or make an additional award as to claims presented but omitted from the award.

2. If the tribunal considers such a request justified, after considering the contentions of the parties, it shall comply with such a request within thirty days after the request.

Costs

Article 32—The tribunal shall fix the costs of arbitration in its award. The tribunal may apportion such costs among the parties if it determines that such apportionment is reasonable, taking into account the circumstances of the case. Such costs may include: (a) the fees and expenses of the arbitrators; (b) the costs of assistance required by the tribunal, including its experts; (c) the fees and expenses of the administrator; (d) the reasonable costs for legal representation of a successful party.

Compensation of Arbitrators

Article 33—Arbitrators shall be compensated based upon their amount of service, taking into account the size and complexity of the case. An appropriate daily or hourly rate, based on such considerations, shall be arranged by the administrator with the parties and the arbitrators prior to the commencement of the arbitration. If the parties fail to agree on the terms of compensation, an appropriate rate shall be established by the administrator and communicated in writing to the parties.

Deposit of Costs

Article 34—1. When claims are filed, the administrator may request the filing party to deposit appropriate amounts, as an advance for the costs referred to in Article 32, paragraphs (a), (b) and (c).

2. During the course of the arbitral proceedings, the tribunal may request supplementary deposits from the parties.

3. If the deposits requested are not paid in full within thirty days after the receipt of the request, the administrator shall so inform the parties, in order that one or the other of them may make the required payment. If such payments are not made, the tribunal may order the suspension or termination of the proceedings.

4. After the award has been made, the administrator shall render an accounting to the parties of the deposits received and return any unexpended balance to the parties.

Confidentiality

Article 35—Confidential information disclosed during the proceedings by the parties or by witnesses shall not be divulged by an arbitrator or by the administrator. Unless otherwise agreed by the parties, or required by applicable law, the members of the tribunal and the administrator shall keep confidential all matters relating to the arbitration or the award.

Exclusion of Liability

Article 36—The members of the tribunal and the administrator shall be liable to any party for any act or omission in connection with any arbitration conducted under these rules, except that they may be liable to a party for the consequences of conscious and deliberate wrongdoing.

Interpretation of Rules

Article 37—The tribunal shall interpret and apply these rules insofar as they relate to its powers and duties. All other rules shall be interpreted and applied by the administrator.

AMERICAN ARBITRATION ASSOCIATION PROCEDURES FOR CASES UNDER THE UNCITRAL ARBITRATION RULES

To facilitate the conduct of arbitration cases that the parties have agreed to conduct under the UNCITRAL Arbitration Rules, the American Arbitration Association will:

1. Perform the functions of the appointing authority as set forth in the UNCITRAL Arbitration Rules whenever the AAA has been so designated by the parties either in the arbitration clause of their contract or in a separate agreement.

2. Perform the administrative services described in this booklet when called for by the contract, or when requested by all parties or by the arbitral tribunal.

Services as Appointing Authority

1. Appointment of Sole or Presiding Arbitrator—When requested to appoint a sole or presiding arbitrator, the AAA will follow the list procedure set forth in the UNCITRAL Arbitration Rules (Article 6, paragraph 3). The AAA has extensive experience in using the list procedure because it utilizes a similar procedure to conduct cases under various other rules.

In selecting arbitrators, the AAA will utilize its extensive panel of arbitrators for commercial cases. That panel includes qualified persons of many different nationalities having varied professional and business backgrounds. The AAA will carefully consider the nature of the case, as described in the notice of arbitration, in order to include in the list persons having appropriate professional or business experience and language ability.

When appointing a sole or presiding arbitrator under the UNCITRAL Arbitration Rules, the AAA will follow its usual practice and, upon the request of either party, designate a person of a nationality other than the nationalities of the parties, unless otherwise provided by written agreement of the parties.

2. Appointment of "Second" Arbitrator in Three-Arbitrator Cases—Under Article 7 of the UNCITRAL Arbitration Rules, when three arbitrators are to be appointed, each party is to appoint one arbitrator; but, if a party fails to do so, the other party may request that the appointment of the second arbitrator be made by the appointing authority.

In accordance with the UNCITRAL Arbitration Rules, the AAA, when appointing a second arbitrator, will exercise its discretion and will not utilize the list procedure. The second arbitrator to be appointed under Article 7, paragraph 2*(a)*, shall be impartial and independent of either party.

3. Decisions on Challenges to Arbitrators—Under Article 10 of the UNCITRAL Arbitration Rules, all arbitrators—including those appointed by one party—are required to be impartial and independent. Article 10 provides that any arbitrator may be challenged if circumstances exist that give rise to justifiable doubts as to the arbitrator's impartiality or independence.

Article 12 of the UNCITRAL Arbitration Rules requires that all contested challenges be decided by the appointing authority. When deciding challenges at the request of any party, the AAA will appoint a special committee to make the decision, consisting of three persons, a majority of whom will be of nationalities different from that of either party.

In deciding challenges, the AAA and any such committee will be guided by the principles set forth in the Code of Ethics for Arbitrators in Commercial Disputes, a code jointly adopted by the AAA and the American Bar Association.

4. Appointment of Substitute Arbitrators—The UNCITRAL Arbitration Rules provide that a substitute arbitrator will be appointed if an arbitrator dies or resigns during an arbitration proceeding, or if a challenge against him is sustained (Article 12, paragraph 2, and Article 13). In such cases, the AAA will perform the same function in appointing a substitute arbitrator as described above with respect to other arbitrators.

5. Consultation on Fees of Arbitrators—The UNCITRAL Arbitration Rules provide that the fees of arbitrators shall be reasonable in amount, taking into consideration the amount in dispute, the complexity of the subject matter, the time spent by the arbitrators, and any other relevant circumstances of the case (Article 39, paragraph 2). The rules provide that parties may request the appointing authority to provide to the arbitrators and parties a statement setting forth the basis for establishing fees that is customarily followed in cases in which the appointing authority acts (Article 39, paragraph 3). The AAA has no schedule of fees for arbitrators, but it will furnish a statement concerning customary fees based on its experience in administering large numbers of cases.

Administrative Services

Upon the request of all parties or the arbitral tribunal, the AAA will provide the following administrative services:

1. Communications—The experience of major arbitration agencies suggests that arbitrations are best served when communications—except at hearings—are transmitted through the arbitration administrator. Upon request, all oral or written communications from a party to the arbitral tribunal—except at hearings—may be directed to the AAA, which will transmit them to the arbitral tribunal and to the other party.

Agreement by the parties that the AAA shall administer a case constitutes consent by the parties that, for purposes of compliance with the time requirements of the UNCITRAL Arbitration Rules, any written communication shall be deemed to have been received by the addressee when received by the AAA. When transmitting communications to a party, the AAA will use the addresses set forth in the notice of arbitration or any other address that has been furnished by a party in writing to the AAA.

2. Hearings—Upon request, the AAA will assist the arbitral tribunal to establish the date, time, and place of hearings, giving such advance notice thereof to the parties as the tribunal may determine pursuant to the UNCITRAL Arbitration Rules (Article 25, paragraph 1).

3. Hearing Rooms—The AAA will provide a room for hearings in the offices of the AAA. If a hearing room is not available in the offices of the AAA, the AAA will arrange a hearing room elsewhere. The cost of hearing rooms outside of AAA offices will be billed separately and excluded from the fee for administrative services.

4. Stenographic Transcripts—Upon request, the AAA will make arrangements for stenographic transcripts of hearings. The cost of stenographic transcripts will be billed separately and excluded from the fee for administrative services.

5. Interpretation—Upon request, the AAA will make arrangements for the services of interpreters at hearings. The cost of interpretation will be billed separately and excluded from the fee for administrative services.

6. Fees of Arbitrators and Deposits—Upon request, the AAA will make all arrangements concerning the amounts of the arbitrators' fees, and advance deposits to be made on account of such fees in consultation with the parties and the arbitrators. The AAA does not fix the amount of fees of arbitrators and has no schedule for arbitrators in international commercial cases.

7. Other Services—Upon request, the AAA will consider providing other appropriate administrative services.

BIBLIOGRAPHY

American Arbitration Association, *International Arbitration Rules As Amended and Effective on May 1, 1992* (New York: American Arbitration Association)

_____, *Procedures for Cases under the UNCITRAL Arbitration Rules* (New York: American Arbitration Association; May, 1992)

_____, *Supplementary Procedures for International Commercial Arbitration As Amended and Effective on February 1, 1986* (New York: American Arbitration Association)

_____, *Survey of International Arbitration Sites* (New York: American Arbitration Association, 1988)

Arbitration & the Law: AAA General Counsel's Annual Report (New York: American Arbitration Association, since 1981)

Berg, Albert Jan van den, *The Netherlands Arbitration Act of 1986* (Deventer, the Netherlands: Kluwer Law and Taxation Publishers, 1987)

Blessing, Marc, "International Arbitration Procedures—I" in *The International Business Lawyer*, Volume 17, Number 9 (October, 1989): 408–417

_____, "International Arbitration Procedures—II" in *The International Business Lawyer*, Volume 17, Number 10 (November, 1989): 451–469

Butler, William E., Editor, *Soviet Commercial and Maritime Arbitration* (Dobbs Ferry, NY: Oceana Publications, Serial from 1980)

Craig, W. Laurence, William W. Park, and Jan Paulsson, *International Chamber of Commerce Arbitration* (Dobbs Ferry, NY: Oceana Publications, Serial since 1984)

El-Ahdab, Abdul Hamid, *Arbitration with the Arab Countries* (Deventer, the Netherlands: Kluwer Law and Taxation Publishers, 1990)

Gaja, Giorgio, Editor, *New York Convention* (Dobbs Ferry, NY: Oceana Publications, Serial since 1978)

German Institute of Arbitration, *Arbitration in US—German Business Relations* (Cologne: Carl Heymanns Verlag, 1985)

Glossner, Ottoarndt, *Commercial Arbitration in the Federal Republic of Germany* (Deventer, the Netherlands: Kluwer Law and Taxation Publishers, 1984)

Graving, Richard J., "The International Commercial Arbitration Institutions: How Good a Job Are They Doing?" *American University Journal of International Law and Policy*, Volume 4, Number 2 (Spring, 1989): 319-376

Hoellering, Michael F., "International Commercial Arbitration: A Peaceful Method of Dispute Settlement" in *The Arbitration Journal*, Volume 40, Number 4 (December, 1985): 19-26

Holtzmann, Howard M., and Joseph E. Neuhaus, *A Guide to the UNCITRAL Model Law on International Commercial Arbitration: Legislative History and Commentary* (Deventer, the Netherlands: Kluwer Law and Taxation Publishers, 1989)

International Commercial Arbitration Law, Procedures and Facilities in India (New Delhi: Singhania, 1985)

International Council for Commercial Arbitration, *International Handbook on Commercial Arbitration*, Edited by Albert Jan van den Berg (Deventer, the Netherlands: Kluwer Law and Taxation Publishers, Serial since 1976)

_____, *Yearbook Commercial Arbitration*, Edited by Albert Jan van den Berg (Deventer, the Netherlands: Kluwer Law and Taxation Publishers, since 1976)

Jones, J. Sorton, "International Arbitration" in *Hastings International and Comparative Law Review*, Volume 8, Number 2 (Winter, 1985): 213-222

Kos-Rabcewicz-Zubkowski, Ludwik, and Paul J. Davidson, *Commercial Arbitration Institutions: An International Directory and Guide* (Dobbs Ferry, NY: Oceana Publications, 1986)

Lamm, Carolyn B., "Recent Developments in International Arbitration" in *Federal Bar News & Journal*, Volume 36, Number 6 (July/August, 1989): 276-279

Lew, Julian D. M., Editor, *Contemporary Problems in International Arbitration* (London: School of International Arbitration, Centre for Commercial Law Studies, Queen Mary College, 1986)

The Parker School of Foreign and Comparative Law, *International Commercial Arbitration and the Courts* (Dobbs Ferry, NY: Transnational Juris Publications, 1990)

_____, *The 1989 Guide to International Arbitration and Arbitrators* (Dobbs Ferry, NY: Transnational Juris Publications, 1989)

_____, *The World Arbitration Reporter*, Edited by Hans Smit and Vratislav Pechota (Boston: Butterworth Legal Publishers, Serial since 1986)

Peter, Wolfgang, *Arbitration and Renegotiation of International Investment Agreements* (Hingham, MA: Martinus Nijhoff Publishers, 1986)

Redfern, Alan, and Martin Hunter, *Law and Practice of International Commercial Arbitration* (London: Sweet & Maxwell, 1986)

Sarcevic, Petar, Editor, *Essays on International Commercial Arbitration* (London: Graham & Trotman, 1989)

Schmitthoff, Clive M., Editor, *International Commercial Arbitration* (Dobbs Ferry, NY: Oceana Publications, Serial since 1974)

Schultsz, Jan C., and Albert Jan van den Berg, Editors, *The Art of Arbitration: Essays on International Arbitration, Liber Amicorum Pieter Sanders, 12 September 1912#1982* (Deventer, the Netherlands: Kluwer, 1982)

Simmonds, Kenneth R., and Brian H. W. Hill, Editors, *Commercial Arbitration Law in Asia and the Pacific* (Dobbs Ferry, NY: Oceana Publications, Serial since 1987)

The Stockholm Chamber of Commerce, *Arbitration in Sweden* (Stockholm: Stockholm Chamber of Commerce, 1984)

APPENDICES

THE CODE OF ETHICS FOR ARBITRATORS IN COMMERCIAL DISPUTES

PREAMBLE

The use of commercial arbitration to resolve a wide variety of disputes has grown extensively and forms a significant part of the system of justice on which our society relies for fair determination of legal rights. Persons who act as commercial arbitrators therefore undertake serious responsibilities to the public as well as to the parties. Those responsibilities include important ethical obligations.

Few cases of unethical behavior by commercial arbitrators have arisen. Nevertheless, the American Bar Association and the American Arbitration Association believe that it is in the public interest to set forth generally accepted standards of ethical conduct for guidance of arbitrators and parties in commercial disputes. By establishing this code, the sponsors hope to contribute to the maintenance of high standards and continued confidence in the process of arbitration.

There are many different types of commercial arbitration. Some cases are conducted under arbitration rules established by various organizations and trade associations, while others are conducted without such rules. Although most cases are arbitrated pursuant to voluntary agreement of the parties, certain types of dispute are submitted to arbitration by reason of particular laws. This code is intended to apply to all such proceedings in which disputes or claims are submitted for decision to one or more arbitrators appointed in a manner provided by an agreement of the parties, by applicable arbitration rules, or by law. In all such cases, the persons who have the power to decide should observe fundamental standards of ethical conduct. In this code all such persons are called "arbitrators" although, in some types of case, they might be called "umpires" or have some other title.

Various aspects of the conduct of arbitrators, including some matters covered by this code, may be governed by agreements of the parties, by arbitration rules to which the parties have agreed, or by applicable law. This code does not take the place of or supersede such agreements, rules, or laws and does not establish new or additional grounds for judicial review of arbitration awards.

While this code is intended to provide ethical guidelines in many types of arbitration, it does not form a part of the arbitration rules of the American Arbitration Association or of any other organization, nor is it intended to apply to mediation or conciliation. Labor arbitration is governed by the Code of Professional Responsibility for Arbitrators of Labor–Management Disputes, not by this code.

Arbitrators, like judges, have the power to decide cases. However, unlike full-time judges, arbitrators are usually engaged in other occupations before, during, and after the time that they serve as arbitrators. Often, arbitrators are purposely chosen from the same trade or industry as the parties in order to bring special knowledge to the task of deciding. This code recognizes these fundamental differences between arbitrators and judges.

In some types of arbitration, there are three or more arbitrators. In such cases, it is sometimes the practice for each party, acting alone, to appoint one arbitrator and for the other arbitrators to be designated by those two, by the parties, or by an independent institution or individual. The sponsors of this code believe that it is preferable for parties to agree that all arbitrators should comply with the same ethical standards. However, it is recognized that there is a long-established practice in some types of arbitration for the arbitrators who are appointed by one party, acting alone, to be governed by special ethical considerations. Those special considerations are set forth in the last section of the code, headed "Ethical Considerations Relating to Arbitrators Appointed by One Party."

Although this code is sponsored by the American Arbitration Association and the American Bar Association, its use is not limited to arbitrations administered by the AAA or to cases in which the arbitrators are lawyers. Rather, it is presented as a public service to provide guidance in all types of commercial arbitration.

CANON I.
AN ARBITRATOR SHOULD UPHOLD THE INTEGRITY AND FAIRNESS OF THE ARBITRATION PROCESS.

A. Fair and just processes for resolving disputes are indispensable in our society. Commercial arbitration is an important method for deciding many types of disputes. In order for commercial arbitration to be effective, there must be broad public confidence in the integrity and fairness of the process. Therefore, an arbitrator has a responsibility not only to the parties but also to the process of arbitration itself, and must observe high standards of conduct so that the integrity and fairness of the process will be preserved. Accordingly, an arbitrator should recognize a responsibility to the public, to the parties whose rights will be decided, and to all other participants in the proceeding. The provisions of this code should be construed and applied to further these objectives.

B. It is inconsistent with the integrity of the arbitration process for persons to solicit appointment for themselves. However, a person may indicate a general willingness to serve as an arbitrator.

C. Persons should accept appointment as arbitrators only if they believe that they can be available to conduct the arbitration promptly.

D. After accepting appointment and while serving as an arbitrator, a person should avoid entering into any financial, business, professional, family or social relationship, or acquiring any financial or personal interest, which is likely to affect impartiality or which might reasonably create the appearance of partiality or bias. For a reasonable period of time after the decision of a case, persons who have served as arbitrators should avoid entering into any such relationship, or acquiring any such interest, in circumstances which might reasonably create the appearance that they had been influenced in the arbitration by the anticipation or expectation of the relationship or interest.

E. Arbitrators should conduct themselves in a way that is fair to all parties and should not be swayed by outside pressure, by public clamor, by fear of criticism or by self-interest.

F. When an arbitrator's authority is derived from an agreement of the parties, the arbitrator should neither exceed that authority nor do less than is required to exercise that authority completely. Where the agreement of the parties sets forth procedures to be followed in conducting the arbitration or refers to rules to be followed, it is the obligation of the arbitrator to comply with such procedures or rules.

G. An arbitrator should make all reasonable efforts to prevent delaying tactics, harassment of parties or other participants, or other abuse or disruption of the arbitration process.

H. The ethical obligations of an arbitrator begin upon acceptance of the appointment and continue throughout all stages of the proceeding. In addition, wherever specifically set forth in this code, certain ethical obligations begin as soon as a person is requested to serve as an arbitrator and certain ethical obligations continue even after the decision in the case has been given to the parties.

CANON II.
AN ARBITRATOR SHOULD DISCLOSE ANY INTEREST OR RELATIONSHIP LIKELY TO AFFECT IMPARTIALITY OR WHICH MIGHT CREATE AN APPEARANCE OF PARTIALITY OR BIAS.

Introductory Note

This code reflects the prevailing principle that arbitrators should disclose the existence of interests or relationships that are likely to affect their impartiality or that might reasonably create an appearance that they are biased against one party or favorable to another. These provisions of the code are intended to be applied realistically so that the burden of detailed disclosure does not become so great that it is impractical for persons in the business world to be arbitrators, thereby depriving parties of the services of those who might be best informed and qualified to decide particular types of case.*

This code does not limit the freedom of parties to agree on whomever they choose as an arbitrator. When parties, with knowledge of a person's interests and relationships, nevertheless desire that individual to serve as an arbitrator, that person may properly serve.

Disclosure

A. Persons who are requested to serve as arbitrators should, before accepting, disclose

  (1) any direct or indirect financial or personal interest in the outcome of the arbitration;

---

* In applying the provisions of this code relating to disclosure, it might be helpful to recall the words of the concurring opinion, in a case decided by the US Supreme Court, that arbitrators "should err on the side of disclosure" because "it is better that the relationship be disclosed at the outset when the parties are free to reject the arbitrator or accept him with knowledge of the relationship." At the same time, it must be recognized that "an arbitrator's business relationships may be diverse indeed, involving more or less remote commercial connections with great numbers of people." Accordingly, an arbitrator "cannot be expected to provide the parties with his complete and unexpurgated business biography," nor is an arbitrator called on to disclose interests or relationships that are merely "trivial" (a concurring opinion in *Commonwealth Coatings Corp. v. Continental Casualty Co.*, 393 US 145, 151–152, 1968).

    (2) any existing or past financial, business, professional, family or social relationships which are likely to affect impartiality or which might reasonably create an appearance of partiality or bias. Persons requested to serve as arbitrators should disclose any such relationships which they personally have with any party or its lawyer, or with any individual whom they have been told will be a witness. They should also disclose any such relationships involving members of their families or their current employers, partners or business associates.

B. Persons who are requested to accept appointment as arbitrators should make a reasonable effort to inform themselves of any interests or relationships described in the preceding paragraph A.

C. The obligation to disclose interests or relationships described in the preceding paragraph A is a continuing duty which requires a person who accepts appointment as an arbitrator to disclose, at any stage of the arbitration, any such interests or relationships which may arise, or which are recalled or discovered.

D. Disclosure should be made to all parties unless other procedures for disclosure are provided in the rules or practices of an institution which is administering the arbitration. Where more than one arbitrator has been appointed, each should inform the others of the interests and relationships which have been disclosed.

E. In the event that an arbitrator is requested by all parties to withdraw, the arbitrator should do so. In the event that an arbitrator is requested to withdraw by less than all of the parties because of alleged partiality or bias, the arbitrator should withdraw unless either of the following circumstances exists.

    (1) If an agreement of the parties, or arbitration rules agreed to by the parties, establishes procedures for determining challenges to arbitrators, then those procedures should be followed; or,

    (2) if the arbitrator, after carefully considering the matter, determines that the reason for the challenge is not substantial, and that he or she can nevertheless act and decide the case impartially and fairly, and that withdrawal would cause unfair delay or expense to another party or would be contrary to the ends of justice.

CANON III.
AN ARBITRATOR IN COMMUNICATING WITH THE PARTIES SHOULD AVOID IMPROPRIETY OR THE APPEARANCE OF IMPROPRIETY.

A. If an agreement of the parties or applicable arbitration rules referred to in that agreement, establishes the manner or content of communications between the arbitrator and the parties, the arbitrator should follow those procedures notwithstanding any contrary provision of the following paragraphs B and C.

B. Unless otherwise provided in applicable arbitration rules or in an agreement of the parties, arbitrators should not discuss a case with any party in the absence of each other party, except in any of the following circumstances.

    (1) Discussions may be had with a party concerning such matters as setting the time and place of hearings or making other arrangements for the conduct of the proceedings. However, the arbitrator should promptly inform each other party of

the discussion and should not make any final determination concerning the matter discussed before giving each absent party an opportunity to express its views.

(2) If a party fails to be present at a hearing after having been given due notice, the arbitrator may discuss the case with any party who is present.

(3) If all parties request or consent to it, such discussion may take place.

C. Unless otherwise provided in applicable arbitration rules or in an agreement of the parties, whenever an arbitrator communicates in writing with one party, the arbitrator should at the same time send a copy of the communication to each other party. Whenever the arbitrator receives any written communication concerning the case from one party which has not already been sent to each other party, the arbitrator should do so.

CANON IV.
AN ARBITRATOR SHOULD CONDUCT THE PROCEEDINGS FAIRLY AND DILIGENTLY.

A. An arbitrator should conduct the proceedings in an evenhanded manner and treat all parties with equality and fairness at all stages of the proceedings.

B. An arbitrator should perform duties diligently and conclude the case as promptly as the circumstances reasonably permit.

C. An arbitrator should be patient and courteous to the parties, to their lawyers and to the witnesses and should encourage similar conduct by all participants in the proceedings.

D. Unless otherwise agreed by the parties or provided in arbitration rules agreed to by the parties, an arbitrator should accord to all parties the right to appear in person and to be heard after due notice of the time and place of hearing.

E. An arbitrator should not deny any party the opportunity to be represented by counsel.

F. If a party fails to appear after due notice, an arbitrator should proceed with the arbitration when authorized to do so by the agreement of the parties, the rules agreed to by the parties or by law. However, an arbitrator should do so only after receiving assurance that notice has been given to the absent party.

G. When an arbitrator determines that more information than has been presented by the parties is required to decide the case, it is not improper for the arbitrator to ask questions, call witnesses, and request documents or other evidence.

H. It is not improper for an arbitrator to suggest to the parties that they discuss the possibility of settlement of the case. However, an arbitrator should not be present or otherwise participate in the settlement discussions unless requested to do so by all parties. An arbitrator should not exert pressure on any party to settle.

I. Nothing in this code is intended to prevent a person from acting as a mediator or conciliator of a dispute in which he or she has been appointed as arbitrator, if requested to do so by all parties or where authorized or required to do so by applicable laws or rules.

J. When there is more than one arbitrator, the arbitrators should afford each other the full opportunity to participate in all aspects of the proceedings.

CANON V.
AN ARBITRATOR SHOULD MAKE DECISIONS IN A JUST, INDEPENDENT AND DELIBERATE MANNER.

A. An arbitrator should, after careful deliberation, decide all issues submitted for determination. An arbitrator should decide no other issues.

B. An arbitrator should decide all matters justly, exercising independent judgment, and should not permit outside pressure to affect the decision.

C. An arbitrator should not delegate the duty to decide to any other person.

D. In the event that all parties agree upon a settlement of issues in dispute and request an arbitrator to embody that agreement in an award, an arbitrator may do so, but is not required to do so unless satisfied with the propriety of the terms of settlement. Whenever an arbitrator embodies a settlement by the parties in an award, the arbitrator should state in the award that it is based on an agreement of the parties.

CANON VI.
AN ARBITRATOR SHOULD BE FAITHFUL TO THE RELATIONSHIP OF TRUST AND CONFIDENTIALITY INHERENT IN THAT OFFICE.

A. An arbitrator is in a relationship of trust to the parties and should not, at any time, use confidential information acquired during the arbitration proceeding to gain personal advantage or advantage for others, or to affect adversely the interest of another.

B. Unless otherwise agreed by the parties, or required by applicable rules or law, an arbitrator should keep confidential all matters relating to the arbitration proceedings and decision.

C. It is not proper at any time for an arbitrator to inform anyone of the decision in advance of the time it is given to all parties. In a case in which there is more than one arbitrator, it is not proper at any time for an arbitrator to inform anyone concerning the deliberations of the arbitrators. After an arbitration award has been made, it is not proper for an arbitrator to assist in postarbitral proceedings, except as is required by law.

D. In many types of arbitration it is customary practice for the arbitrators to serve without pay. However, in some types of cases it is customary for arbitrators to receive compensation for their services and reimbursement for their expenses. In cases in which any such payments are to be made, all persons who are requested to serve, or who are serving as arbitrators, should be governed by the same high standards of integrity and fairness as apply to their other activities in the case. Accordingly, such persons should scrupulously avoid bargaining with parties over the amount of payments or engaging in any communications concerning payments which would create an appearance of coercion or other impropriety. In the absence of governing provisions in the agreement of the parties or in rules agreed to by the parties or in applicable law, certain practices, relating to payments are generally recognized as being preferable in order to preserve the integrity and fairness of the arbitration process. These practices include the following.

    (1) It is preferable that before the arbitrator finally accepts appointment the basis of payment be established and that all parties be informed thereof in writing.

(2) In cases conducted under the rules or administration of an institution that is available to assist in making arrangements for payments, the payments should be arranged by the institution to avoid the necessity for communication by the arbitrators directly with the parties concerning the subject.

(3) In cases where no institution is available to assist in making arrangement for payments, it is preferable that any discussions with arbitrators concerning payments should take place in the presence of all parties.

CANON VII.
ETHICAL CONSIDERATIONS RELATING
TO ARBITRATORS APPOINTED BY ONE PARTY

Introductory Note

In some types of arbitration in which there are three arbitrators, it is customary for each party, acting alone, to appoint one arbitrator. The third arbitrator is then appointed by agreement either of the parties or of the two arbitrators, or, failing such agreement, by an independent institution or individual. In some of these types of arbitration, all three arbitrators are customarily considered to be neutral and are expected to observe the same standards of ethical conduct. However, there are also many types of tripartite arbitration in which it has been the practice that the two arbitrators appointed by the parties are not considered to be neutral and are expected to observe many—but not all—of the same ethical standards as the neutral third arbitrator. For the purposes of this code, an arbitrator appointed by one party who is not expected to observe all of the same standards as the third arbitrator is called a "nonneutral arbitrator." This Canon VII describes the ethical obligations that nonneutral party-appointed arbitrators should observe and those that are not applicable to them.

In all arbitrations in which there are two or more party-appointed arbitrators, it is important for everyone concerned to know from the start whether the party-appointed arbitrators are expected to be neutrals or nonneutrals. In such arbitrations, the two party-appointed arbitrators should be considered nonneutrals unless both parties inform the arbitrators that all three arbitrators are to be neutral or unless the contract, the applicable arbitration rules, or any governing law requires that all three arbitrators be neutral.

It should be noted that, in cases conducted outside the United States, the applicable law might require that all arbitrators be neutral. Accordingly, in such cases, the governing law should be considered before applying any of the following provisions relating to nonneutral party-appointed arbitrators.

A. *Obligations under Canon I*

Nonneutral party-appointed arbitrators should observe all of the obligations of Canon I to uphold the integrity and fairness of the arbitration process, subject only to the following provisions.

(1) Nonneutral arbitrators may be predisposed toward the party who appointed them but in all other respects are obligated to act in good faith and with integrity and fairness. For example, nonneutral arbitrators should not engage in delaying tactics or harassment of any party or witness and should not knowingly make untrue or misleading statements to the other arbitrators.

(2) The provisions of Canon I.D relating to relationships and interests are not applicable to nonneutral arbitrators.

B. *Obligations under Canon II*

Nonneutral party-appointed arbitrators should disclose to all parties, and to the other arbitrators, all interests and relationships which Canon II requires be disclosed. Disclosure as required by Canon II is for the benefit not only of the party who appointed the nonneutral arbitrator, but also for the benefit of the other parties and arbitrators so that they may know of any bias which may exist or appear to exist. However, this obligation is subject to the following provisions.

(1) Disclosure by nonneutral arbitrators should be sufficient to describe the general nature and scope of any interest or relationship, but need not include as detailed information as is expected from persons appointed as neutral arbitrators.

(2) Nonneutral arbitrators are not obliged to withdraw if requested to do so by the party who did not appoint them, notwithstanding the provisions of Canon II.E.

C. *Obligations under Canon III*

Nonneutral party-appointed arbitrators should observe all of the obligations of Canon III concerning communications with the parties, subject only to the following provisions.

(1) In an arbitration in which the two party-appointed arbitrators are expected to appoint the third arbitrator, nonneutral arbitrators may consult with the party who appointed them concerning the acceptability of persons under consideration for appointment as the third arbitrator.

(2) Nonneutral arbitrators may communicate with the party who appointed them concerning any other aspect of the case, provided they first inform the other arbitrators and the parties that they intend to do so. If such communication occurred prior to the time the person was appointed as arbitrator, or prior to the first hearing or other meeting of the parties with the arbitrators, the nonneutral arbitrator should, at the first hearing or meeting, disclose the fact that such communication has taken place. In complying with the provisions of this paragraph, it is sufficient that there be disclosure of the fact that such communication has occurred without disclosing the content of the communication. It is also sufficient to disclose at any time the intention to follow the procedure of having such communications in the future and there is no requirement thereafter that there be disclosure before each separate occasion on which such a communication occurs.

(3) When nonneutral arbitrators communicate in writing with the party who appointed them concerning any matter as to which communication is permitted under this code, they are not required to send copies of any such written communication to any other party or arbitrator.

D. *Obligations under Canon IV*

Nonneutral party-appointed arbitrators should observe all of the obligations of Canon IV to conduct the proceedings fairly and diligently.

E. *Obligations under Canon V*

Nonneutral party-appointed arbitrators should observe all of the obligations of Canon V concerning making decisions, subject only to the following provision.

(1) Nonneutral arbitrators are permitted to be predisposed toward deciding in favor of the party who appointed them.

F. *Obligations under Canon VI*

Nonneutral party-appointed arbitrators should observe all of the obligations of Canon VI to be faithful to the relationship of trust inherent in the office of arbitrator, subject only to the following provision.

(1) Nonneutral arbitrators are not subject to the provisions of Canon VI.D with respect to any payments by the party who appointed them.

CHECKLIST FOR COMMERCIAL ARBITRATION*

This is a brief summary of commercial arbitration principles and procedure in general. There are specialized rules for various types of commercial arbitrations, and these rules may differ in certain respects from the general commercial arbitration rules referred to in this checklist. These specialized rules should be consulted when dealing with such cases. The following abbreviations are used in this checklist: CAR: Commercial Arbitration Rules of the American Arbitration Association (January 1, 1991); UAA: Uniform Arbitration Act (adopted in whole or in part by 35 states plus Puerto Rico and the District of Columbia); and USC: United States Code. In addition to the 35 states that have adopted the Uniform Arbitration Act, there are 13 that have enacted so-called modern arbitration statutes that are similar to the UAA.

Nature of arbitration as contrasted with judicial proceedings.
A. Particular arbitrator with expertise selected for specific dispute, instead of permanent tribunal for all disputes. (CAR §4.)
B. Substantive principles of law not necessarily followed. *Burchell v. Marsch*, 58 US (17 How) 344 (1854).
C. Proceedings private and usually without recorded transcript. (CAR §§23, 25.)
D. Arbitrators not bound by rules of evidence. (CAR §§31, 32.)
E. Reasons need not be given in support of determination. (CAR §§42, 43.)
F. Award subject to limited appellate review. (9 USC§§10, 15; UAA § 12).
G. Proceedings expeditious and relatively inexpensive. (CAR Administrative Fee Schedule, p 22.)

Areas of dispute adaptable to arbitration.
A. General commercial disputes:
    1. Contracts.
        a. Interpretation.
        b. Performance.
    2. Accounting.
    3. Intrabusiness disputes.
    4. Matters of trade custom and usage.
    5. Valuation issues.
    6. Small claims.

---

*Prepared by the American Arbitration Association. Reprinted with permission from LEGAL CHECK-LISTS, published by Callaghan & Co., 3201 Old Glenview Road, Wilmette, Illinois 60091.

B. Specialized commercial disputes:
1. Construction.
2. Homeowner's warranty.
3. Textile.
4. Seed and grain.
5. International.
6. No-fault.
7. Real estate valuation.
8. Uninsured motorist.
9. Maritime.
10. Fats and oils.
11. Patents validity and infringement. 35 USC §294. See also American Arbitration Association, Patent Arbitration Rules (Nov. 1, 1988).
12. Foreign antitrust. *Mitsubishi Motors Corp. v. Soler Chrysler–Plymouth*, 473 US 614, 87 L Ed 2d 444, 105 S Ct 3346 (1985).
13. Securities fraud, under the 1934 Securities Exchange Act. *Shearson/American Express v. McMahon*, 482 US 220, 96 L Ed 2d 185, 107 S Ct 2332 (1987). See also the American Arbitration Association Security Arbitration Rules (January 1, 1989).
14. Cases brought under §12(2) of the Securities Act of 1933 (misstatements in initial public offerings). *Rodriguez de Quijas v. Shearson/American Express, Inc.*, __ US __, __ L Ed 2d __, 109 S Ct 1917 (1989), revg *Wilko v. Swan*, 346 US 427, 98 L Ed 168, 74 S Ct 182 (1953).

C. Disputes not arbitrable.
1. Statutes may reserve jurisdiction over dispute to courts or prohibit waiver of person's right to sue in court (e.g., certain violations of federal securities laws, bankruptcy laws).
2. Courts may prohibit arbitration of certain disputes (e.g., domestic antitrust matters).
See Hoellering, Arbitrability of Disputes, 41 *Bus Law* 125 (1985).

Methods of obtaining arbitration of disputes.

A. Future disputes.
1. Contract provisions suggested by American Arbitration Association:
2. Any controversy or claim arising out of or relating to this contract, or any breach thereof, shall be settled in accordance with the rules of the American Arbitration Association, and judgment upon the award rendered by the arbitrator(s) may be entered in any court having jurisdiction thereof.

B. Existing disputes.
1. Submission form suggested by American Arbitration Association:
2. We, the undersigned parties, hereby agree to submit to arbitration under the . . . Arbitration Rules of the American Arbitration Association the following controversy: (describe dispute briefly and state amount involved).
3. We further agree that the above controversy be submitted to (one)(three) arbitrators selected from the panels of arbitrators of the American Arbitration Association.

4. We further agree that we will faithfully observe this agreement and the rules and that we will abide by and perform any award rendered by the arbitrator(s) and that a judgment of any court having jurisdiction may be entered upon the award. (See Form G1.)

Prerequisites to arbitration.

A. Arbitrable controversy.
   1. Justiciable dispute or one subject to judicial action.
   2. Dispute the resolution of which would not contravene public policy.

B. Formal writing.
   1. Contract clause providing for arbitration of future disputes. (UAA §1; CAR §1), or
   2. Submission of a pending dispute. (CAR §7.)

C. Arbitration procedure:
   1. Locale. (CAR §11.)
   2. Method of selecting arbitrators (9 USC §5; UAA §3; CAR §§13–15) and of filling vacancies. (UAA §3; CAR §20.) Arbitrator must disclose any information about circumstances likely to affect impartiality. (CAR §19.)
   3. Number of arbitrators. (9 USC §5; CAR §17.) Generally one arbitrator unless otherwise agreed by parties or the AAA, in its discretion, directs that a greater number of arbitrators be appointed. (*Id.*)
   4. Date, time, place of hearing. (UAA §5(a); CAR §21.)
      a. Generally set by arbitrator. (*Id.*)
      b. Administrative conference or preliminary hearing may be available at the request of any party or at the discretion of the AAA or the arbitrator. (CAR §10.)
   5. Provision for costs and fees. (UAA §10; CAR §§43, 48–51.)
   6. Provision as to whether judgment may be entered on award. (UAA §11.)
   7. Arbitration may be available on a class basis in some jurisdictions. *Keating v. Superior Court (Southland)*, 31 Cal 3d 628, 183 Cal Rptr 360, 645 P2d 1192 (1982), affd sub nom. *Southland Corp. v. Keating*, 465 US 1, 79 L Ed 2d 1, 104 S Ct 851 (1984).

Initiation of arbitration proceedings.

A. Without court order.
   1. Demand for arbitration (Form G2), filed by one party to dispute, listing names of parties, contract involved, nature of dispute, amount involved, if any, remedy sought, and hearing locale requested. (CAR §6.)
   2. Submission agreement. (CAR §7; Form C1.)
   3. Answering statement and/or counterclaim are like pleadings and ordinarily define and limit scope of arbitrable issues. (CAR §6.) No new or different claims after filing period without consent of arbitrator. (CAR §8.)

B. By court order.
   1. If either party refuses to arbitrate, the other party may apply for a court order compelling arbitration. (9 USC §4; UAA §2(a).)
   2. Under United States Arbitration Act, notice of application for court order must be served in accordance with Federal Rules of Civil Procedure. (9 USC §4.)

C. Stay of action.
  1. If one party brings judicial action of an arbitrable issue, other party may obtain a stay in court in which action is brought. (9 USC §3; UAA §2(c).)
  2. Failure of party to seek a stay may result in waiver of right to arbitrate. (9 USC §§3, 4.)

Issues available to party opposing arbitration.
A. Party opposing arbitration may raise:
  1. Questions of fact.
    a. No valid contract or submission for arbitration exists.
    b. Other party has failed to comply with conditions precedent to arbitration.
    c. No issue referable to arbitration exists.
    d. Fraud in inducement of arbitration provision. Most courts distinguish between fraud in inducement of contract, which is arbitrable, and fraud in inducement of arbitration provision, which is not arbitrable.
  2. Questions of law.
    a. Existence of bona fide controversy.
    b. Waiver.
      (1) By filing judicial action.
      (2) By answering or counterclaiming to judicial action.
      (3) Other conduct inconsistent with arbitration.
    c. Illegal contract.
    d. Contract impossible of performance.
    e. Existence of subsequent written contract superseding, or releasing parties from requirements of, arbitration contract.
    f. Nonarbitrable issue.
      (1) It is error for a federal district court to deny a motion to compel arbitration of arbitrable state law claims because they are intertwined with nonarbitrable federal law claims. Under the United States Arbitration Act, courts must compel arbitration of all arbitrable claims at the request of a party to the agreement, where there is a valid agreement to arbitrate. See *Dean Witter Reynolds, Inc. v. Byrd*, 470 US 213, 84 L Ed 2d 158, 105 S Ct 1238 (1985).
      (2) Bankruptcy court has discretion to permit or deny arbitration of claim.

B. If substantial issue of fact exists, court in which action to enforce right to arbitration is brought will proceed with trial on such issue. (9 USC §4; UAA §2(b).)
  1. Court hearing is similar to hearing on motion for summary judgment. (9 USC §4; UAA §2(b).)
  2. Party opposing arbitration may seek jury trial under United States Arbitration Act. (9 USC §4.)

C. Ordinarily, participation in the selection of arbitrators or in any proceedings before them constitutes a waiver of the issue of validity of the arbitration submission or contract.
  1. Party seeking to raise issues opposing arbitration should avoid any participation in the arbitration proceedings.

2. When party claims arbitrators were improperly selected, he or she should not continue with arbitration, in order to avoid a charge of waiver.

D. Section 2 of Federal Arbitration Act (9 USC §2) preempts states from requiring judicial proceeding to resolve issues that parties have agreed to resolve by arbitration. *Southland Corp. v. Keating*, 465 US 1, 79 L Ed 2d 1, 104 S Ct 852 (1984).
See Hoellering, Arbitrability of Disputes, 41 *Bus Law* 125 (1985).

Arbitration hearing.

A. Any party may be represented by counsel or other authorized representative. (UAA §6; CAR §22.)

B. Hearings are ordinarily set promptly. (UAA §5(a); CAR §21.)

C. Notice of hearing must be given to all parties. (CAR §21.) Facsimile transmission, telex, telegram, or other written forms of electronic communication may be used to give notices required by rules. (CAR §40.)

D. Arbitrators may be empowered to proceed in the absence of party that fails to appear. (UAA §5(a); CAR §30.)

E. All parties having a direct interest in the case may attend. (UAA §5(b); CAR §25.)

F. Arbitrators may adjourn hearing for good cause shown. (UAA §5(a); CAR §26.)

G. In some jurisdictions, the arbitrator, or other persons authorized by law, may issue subpoenas. (9 USC §7; UAA §7(a); CAR §31.) (See Form C7.)

H. Rules of evidence do not control, although sometimes relevant as guides. (CAR §§31, 32.)

I. Party bringing the arbitrtion generally opens and closes hearing. (CAR §29.)

J. No stenographic record kept unless requested by one or more parties. (CAR §23.)

K. Refusal of arbitrator to hear material evidence may constitute ground for vacating award. (9 USC §10(c); UAA §12(a)(4).)

L. Party that proceeds with arbitration after knowledge that rules have not been complied with, and fails to state objection in writing, is deemed to have waived right to object. (CAR §38.)

M. No ex parte communication by party with arbitrator. (CAR §29(a).)

N. Parties may stipulate to vary procedure. (See Form C7.)

O. Arbitrator is empowered to vary hearing procedure. (CAR §29.)

Arbitration award.

A. Award must be rendered within specified time after close of hearings (usually 30 days). (UAA §8(b); CAR §41.)

B. Award must be in writing (9 USC §13(b); UAA §8(a); CAR §42), signed by a majority. (UAA §5(c); CAR §42.)

C. Interest is assessable at discretion of arbitrator. (CAR §43.) Punitive damages may be awarded in some jurisdictions. *Baker v. Sadick*, 162 Cal App 3d 618, 208 Cal Rptr 676 (1984).

D. Award may be confirmed by court, if either party so desires (9 USC §13; UAA §11), within one year after award. (9 USC §9.)

E. Award may be vacated by court only:
   1. If procured by corruption, fraud, or undue means. (9 USC §10(a); UAA §12(a)(1).)
   2. Because of partiality or corruption of the arbitrator. (9 USC §10(b); UAA §12(a)(2).)
   3. Where the arbitrator:
      a. Refused to hear pertinent or material evidence. (9 USC §10(c); UAA §12(a)(4).)
      b. Refused to postpone hearing upon sufficient cause shown. (9 USC §10(c); UAA §12(a)(4).)
      c. Was guilty of other misbehavior prejudicing the rights of parties. (9 USC §10(c); UAA §12(a)(4).)
      d. Exceeded powers. (9 USC §10(d); UAA §12(a)(3).)
      e. Imperfectly executed powers. (9 USC §10(d).)

F. An award may be modified or corrected by a court:
   1. Where there was a miscalculation of figures or a mistake in description of person, thing, or property. (9 USC §11(a); UAA §13(a)(1).)
   2. Where arbitrator awarded upon a matter not submitted to arbitration. (9 USC §11(b); UAA §13(a)(2).)
   3. Where the award is imperfect in form. (9 USC §11(c); UAA §13(a)(3).)

G. Arbitrator may be empowered to modify award for reasons set forth in (F), above, upon timely application by party. (UAA §9.)

Effect of arbitration judgment.

A. Res judicata applies to every arbitration award confirmed by a court. *Rembrandt Industries v. Hodges International*, 38 NY2d 502, 381 NYS2d 451, 344 NE2d 383 (1970).

B. An appeal from a confirmed award is limited to defects in the arbitration procedure as outlined above. (9 USC §10.)

Liability of arbitrators.

A. Arbitrators immune from *civil* liability for damages arising out of their conduct as arbitrators. *Hill v. Aro*, 263 F Supp 324 (ND Ohio, 1967). See also CAR §47(b). But see *Baar v. Tigerman*, 140 Cal App 3d 979, 189 Cal Rptr 834 (1983), holding that an arbitrator may be liable for breaching contract to render timely award. See also *York International v. Alabama Oxygen Co., Inc.*, 465 US 1016, 79 L Ed 2d 668, 104 S Ct 1260 (1984).

B. Arbitrators not liable for acts of omission. (CAR §47.)

Liability of administering agencies.

Administering agencies generally immune from civil liability for damages arising out of their conduct in administration of arbitrations. *Corey v. New York Stock Exchange*, 493 F Supp 51 (WD Mich, 1980), affd 691 F2d 1205 (CA6, 1982). See also CAR §47(b).

International arbitration.

A. United States Supreme Court has approved arbitration of statutory antitrust claims under international contract. *Mitsubishi Motors Corp. v. Soler Chrysler-Plymouth Inc.*, 473 US 614, 87 L Ed 2d 444, 105 S Ct 3346 (1985).

B. Important to specify that arbitration is desired and what rules should govern (e.g., Rules of Conciliation and Arbitration of the International Chamber of Commerce).

C. Consider giving arbitrator broad authority.

D. Specify number, nationality, and qualifications of arbitrators. Consider arbitral institutions such as the International Chamber of Commerce, American Arbitration Association, London Court of Arbitration, Stockholm Chamber of Commerce Arbitration Institute, or International Centre for Settlement of Investment Disputes.

E. Choose language.

F. Specify governing law. Important to make it clear that law chosen applies to merits of dispute, not just to choice of law question. Sometimes parties stipulate lex mercatoria (international law merchant).

G. Consider authorizing arbitrator to be "amiable compositeur." Arbitrator decides disputes using equitable principles.

H. Waiver of sovereign immunity if contract involves nation or national agency.

I. Place of arbitration. Best to select place where court intervention unlikely. Choice might be left to institution dealing with arbitration if fear that political climate might change by time dispute occurs.
   1. Advisable to choose country party to the 1958 New York Convention on Recognition and Enforcement of Foreign Arbitral Awards. (United States ratified in 1970; see 9 USC §201 et seq).
   2. 1961 European Convention on International Commercial Arbitration.
   See Park, Arbitration of International Contract Disputes, 39 *Bus Law* 1783 (1984); Craig, Park & Paulsson, International Chamber of Commerce Arbitration; American Arbitration Association Supplementary Procedures for International Arbitration (discussed infra).

Alternatives to traditional arbitration.
A. Expedited Procedures.
   1. Under CAR §9, expedited procedures are applied in any case where no disclosed claim or counterclaim exceeds $50,000, exclusive of interest and costs.
   2. Parties accept all notices from AAA by telephone (generally confirmed later in writing). (CAR § 53.)
   3. Five names submitted on AAA list of arbitrators; each party may strike up to two names.
   4. Hearing set by telephone; confirmed later in writing. Seven-day notice given. (CAR § 55.)
   5. Award rendered within 14 days of close of hearing. (CAR §57.)
B. Mini-trial.
   1. Confidential, nonbinding settlement procedure. See Hoellering, The Mini-trial, 37:4 *Arb J* (1982); American Arbitration Association Mini-trial Procedures (Dec. 1986).
   2. Abbreviated discovery.
   3. Case presented by counsel, usually in one day, to the mini-trial judge who has been mutually selected by the parties. Key executives involved in dispute are present.

4. Judge issues nonbinding advisory decision, with written opinion detailing strengths and weaknesses in parties' cases.

5. Parties attempt to settle dispute after receipt of judge's decision and opinion.

C. Mediation

1. Confidential, nonbinding settlement procedure. See Coulson, *Professional Mediation of Civil Disputes* 6–10 (1984).

2. Dispute submitted to impartial individual who attempts to bring parties to a settlement.

3. Mediator may suggest ways of resolving dispute but cannot impose a settlement. American Arbitration Association, Commercial Mediation Rules Sec 10 (Oct. 1, 1987).

4. Mediation is strictly confidential; no stenographic record kept; statements made at mediation sessions cannot be used against a party to the mediation. American Arbitration Association, Commercial Mediation Rules §§10, 13 (Oct. 1, 1987).

5. See the American Arbitration Association Guide to Mediation for Business People.

6. Pursuant to CAR §10, parties to a pending arbitration may agree to mediate under the AAA's Mediation Rules without additional administrative fee.

D. Alternative Dispute Resolution Procedures.

1. Prompt, inexpensive means of settling disputes where there is no arbitration agreement existing at the time a dispute arises. Used primarily for insurance claims disputes. American Arbitration Association Alternative Dispute Resolution Procedures for Insurance Claims (Jan. 1, 1989).

2. Party desiring to initiate proceedings advises American Arbitration Association of its willingness to submit a particular matter to resolution under the alternative dispute resolution procedures.

3. American Arbitration Association contacts other involved parties and attempts to obtain their agreement to use alternative dispute resolution procedures.

4. Parties can agree to use mediation or arbitration.

Special procedures.

A. Guidelines for expediting large, complex commercial (construction) cases.

1. Designed to facilitate the arbitration of such cases. Parties may wish to adopt any or all of the guidelines in their arbitration.

2. Provides extensive guidelines for administrative conference and/or preliminary hearing.

3. Provides for three arbitrators, unless the parties agree otherwise.

4. Parties may agree to the neutrality of party-appointed arbitrators.

B. Supplementary procedures for international commercial arbitration.

1. Designed to deal with the unique procedural problems often present in international arbitration cases. Will be applied by the AAA absent the objections of a party.

2. Contains provisions for nonnational arbitrators; challenge of arbitrators; exchange of documents, advance filing of documents; hearings; language of arbitration; opinions; fees of arbitrators and deposits.

REFERENCES

Statutes and Rules

American Arbitration Association, Commercial Arbitration Rules of the American Arbitration Association: As Amended and in Effect January 1, 1991.

American Arbitration Association, Guidelines for Expediting Larger, Complex Commercial Arbitrations (1987).

American Arbitration Association, Supplementary Procedures for International Commercial Arbitration (1987).

Uniform Arbitration Act (reprint) (1985).

Texts and Services

Arbitration & the Law, AAA General Counsel's Report, annual series from 1981 to the present.

Coulson, *Business Arbitration—What You Need To Know* (Revised 3rd Ed, 1987).

De Seife, *Solving Disputes Through Commercial Arbitration* (1987).

Domke, *Domke on Commercial Arbitration* (Rev Ed Wilner, 1984).

Goldberg, *A Lawyer's Guide to Commercial Arbitration* (2nd Ed, 1983).

A Guide for Commercial Arbitrators (1990).

Rodman, *Commercial Arbitration with Forms* (1985).

Articles

Barrett, Arbitration of a Complex Commercial Case: Practical Guidelines for Arbitrators and Counsel, 41 *Arbitration Journal* 15 (1986).

Coulson, Dispute Management under Modern Construction Systems, 46 *Law & Contemporary Problems* 127 (Winter 1983).

Friedman, Correcting Arbitrator Error: The Limited Scope of Judicial Review, 33 *Arbitration Journal* 9–16 (Dec. 1978).

SIGNIFICANT COURT DECISIONS

Amtorg Trading Corp. v. *Camden Fibre Mills*, 304 N.Y. 519, 109 N.E.2d 606 (1952): a company that agreed to do business with a trading agent for a foreign country waived the right to assert that the arbitrators could not be impartial because they were controlled by a foreign country.

Anaconda v. *American Sugar Refining Co.*, 332 U.S. 42 (1944): the statutory remedy provided in the United States Arbitration Act (9 U.S.C. §1 *et seq.*) for libel and seizure in admiralty cases cannot be eliminated by the agreement of the parties.

Astoria Medical Group v. *Health Insurance Plan of Greater New York*, 11 N.Y.2d 128, 227 N.Y.S.2d 401 (1962): established criteria by which to judge a party-appointed arbitrator.

Baar v. *Tigerman*, Cal. Rptr. 834 (App. 1983): an arbitrator who breaches his or her contract by failing to render a timely award is not protected by the doctrine of quasi-judicial immunity. Arbitration associations performing ministerial functions, as well, are not immune from suit.

Bernhardt v. *Polygraphic Company of America*, 350 U.S. 198 (1956): the Federal Arbitration Act applied to two types of claims: (1) admiralty and (2) those involving interstate commerce.

The Bremen v. *Zapata Off-Shore Co.*, 407 U.S. 1 (1972): a forum selection clause may not be disregarded solely on the ground of *forum non conveniens.*

Commonwealth Coatings Corp. v. *Continental Casualty Co.*, 393 U.S. 145 (1968): established a standard for determining the extent to which the United States Arbitration Act requires disclosure of the arbitrator's prior business relationships with either party to the arbitration agreement. Arbitrators must not only be unbiased but must avoid the appearance of bias.

Dean Witter Reynolds, Inc. v. *Byrd*, 470 U.S. 213 (1985): it is error for a federal district court to deny a motion to compel arbitration of arbitrable state law claims because they are intertwined with nonarbitrable federal law claims. Rather, the courts must compel arbitration of arbitrable claims at the request of a party to the agreement where there is a valid agreement to arbitrate, under the U.S. Arbitration Act (9 U.S.C. §1 *et seq.*).

Dormitory Authority of the State of New York v. *Span Electric Corp.*, 18 N.Y.2d 114, 271 N.Y.S.2d 983 (1966): the state itself is not insulated against the operation of an arbitration clause because the power to contract implies the power to agree to arbitrate.

Ericksen, Arbuthnot, McCarthy, Kearney & Walsh v. *100 Oak Street*, 35 Cal. 3d 312, 197 Cal. Rptr. 581, 673 P.2d 251 (1983): under a broad arbitration clause, unless the parties specifically exclude from arbitration claims of fraud in the inducement of the contract, as distinguished from fraud in the inducement of the arbitration clause itself, claims are arbitrable.

Florasynth, Inc. v. *Pickholz*, 598 F. Supp. 17 (S.D.N.Y. 1984), *aff'd*, 750 F.2d 171 (2d Cir. 1984): under the Federal Arbitration Act, motions to vacate arbitration awards must be brought within the three-month limitation period specified in the statute. Such motions will not be timely when brought in answer to a motion to confirm made after the three-month period has expired.

H. W. Moseley v. *Electronic & Missile Facilities*, 374 U.S. 167 (1963): fraud in the inducement of the arbitration clause is an issue for the court to decide.

Just In-Material Designs, Ltd. v. *I.T.A.D. Associates, Inc.*, 61 N.Y.2d 882, 464 N.E.2d 1188, 474 N.Y.S.2d 47 (1984), *aff'g* 94 A.D.2d 103, 463 N.Y.S.2d 202 (1983): retention without objection for a reasonable period of time of a sales note executed by a broker authorized to act for both parties establishes an agreement to arbitrate, where the sales note contains an arbitration provision.

Kalman Floor Co., Inc. v. *Jos. L. Muscarelle, Inc.*, 196 N.J. Super. 16, 481 A.2d 553 (1984): the American Arbitration Association has the right to submit the consolidation question to the arbitrator without party consent or judicial decree.

Merit Insurance Co. v. *Leatherby Insurance Co.*, 714 F.2d 673 (7th Cir. 1983): an arbitration award will not be set aside for allegations of arbitrator bias unless the bias is adequately proven.

Mitsubishi Motors Corp. v. *Soler Chrysler–Plymouth, Inc.*, 473 U.S. 614 (1985): antitrust claims raised in cases involving international trade are arbitrable despite a domestic public policy reserving antitrust matters to the courts.

Moses H. Cone Memorial Hospital v. *Mercury Construction Corp.*, 460 U.S. 1 (1983): the district court abused its discretion in granting a stay of the federal court proceedings pending resolution of the issue of arbitrability in the state court, and the stay order was appealable.

Prima Paint Corp. v. *Flood & Conklin Manufacturing Co.*, 338 U.S. 395 (1967): as long as the arbitration clause was not fraudulently induced, the question of fraud in the inducement of the contract was for the arbitrators, not the courts, to decide, under the U.S. Arbitration Act.

Raytheon Co. v. *Automated Business Systems*, 882 F.2d 6 (1st Cir. 1989): the appellate court held that the lower court correctly ruled that the arbitrators were authorized to award punitive damages.

Rodriguez de Quijas v. *Shearson/American Express, Inc.*, __ U.S. __, 109 S. Ct. 1917 (1989): the U.S. Supreme Court held that an agreement to arbitrate claims arising under the Securities Act of 1933 is enforceable, thereby overruling *Wilko v. Swan*, which it deemed was incorrectly decided and inconsistent with the prevailing uniform construction of other federal statutes governing arbitration agreements in business transactions.

Securities Industry Association v. *Connolly*, 883 F.2d 1114 (1st Cir. 1989): the court affirmed the lower court's determination that a state's regulations concerning predispute arbitration agreements were preempted by federal law.

Scherk v. *Alberto-Culver Co.*, 417 U.S. 506 (1974): an international contract for the sale of stock was arbitrable under the Convention on the Recognition and Enforcement of Foreign Arbitral Awards.

Shearson/American Express, Inc. v. *McMahon*, 482 U.S. 220 (1987): agreements to arbitrate future disputes raising statutory claims, such as those under the Securities Exchange Act of 1934 and the Racketeer Influenced and Corrupt Organizations Act, are enforceable under the Federal Arbitration Act absent a clear expression of congressional intent to the contrary.

Silverman v. *Benmor Coats, Inc.*, 61 N.Y.2d 299, 461 N.E.2d 1261, 473 N.Y.S.2d 774 (1984): under a broad arbitration clause, questions of fraud in inducement are for the arbitrator, except as related to the arbitration clause itself. Arbitration will be stayed only if the entire controversy is nonarbitrable.

Southland Corp. v. *Keating*, 465 U.S. 1 (1984): the U.S. Arbitration Act creates federal substantive law that is applicable in both federal and state courts and supersedes conflicting state law in transactions evidencing commerce, under the Supremacy Clause of the U.S. Constitution.

Volt Information Sciences, Inc. v. *Board of Trustees of Leland Stanford Junior University*, 109 S. Ct. 1248 (1989): the U.S. Supreme Court declined to set aside a ruling by the California Court of Appeal that raised the question of whether the state arbitration law was preempted by the Federal Arbitration Act.

Willoughby Roofing & Supply Co., Inc. v. *Kajima International Inc.*, 598 F. Supp. 353 (N.D. Ala. 1984): under a broad arbitration clause, arbitrators have authority to award punitive damages, and such awards do not violate public policy.

York International v. *Alabama Oxygen Co., Inc.*, 465 U.S. 1016 (1984), *rev'g Ex Parte Alabama Oxygen Co., Inc.*, 433 So. 2d 1158 (Ala. 1983): the Supreme Court summarily reversed a decision of the Alabama Supreme Court that the U.S. Arbitration Act does not preempt contradictory state law in state courts, even if the transaction involves interstate commerce.

THE UNITED STATES ARBITRATION ACT

Title 9, US Code, §§ 1–14, was first enacted February 12, 1925 (43 Stat. 883), codified July 30, 1947 (61 Stat. 669), and amended September 3, 1954 (68 Stat. 1233). Chapter 2 was added July 31, 1970 (84 Stat. 692); two new Sections 15 were passed by the Congress in October of 1988 and renumbered on December 1, 1990 (PLs 669 and 702); Chapter 3 was added on May 31 (PL 101–369), and Section 10 was amended on November 15, 1990.

Chapter 1. GENERAL PROVISIONS

§ 1. "Maritime transactions" and "commerce" defined; exceptions to operation of title

§ 2. Validity, irrevocability, and enforcement of agreements to arbitrate

§ 3. Stay of proceedings where issue therein referable to arbitration

§ 4. Failure to arbitrate under agreement; petition to United States court having jurisdiction for order to compel arbitration; notice and service thereof; hearing and determination

§ 5. Appointment of arbitrators or umpire

§ 6. Application heard as motion

§ 7. Witnesses before arbitrators; fees; compelling attendance

§ 8. Proceedings begun by libel in admiralty and seizure of vessel or property

§ 9. Award of arbitrators; confirmation; jurisdiction; procedure

§ 10. Same; vacation; grounds; rehearing.

§ 11. Same; modification or correction; grounds; order

§ 12. Notice of motions to vacate or modify; service; stay of proceedings

§ 13. Papers filed with order on motions; judgment; docketing; force and effect; enforcement

§ 14. Contracts not affected

§ 15. Inapplicability of the Act of State doctrine

§ 16. Appeals

Chapter 2. CONVENTION ON THE RECOGNITION AND ENFORCEMENT OF FOREIGN ARBITRAL AWARDS

§ 201. Enforcement of Convention

§ 202. Agreement or award falling under the Convention

§ 203. Jurisdiction; amount in controversy

§ 204. Venue

§ 205. Removal of cases from State courts

§ 206. Order to compel arbitration; appointment of arbitrators

§ 207. Award of arbitrators; confirmation; jurisdiction; proceeding

§ 208. Chapter 1; residual application

Chapter 3. INTER-AMERICAN CONVENTION ON INTERNATIONAL COMMERCIAL ARBITRATION

Chapter 1. GENERAL PROVISIONS

§ 1. "MARITIME TRANSACTIONS" AND "COMMERCE" DEFINED; EXCEPTIONS TO OPERATION OF TITLE—"Maritime transaction", as herein defined, means charter parties, bills of lading of water carriers, agreements relating to wharfage, supplies furnished vessels or repairs to vessels, collisions, or any other matters in foreign commerce which, if the subject of controversy, would be embraced within admiralty jurisdiction; "commerce", as herein defined, means commerce among the several States or with foreign nations, or in any Territory of the United States or in the District of Columbia, or between any such Territory and another, or between any such Territory and any State or foreign nation, or between the District of Columbia and any State or Territory or foreign nation, but nothing herein contained shall apply to contracts of employment of seamen, railroad employees, or any other class of workers engaged in foreign or interstate commerce.

§ 2. VALIDITY, IRREVOCABILITY, AND ENFORCEMENT OF AGREEMENTS TO ARBITRATE—A written provision in any maritime transaction or a contract evidencing a transaction involving commerce to settle by arbitration a controversy thereafter arising out of such contract or transaction, or the refusal to perform the whole or any part thereof, or an agreement in writing to submit to arbitration an existing controversy arising out of such a contract, transaction, or refusal, shall be valid, irrevocable, and enforceable, save upon such grounds as exist at law or in equity for the revocation of any contract.

§ 3. STAY OF PROCEEDINGS WHERE ISSUE THEREIN REFERABLE TO ARBITRATION—If any suit or proceeding be brought in any of the courts of the United States upon any issue referable to arbitration under an agreement in writing for such arbitration, the court in which such suit is pending, upon being satisfied that the issue involved in such suit or proceeding is referable to arbitration under such an agreement, shall on application of one of the parties stay the trial of the action until such arbitration has been had in accordance with the terms of the agreement, providing the applicant for the stay is not in default in proceeding with such arbitration.

§ 4. FAILURE TO ARBITRATE UNDER AGREEMENT; PETITION TO UNITED STATES COURT HAVING JURISDICTION FOR ORDER TO COMPEL ARBITRATION; NOTICE AND SERVICE THEREOF; HEARING AND DETERMINATION—A party aggrieved by the alleged failure, neglect, or refusal of another to arbitrate under a written agreement for arbitration may petition any United States district court which, save for such agreement, would have jurisdiction under Title 28, in a civil action or in admiralty of the subject matter of a suit arising out of the controversy between the parties, for an order directing that such arbitration proceed in the manner provided for in such agreement. Five days' notice in writing of such application shall be served upon the party in default. Service thereof shall be made in the manner provided by the Federal Rules of Civil Procedure. The court shall hear the parties, and upon being satisfied that the making of the agreement for arbitration or the failure to comply therewith is not in issue, the court shall make an order directing the parties to proceed to arbitration in accordance with the terms of the agreement. The hearing and proceedings, under such agreement, shall be within the district in which the petition for an order directing such arbitration is filed. If the making of the arbitration agreement or the failure, neglect, or refusal to perform the same be in issue, the court shall proceed summarily to the trial thereof. If no jury trial be demanded by the party alleged to be in default, or if the matter in dispute is within admiralty jurisdiction, the court shall hear and determine such issue. Where such an issue is raised, the party alleged to be in default may, except in cases of admiralty, on or before the return day of the notice of application, demand a jury trial of such issue, and upon such demand the court shall make an order referring the issue or issues to a jury in the manner provided by the Federal Rules of Civil Procedure, or may specially call a jury for that purpose. If the jury find that no agreement in writing for arbitration was made or that there is no default in proceeding thereunder, the proceeding shall be dismissed. If the jury find that an agreement for arbitration was made in writing and that there is a default in proceeding thereunder, the court shall make an order summarily directing the parties to proceed with the arbitration in accordance with the terms thereof.

§ 5. APPOINTMENT OF ARBITRATORS OR UMPIRE—If in the agreement provision be made for a method of naming or appointing an arbitrator or arbitrators or an umpire, such method shall be followed; but if no method be provided therein, or if a method be provided and any party thereto shall fail to avail himself of such method, or if for any other reason there shall be a lapse in the naming of an arbitrator or arbitrators or umpire, or in filling a vacancy, then upon the application of either party to the controversy the court shall designate and appoint an arbitrator or arbitrators or umpire, as the case may require, who shall act under the said agreement with the same force and effect as if he or they had been specifically named therein; and unless otherwise provided in the agreement the arbitration shall be by a single arbitrator.

§ 6. APPLICATION HEARD AS MOTION—Any application to the court hereunder shall be made and heard in the manner provided by law for the making and hearing of motions, except as otherwise herein expressly provided.

§ 7. WITNESSES BEFORE ARBITRATORS; FEES; COMPELLING ATTENDANCE —The arbitrators selected either as prescribed in this title or otherwise, or a majority of them, may summon in writing any person to attend before them or any of them as a witness and in a proper case to bring with him or them any book, record, document, or paper which may be deemed material as evidence in the case. The fees for such attendance shall be the same as the fees of witnesses before masters of the United States courts. Said summons shall issue in the name of the arbitrator or arbitrators, or a majority of them, and shall be signed by the arbitrators, or a majority of them, and shall be directed to the said person and shall be served in the same manner as subpoenas to appear and testify before the court; if any person or persons so summoned to testify shall refuse or neglect to obey said summons, upon petition the United States district court for the district in which such arbitrators, or a majority of them, are sitting may compel the attendance of such person or persons before said arbitrator or arbitrators, or punish said person or persons for contempt in the same manner provided by law for securing the attendance of witnesses or their punishment for neglect or refusal to attend in the courts of the United States.

§ 8. PROCEEDINGS BEGUN BY LIBEL IN ADMIRALTY AND SEIZURE OF VESSEL OR PROPERTY—If the basis of jurisdiction be a cause of action otherwise justiciable in admiralty, then, notwithstanding anything herein to the contrary, the party claiming to be aggrieved may begin his proceeding hereunder by libel and seizure of the vessel or other property of the other party according to the usual course of admiralty proceedings, and the court shall then have jurisdiction to direct the parties to proceed with the arbitration and shall retain jurisdiction to enter its decree upon the award.

§ 9. AWARD OF ARBITRATORS; CONFIRMATION; JURISDICTION; PROCEDURE—If the parties in their agreement have agreed that a judgment of the court shall be entered upon the award made pursuant to the arbitration, and shall specify the court, then at any time within one year after the award is made any party to the arbitration may apply to the court so specified for an order confirming the award, and thereupon the court must grant such an order unless the award is vacated, modified, or corrected as prescribed in sections 10 and 11 of this title. If no court is specified in the agreement of the parties, then such application may be made to the United States court in and for the district within which such award was made. Notice of the application shall be served upon the adverse party, and thereupon the court shall have jurisdiction of such party as though he had appeared generally in the proceeding. If the adverse party is a resident of the district within which the award was made, such service shall be made upon the adverse party or his attorney as prescribed by law for service of notice of motion in an action in the same court. If the adverse party shall be a nonresident, then the notice of the application shall be served by the marshal of any district within which the adverse party may be found in like manner as other process of the court.

§ 10. SAME; VACATION; GROUNDS; REHEARING—(a) In any of the following cases the United States court in and for the district wherein the award was made may make an order vacating the award upon the application of any party to the arbitration—

(1) Where the award was procured by corruption, fraud, or undue means.

(2) Where there was evident partiality or corruption in the arbitrators, or either of them.

(3) Where the arbitrators were guilty of misconduct in refusing to postpone the hearing, upon sufficient cause shown, or in refusing to hear evidence pertinent and material to the controversy; or of any other misbehavior by which the rights of any party have been prejudiced.

(4) Where the arbitrators exceeded their powers, or so imperfectly executed them that a mutual, final, and definite award upon the subject matter submitted was not made.

(5) Where an award is vacated and the time within which the agreement required the award to be made has not expired the court may, in its discretion, direct a rehearing by the arbitrators.

(b) The United States district court for the district wherein an award was made that was issued pursuant to section 590 of title 5 may make an order vacating the award upon the application of a person, other than a party to the arbitration, who is adversely affected or aggrieved by the award, if the use of arbitration or the award is clearly inconsistent with the factors set forth in section 582 of title 5.

§ 11. SAME; MODIFICATION OR CORRECTION; GROUNDS; ORDER—In either of the following cases the United States court in and for the district wherein the award was made may make an order modifying or correcting the award upon the application of any party to the arbitration—

(a) Where there was an evident material miscalculation of figures or an evident material mistake in the description of any person, thing, or property referred to in the award.

(b) Where the arbitrators have awarded upon a matter not submitted to them, unless it is a matter not affecting the merits of the decision upon the matter submitted.

(c) Where the award is imperfect in matter of form not affecting the merits of the controversy.

The order may modify and correct the award, so as to effect the intent thereof and promote justice between the parties.

§ 12. NOTICE OF MOTIONS TO VACATE OR MODIFY; SERVICE; STAY OF PROCEEDINGS—Notice of a motion to vacate, modify, or correct an award must be served upon the adverse party or his attorney within three months after the award is filed or delivered. If the adverse party is a resident of the district within which the award was made, such service shall be made upon the adverse party or his attorney as prescribed by law for service of notice of motion in an action in the same court. If the adverse party shall be a nonresident then the notice of the application shall be served by the marshal of any district within which the adverse party may be found in like manner as other process of the court. For the purposes of the motion any judge who might make an order to stay the proceedings in an action brought in the same court may make an order, to be served with the notice of motion, staying the proceedings of the adverse party to enforce the award.

§ 13. PAPERS FILED WITH ORDER ON MOTONS; JUDGMENT; DOCKETING; FORCE AND EFFECT; ENFORCEMENT—The party moving for an order confirming, modifying, or correcting an award shall, at the time such order is filed with the clerk for the entry of judgment thereon, also file the following papers with the clerk:

(a) The agreement; the selection or appointment, if any, of an additional arbitrator or umpire; and each written extension of the time, if any, within which to make the award.

(b) The award.

(c) Each notice, affidavit, or other paper used upon an application to confirm, modify, or correct the award, and a copy of each order of the court upon such an application.

The judgment shall be docketed as if it was rendered in an action.

The judgment so entered shall have the same force and effect, in all respects, as, and be subject to all the provisions of law relating to, a judgment in an action; and it may be enforced as if it had been rendered in an action in the court in which it is entered.

§ 14. CONTRACTS NOT AFFECTED—This title shall not apply to contracts made prior to January 1, 1926.

§ 15. INAPPLICABILITY OF THE ACT OF STATE DOCTRINE—Enforcement of arbitral agreements, confirmation of arbitral awards, and execution upon judgments based on orders confirming such awards shall not be refused on the basis of the Act of State doctrine.

§ 16. APPEALS

(a) An appeal may be taken from—

    (1) an order—

        (A) refusing a stay of any action under section 3 of this title,

        (B) denying a petition under section 4 of this title to order arbitration to proceed,

        (C) denying an application under section 206 of this title to compel arbitration,

        (D) confirming or denying confirmation of an award or partial award, or

        (E) modifying, correcting, or vacating an award;

    (2) an interlocutory order granting, continuing, or modifying an injunction against an arbitration that is subject to this title; or

    (3) a final decision with respect to an arbitration that is subject to this title.

(b) Except as otherwise provided in section 1292(b) of title 28, an appeal may not be taken from an interlocutory order—

    (1) granting a stay of any action under section 3 of this title;

    (2) directing arbitration to proceed under section 4 of this title;

    (3) compelling arbitration under section 206 of this title; or

    (4) refusing to enjoin an arbitration that is subject to this title.

Chapter 2. CONVENTION ON THE RECOGNITION AND ENFORCEMENT OF FOREIGN ARBITRAL AWARDS

§ 201. ENFORCEMENT OF CONVENTION—The Convention on the Recognition and Enforcement of Foreign Arbitral Awards of June 10, 1958, shall be enforced in United States courts in accordance with this chapter.

§ 202. AGREEMENT OR AWARD FALLING UNDER THE CONVENTION—An arbitration agreement or arbitral award arising out of a legal relationship, whether contractual or not, which is considered as commercial, including a transaction, contract, or agreement described in section 2 of this title, falls under the Convention. An agreement or award arising out of such a relationship which is entirely between citizens of the United States shall be deemed not to fall under the Convention unless that relationship involves property located abroad, envisages performance or enforcement abroad, or has some other reasonable relation with one or more foreign states. For the purpose of this section a corporation is a citizen of the United States if it is incorporated or has its principal place of business in the United States.

§ 203. JURISDICTION; AMOUNT IN CONTROVERSY—An action or proceeding falling under the Convention shall be deemed to arise under the laws and treaties of the United States. The district courts of the United States (including the courts enumerated in section 460 of title 28) shall have original jurisdiction over such an action or proceeding, regardless of the amount in controversy.

§ 204. VENUE—An action or proceeding over which the district courts have jurisdiction pursuant to section 203 of this title may be brought in any such court in which save for the arbitration agreement an action or proceeding with respect to the controversy between the parties could be brought, or in such court for the district and division which embraces the place designated in the agreement as the place of arbitration if such place is within the United States.

§ 205. REMOVAL OF CASES FROM STATE COURTS—Where the subject matter of an action or proceeding pending in a State court relates to an arbitration agreement or award falling under the Convention, the defendant or the defendants may, at any time before the trial thereof, remove such action or proceeding to the district court of the United States for the district and division embracing the place where the action or proceeding is pending. The procedure for removal of causes otherwise provided by law shall apply, except that the ground for removal provided in this section need not appear on the face of the complaint but may be shown in the petition for removal. For the purposes of Chapter 1 of this title any action or proceeding removed under this section shall be deemed to have been brought in the district court to which it is removed.

§ 206. ORDER TO COMPEL ARBITRATION; APPOINTMENT OF ARBITRATORS —A court having jurisdiction under this chapter may direct that arbitration be held in accordance with the agreement at any place therein provided for, whether that place is within or without the United States. Such court may also appoint arbitrators in accordance with the provisions of the agreement.

§ 207. AWARD OF ARBITRATORS; CONFIRMATION; JURISDICTION; PRO-CEEDING—Within three years after an arbitral award falling under the Convention is made, any party to the arbitration may apply to any court having jurisdiction under this chapter for an order confirming the award as against any other party to the arbitration. The court shall confirm the award unless it finds one of the grounds for refusal or deferral of recognition or enforcement of the award specified in the said Convention.

§ 208. CHAPTER 1; RESIDUAL APPLICATION—Chapter 1 applies to actions and proceedings brought under this chapter to the extent that chapter is not in conflict with this chapter or the Convention as ratified by the United States.

Chapter 3. INTER-AMERICAN CONVENTION ON INTERNATIONAL COMMERCIAL ARBITRATION

§ 301. ENFORCEMENT OF CONVENTION—The Inter-American Convention on International Commercial Arbitration of January 30, 1975, shall be enforced in United States courts in accordance with this chapter.

§ 302. INCORPORATION BY REFERENCE—Sections 202, 203, 204, 205, and 207 of this title shall apply to this chapter as if specifically set forth herein, except that for the purposes of this chapter "the Convention" shall mean the Inter-American Convention.

§ 303. ORDER TO COMPEL ARBITRATION; APPOINTMENT OF ARBITRATORS; LOCALE

(a) A court having jurisdiction under this chapter may direct that arbitration be held in accordance with the agreement at any place therein provided for, whether that place is within or without the United States. The court may also appoint arbitrators in accordance with the provisions of the agreement.

(b) In the event the agreement does not make provision for the place of arbitration or the appointment of arbitrators, the court shall direct that the arbitration shall be held and the arbitrators be appointed in accordance with Article 3 of the Inter-American Convention.

§ 304. RECOGNITION AND ENFORCEMENT OF FOREIGN ARBITRAL DECISIONS AND AWARDS; RECIPROCITY—Arbitral decisions or awards made in the territory of a foreign State shall, on the basis of reciprocity, be recognized and enforced under this chapter only if that State has ratified or acceded to the Inter-American Convention.

§ 305. RELATIONSHIP BETWEEN THE INTER-AMERICAN CONVENTION AND THE CONVENTION ON THE RECOGNITION AND ENFORCEMENT OF FOREIGN ARBITRAL AWARDS OF JUNE 10, 1958—When the requirements for application of both the Inter-American Convention and the Convention on the Recognition and Enforcement of Foreign Arbitral Awards of June 10, 1958, are met, determination as to which Convention applies shall, unless otherwise expressly agreed, be made as follows:

(1) If a majority of the parties to the arbitration agreement are citizens of a State or States that have ratified or acceded to the Inter-American Convention and are member States of the Organization of American States, the Inter-American Convention shall apply.

(2) In all other cases the Convention on the Recognition and Enforcement of Foreign Arbitral Awards of June 10, 1958, shall apply.

§ 306. APPLICABLE RULES OF INTER-AMERICAN COMMERCIAL ARBITRATION COMMISSION

(a) For the purposes of this chapter the rules of procedure of the Inter-American Commercial Arbitration Commission referred to in Article 3 of the Inter-American Convention shall, subject to subsection (b) of this section, be those rules as promulgated by the Commission on July 1, 1988.

(b) In the event the rules of procedure of the Inter-American Commercial Arbitration Commission are modified or amended in accordance with the procedures for amendment of the rules of that Commission, the Secretary of State, by regulation in accordance with section 553 of title 5, consistent with the aims and purposes of this Convention, may prescribe that such modifications or amendments shall be effective for purposes of this chapter.

§ 307. CHAPTER 1; RESIDUAL APPLICATION—Chapter 1 applies to actions and proceedings brought under this chapter to the extent chapter 1 is not in conflict with this chapter or the Inter-American Convention as ratified by the United States.

THE UNIFORM ARBITRATION ACT

ACT RELATING TO ARBITRATION AND TO MAKE UNIFORM THE LAW WITH REFERENCE THERETO

Section 1. VALIDITY OF ARBITRATION AGREEMENT—A written agreement to submit any existing controversy to arbitration or a provision in a written contract to submit to arbitration any controversy thereafter arising between the parties is valid, enforceable and irrevocable, save upon such grounds as exist at law or in equity for the revocation of any contract. This act also applies to arbitration agreements between employers and employees or between their respective representatives [unless otherwise provided in the agreement].

Section 2. PROCEEDINGS TO COMPEL OR STAY ARBITRATION—

(a) On application of a party showing an agreement described in Section 1, and the opposing party's refusal to arbitrate, the Court shall order the parties to proceed with arbitration, but if the opposing party denies the existence of the agreement to arbitrate, the Court shall proceed summarily to the determination of the issue so raised and shall order arbitration if found for the moving party, otherwise, the application shall be denied.

(b) On application, the court may stay an arbitration proceeding commenced or threatened on a showing that there is no agreement to arbitrate. Such an issue, when in substantial and bona fide dispute, shall be forthwith and summarily tried and the stay ordered if found for the moving party. If found for the opposing party, the court shall order the parties to proceed to arbitration.

(c) If an issue referable to arbitration under the alleged agreement is involved in an action or proceeding pending in a court having jurisdiction to hear applications under subdivision (a) of this Section, the application shall be made therein. Otherwise and subject to Section 18, the application may be made in any court of competent jurisdiction.

(d) Any action or proceeding involving an issue subject to arbitration shall be stayed if an order for arbitration or an application therefor has been made under this section or, if the issue is severable, the stay may be with respect thereto only. When the application is made in such action or proceeding, the order for arbitration shall include such stay.

(e) An order for arbitration shall not be refused on the ground that the claim in issue lacks merit or bona fides or because any fault or grounds for the claim sought to be arbitrated have not be shown.

Section 3. APPOINTMENT OF ARBITRATORS BY COURT—If the arbitration agreement provides a method of appointment of arbitrators, this method shall be followed. In the absence thereof, or if the agreed method fails or for any reason cannot be followed, or when an arbitrator appointed fails or is unable to act and his successor has not been duly appointed, the court on application of a party shall appoint one or more arbitrators. An arbitrator so appointed has all the powers of one specifically named in the agreement.

Section 4. MAJORITY ACTION BY ARBITRATORS—The powers of the arbitrators may be exercised by a majority unless otherwise provided by the agreement or by this act.

Section 5. HEARING. UNLESS OTHERWISE PROVIDED BY THE AGREEMENT—

(a) The arbitrators shall appoint a time and place for the hearing and cause notification to the parties to be served personally or by registered mail not less than five days before the hearing. Appearance at the hearing waives such notice. The arbitrators may adjourn the hearing from time to time as necessary and, on request of a party and for good cause, or upon their own motion may postpone the hearing to a time not later than the date fixed by the agreement for making the award unless the parties consent to a later date. The arbitrators may hear and determine the controversy upon the evidence produced notwithstanding the failure of a party duly notified to appear. The court on application may direct the arbitrators to proceed promptly with the hearing and determination of the controversy.

(b) The parties are entitled to be heard, to present evidence material to the controversy and to cross-examine witnesses appearing at the hearing.

(c) The hearing shall be conducted by all the arbitrators but a majority may determine any question and render a final award. If, during the course of the hearing, an arbitrator for any reason ceases to act, the remaining arbitrator or arbitrators appointed to act as neutrals may continue with the hearing and determination of the controversy.

Section 6. REPRESENTATION BY ATTORNEY—A party has the right to be represented by an attorney at any proceeding or hearing under this act. A waiver thereof prior to the proceeding or hearing is ineffective.

Section 7. WITNESSES, SUBPOENAS, DEPOSITIONS—

(a) The arbitrators may issue (cause to be issued) subpoenas for the attendance of witnesses and for the production of books, records, documents and other evidence, and shall have the power to administer oaths. Subpoenas so issued shall be served, and upon application to the Court by a party or the arbitrators, enforced, in the manner provided by law for the service and enforcement of subpoenas in a civil action.

(b) On application of a party and for use as evidence, the arbitrators may permit a deposition to be taken, in the manner and upon the terms designated by the arbitrators, of a witness who cannot be subpoenaed or is unable to attend the hearing.

(c) All provisions of law compelling a person under subpoena to testify are applicable.

(d) Fees for attendance as a witness shall be the same as for a witness in the _____ Court.

Section 8. AWARD—

(a) The award shall be in writing and signed by the arbitrators joining in the award. The arbitrators shall deliver a copy to each party personally or by registered mail, or as provided in the agreement.

(b) An award shall be made within the time fixed therefor by the agreement or, if not so fixed, within such time as the court orders on application of a party. The parties may extend the time in writing either before or after the expiration thereof. A party waives the objection that an award was not made within the time required unless he notifies the arbitrators of his objection prior to the delivery of the award to him.

Section 9. CHANGE OF AWARD BY ARBITRATORS—On application of a party or, if an application to the court is pending under Sections 11, 12 or 13, on submission to the arbitrators by the court under such conditions as the court may order, the arbitrators may modify or correct the award upon the grounds stated in paragraphs (1) and (3) of subdivision (a) of Section 13, or for the purpose of clarifying the award. The application shall be made within twenty days after delivery of the award to the applicant. Written notice thereof shall be given forthwith to the opposing party, stating he must serve his objections thereto, if any, within ten days from the notice. The award so modified or corrected is subject to the provisions of Sections 11, 12 and 13.

Section 10. FEES AND EXPENSES OF ARBITRATION—Unless otherwise provided in the agreement to arbitrate, the arbitrators' expenses and fees, together with other expenses, not including counsel fees, incurred in the conduct of the arbitration, shall be paid as provided in the award.

Section 11. CONFIRMATION OF AN AWARD—Upon application of a party, the Court shall confirm an award, unless within the time limits hereinafter imposed grounds are urged for vacating or modifying or correcting the award, in which case the court shall proceed as provided in Sections 12 and 13.

Section 12. VACATING AN AWARD—

(a) Upon application of a party, the court shall vacate an award where:
    (1) The award was procured by corruption, fraud or other undue means;
    (2) There was evident partiality by an arbitrator appointed as a neutral or corruption in any of the arbitrators or misconduct prejudicing the rights of any party;
    (3) The arbitrators exceeded their powers;
    (4) The arbitrators refused to postpone the hearing upon sufficient cause being shown therefor or refused to hear evidence material to the controversy or otherwise so conducted the hearing, contrary to the provisions of Section 5, as to prejudice substantially the rights of a party; or
    (5) There was no arbitration agreement and the issue was not adversely determined in proceedings under Section 2 and the party did not participate in the arbitration hearing without raising the objection;
but the fact that the relief was such that it could not or would not be granted by a court of law or equity is not ground for vacating or refusing to confirm the award.

(b) An application under this Section shall be made within ninety days after delivery of a copy of the award to the applicant, except that, if predicated upon corruption, fraud or other undue means, it shall be made within ninety days after such grounds are known or should have been known.

(c) In vacating the award on grounds other than stated in clause (5) of Subsection (a) the court may order a rehearing before new arbitrators chosen as provided in the agreement, or in the absence thereof, by the court in accordance with Section 3, or if the award is vacated on grounds set forth in clauses (3), and (4) of Subsection (a) the court may order a rehearing before the arbitrators who made the award or their successors appointed in accordance with Section 3. The time within which the agreement requires the award to be made is applicable to the rehearing and commences from the date of the order.

(d) If the application to vacate is denied and no motion to modify or correct the award is pending, the court shall confirm the award.

Section 13. MODIFICATION OR CORRECTION OF AWARD—

(a) Upon application made within ninety days after delivery of a copy of the award to the applicant, the court shall modify or correct the award where:

> (1) There was an evident miscalculation of figures or an evident mistake in the description of any person, thing or property referred to in the award;
>
> (2) The arbitrators have awarded upon a matter not submitted to them and the award may be corrected without affecting the merits of the decision upon the issues submitted; or
>
> (3) The award is imperfect in a matter of form, not affecting the merits of the controversy.

(b) If the application is granted, the court shall modify and correct the award so as to effect its intent and shall confirm the award as so modified and corrected. Otherwise, the court shall confirm the award as made.

(c) An application to modify or correct an award may be joined in the alternative with an application to vacate the award.

Section 14. JUDGMENT OR DECREE ON AWARD—

Upon the granting of an order confirming, modifying or correcting an award, judgment or decree shall be entered in conformity therewith and be enforced as any other judgment or decree. Costs of the application and of the proceedings subsequent thereto, and disbursements may be awarded by the court.

Section 15. JUDGMENT ROLL, DOCKETING—

(a) On entry of judgment or decree, the clerk shall prepare the judgment roll consisting, to the extent filed, of the following:

> (1) The agreement and each written extension of the time within which to make the award;
>
> (2) The award;
>
> (3) A copy of the order confirming, modifying or correcting the award; and
>
> (4) A copy of the judgment or decree.

(b) The judgment or decree may be docketed as if rendered in an action.]

Section 16. APPLICATIONS TO COURT—

Except as otherwise provided, an application to the court under this act shall be by motion and shall be heard in the manner and upon the notice provided by law or rule of court for the making and hearing of motions. Unless the parties have agreed otherwise, notice of an initial application for an order shall be served in the manner provided by law for the service of a summons in an action.

Section 17. COURT, JURISDICTION—

The term "court" means any court of competent jurisdiction of this State. The making of an agreement described in Section 1 providing for arbitration in this State confers jurisdiction on the court to enforce the agreement under this Act and to enter judgment on an award thereunder.

Section 18. VENUE—

An initial application shall be made to the court of the [county] in which the agreement provides the arbitration hearing shall be held or, if the hearing has been held, in the county in which it was held. Otherwise the application shall be made in the [county] where the adverse party resides or has a place of business or, if he has no residence or place of business in this State, to the court of any [county]. All subsequent applications shall be made to the court hearing the initial application unless the court otherwise directs.

Section 19. APPEALS—

(a) An appeal may be taken from:

   (1) An order denying an application to compel arbitration made under Section 2;

   (2) An order granting an application to stay arbitration made under Section 2(b);

   (3) An order confirming or denying confirmataion of an award;

   (4) An order modifying or correcting an award;

   (5) An order vacating an award without directing a rehearing; or

   (6) A judgment or decree entered pursuant to the provisions of this act.

(b) The appeal shall be taken in the manner and to the same extent as from orders or judgments in a civil action.

Section 20. ACT NOT RETROACTIVE—This act applies only to agreements made subsequent to the taking effect of this act.

Section 21. UNIFORMITY OF INTERPRETATION—This act shall be so construed as to effectuate its general purpose to make uniform the law of those states which enact it.

Section 22. CONSTITUTIONALITY—If any provision of this act or the application thereof to any person or circumstance is held invalid, the invalidity shall not affect other provisions or applications of the act which can be given without the invalid provision or application, and to this end the provisions of this act are severable.

Section 23. SHORT TITLE—This act may be cited as the Uniform Arbitration Act.

Section 24. REPEAL—All acts or parts of acts which are inconsistent with the provisions of this act are hereby repealed.

Section 25. TIME OF TAKING EFFECT—This act shall take effect _____.

MODERN ARBITRATION STATUTES IN THE UNITED STATES

United States Arbitration Act, 9 USC §§ 1 et seq.

Alaska Statutes, §§ 09.43.010 *et seq.**
Arizona Revised Statutes, §§ 12–1501 *et seq.**
Arkansas Statutes Annotated, §§ 34–511 *et seq.**
California Code of Civil Procedure, §§ 1280 *et seq.*
Colorado Revised Statutes, §§ 13–22–201 *et seq.**
Connecticut General Statutes Annotated, §§ 52–408 *et seq.*
Delaware Code Annotated, Title 10, §§ 5701 *et seq.**
District of Columbia Code, Title 16, §§ 16–4301 *et seq.**
Florida Statutes Annotated, §§ 682.01 *et seq.*
Code of Georgia, §§ 9–9–80 *et seq.*†
Hawaii Revised Statutes, §§ 658–1 *et seq.**
Idaho Code, §§ 7–901 *et seq.**
Illinois Revised Statutes, Chapter 10, §§ 101 *et seq.**
Indiana Code Annotated, §§ 34–4–2–1 *et seq.**
Code of Iowa, §§ 679A.1 *et seq.**
Kansas Statutes, §§ 5–401 *et seq.**
Kentucky Revised Statutes, §§ 417.045 *et seq.**
Louisiana Revised Statutes, §§ 9:4201 *et seq.**
Maine Revised Statutes Annotated, Title 14, §§ 5927 *et seq.**
Maryland Courts & Judicial Procedure Code Annotated, §§ 3–201 *et seq.**
Annotated Laws of Massachusetts, Chapter 251, §§ 1 *et seq.**
Michigan Compiled Laws, §§ 600.5001 *et seq.*
Minnesota Statutes, §§ 572.08 *et seq.**
Mississippi Code Annotated, §§ 11–15–1 *et seq.**†
Annotated Missouri Statutes, §§ 435.350 *et seq.**
Revised Montana Code Annotated, §§ 27–5–111 *et seq.**
Revised Statutes of Nebraska, §§ 25–2601 *et seq.**
Nevada Revised Statutes, §§ 38.015 *et seq.**
New Hampshire Revised Statutes Annotated, §§ 542:1 *et seq.**
New Jersey Statutes Annotated, §§ 2A:24–1 *et seq.*
New Mexico Statutes Annotated, §§ 44–7–1 *et seq.**

Modern statutes are those enforcing agreements to arbitrate existing controversies and any arising in the future. The other state arbitration statutes (those of Alabama and West Virginia) apply to existing controversies only (the Code of Alabama, § 6, and the West Virginia Code, § 55).
* Incorporating the Uniform Arbitration Act.
† Applicable to construction disputes only.

New York Civil Practice Law and Rules, §§ 7501 *et seq.*
General Statutes of North Carolina, §§ 1-567.1 *et seq.**
North Dakota Century Code, §§ 32-29.2-01 *et seq.**
Ohio Revised Code Annotated, §§ 2711.01 *et seq.*
Oklahoma Statutes Annotated, Title 15, §§ 801 *et seq.**
Oregon Revised Statutes, §§ 33.210 *et seq.*
Pennsylvania Statutes Annotated, Title 42, §§ 7301 *et seq.**
Laws of Puerto Rico Annotated, Title 32, §§ 3201 *et seq.*
General Laws of Rhode Island, §§ 10-3-1 *et seq.*
Code of Laws of South Carolina, §§ 15-48-10 *et seq.**
South Dakota Codified Laws Annotated, §§ 21-25A-1 *et seq.**
Tennessee Code Annotated, §§ 29-5-302 *et seq.**
Texas Revised Civil Statutes Annotated, Title 10, Articles 224 *et seq.**
Utah Code Annotated, §§ 78-31a-1 *et seq.*
Vermont Statutes Annotated, Title 12, §§ 5651 *et seq.**
Code of Virginia Annotated, §§ 8.01-577 *et seq.**
Washington Revised Code Annotated, §§ 7.04.010 *et seq.*
Wisconsin Statutes Annotated, §§ 788.01 *et seq.*
Wyoming Statutes, §§ 1-36-101 *et seq.**

OFFICES OF THE AMERICAN ARBITRATION ASSOCIATION

AZ **Phoenix (85012–2365) • Harry Kaminsky**
333 East Osborn Road, Suite 310 • (602) 234–0950/230–2151 (Fax)

CA **Irvine (92714–7240) • Lori S. Markowicz**
2030 Main Street, Suite 1650 • (714) 474–5090/474–5087 (Fax)

Los Angeles (90010–1108) • Rocco M. Scanza
3055 Wilshire Boulevard, Floor 7 • (213) 383–6516/386–2251 (Fax)

San Diego (92101–4586) • Dennis Sharp
600 B Street, Suite 1450 • (619) 239–3051/239–3807 (Fax)

San Francisco (94104–1113) • Charles A. Cooper
417 Montgomery Street • (415) 981–3901/781–8426 (Fax)

CO **Denver (80264–2101) • Mark Appel**
1660 Lincoln Street, Suite 2150 • (303) 831–0823/832–3626 (Fax)

CT **East Hartford (06108–3240) • Karen M. Jalkut**
111 Founders Plaza, Floor 17 • (203) 289–3993/282–0459 (Fax)

DC **Washington (20036–4104) • Garylee Cox**
1150 Connecticut Avenue, NW, Floor 6 • (202) 296–8510/872–9574 (Fax)

* **Office of National Affairs • Thomas R. Colosi**
1730 Rhode Island Avenue, NW, Suite 512 • (202) 331–7073/331–3356 (Fax)

FL **Miami (33131–2501) • René Grafals**
99 SE Fifth Street, Suite 200 • (305) 358–7777/358–4931 (Fax)

Orlando (32801–2742) • Mark Sholander
201 East Pine Street, Suite 800 • (407) 648–1185/649–8668 (Fax)

GA **Atlanta (30345–3203) • India Johnson**
1975 Century Boulevard, NE, Suite 1 • (404) 325–0101/325–8034 (Fax)

HI **Honolulu (96813–4714) • Keith W. Hunter**
810 Richards Street, Suite 641 • (808) 531–0541/533–2306 (Fax)
In Guam, (671) 477–1845/477–3178 (Fax)

IL **Chicago (60601–7601) • David Scott Carfello**
225 North Michigan Avenue, Suite 2527 • (312) 616–6560/819–0404 (Fax)

LA **New Orleans (70130–6101) • Deann Gladwell**
650 Poydras Street, Suite 1535 • (504) 522–8781/561–8041 (Fax)

MA **Boston (02110–1703) • Richard M. Reilly**
133 Federal Street • (617) 451–6600/451–0763 (Fax)

MI **Southfield (48076–3728) • Mary A. Bedikian**
One Towne Square, Suite 1600 • (313) 352–5500/352–3147 (Fax)

MN **Minneapolis (55402–1092) • James R. Deye**
514 Nicollet Mall, Suite 670 • (612) 332–6545/342–2334 (Fax)

MO **Kansas City (64106–2110) • Lori A. Madden**
1101 Walnut Street, Suite 903 • (816) 221–6401/471–5264 (Fax)

St. Louis (63101–1614) • **Neil Moldenhauer**
One Mercantile Center, Suite 2512 • (314) 621-7175/621-3730 (Fax)

NV Las Vegas (89102–8719) • **Kelvin Chin**
4425 Spring Mountain Road, Suite 310 • (702) 364-8009/364-8084 (Fax)
From Reno, (702) 786-6688

NJ Somerset (08873–4120) • **Richard Naimark**
265 Davidson Avenue, Suite 140 • (908) 560-9560/560-8850 (Fax)

NY Garden City (11530–2004) • **Mark A. Resnick**
666 Old Country Road, Suite 603 • (516) 222-1660/745-6447 (Fax)

New York (10020–1203) • **Florence M. Peterson**
140 West 51st Street • (212) 484-4000/307-4387 (Fax)

Syracuse (13202–1376) • **Deborah A. Brown**
205 South Salina Street • (315) 472-5483/472-0966 (Fax)

White Plains (10603–1916) • **Marion J. Zinman**
399 Knollwood Road, Suite 116 • (914) 946-1119/946-2661 (Fax)

NC Charlotte (28202–2431) • **Neil Carmichael**
428 East Fourth Street, Suite 300 • (704) 347-0200/347-2804 (Fax)

OH Cincinnati (45202–2809) • **Philip S. Thompson**
441 Vine Street, Suite 3308 • (513) 241-8434/241-8437 (Fax)

Middleburg Heights (44130–3490) • **Eileen B. Vernon**
17900 Jefferson Road, Suite 101 • (216) 891-4741/891-4740 (Fax)

PA Philadelphia (19102–4106) • **Kenneth Egger**
230 South Broad Street, Floor 6 • (215) 732-5260/732-5002 (Fax)

Pittsburgh (15222–1207) • **John F. Schano**
Four Gateway Center, Room 419 • (412) 261-3617/261-6055 (Fax)

RI Providence (02903–1082) • **Mark Bayliss**
115 Cedar Street • (401) 453-3250/453-6194 (Fax)

TN Nashville (37219–2111) • **Sheila R. Davy**
221 Fourth Avenue North • (615) 256-5857/244-8570 (Fax)

TX Dallas (75240–6620) • **Helmut O. Wolff**
13455 Noel Road, Suite 1440 • (214) 702-8222/490-9008 (Fax)

Houston (77002–6708) • **Therese Tilley**
1001 Fannin Street, Suite 1005 • (713) 739-1302/739-1702 (Fax)

UT Salt Lake City (84111–3834) • **Diane Abegglen**
645 South 200 East, Suite 203 • (801) 531-9748/531-0660 (Fax)

WA Seattle (98101–2511)
1325 Fourth Avenue, Suite 1414 • (206) 622-6435/343-5679 (Fax)

* Does not administer cases.

Also in the "What You Need to Know" series on dispute resolution . . .

Mediation is increasingly being recognized as a viable method of resolving business disputes. In mediation, the parties attempt to settle their dispute with the aid of a neutral third party while retaining full control over any settlement reached. Mediation proceedings are confidential and private. *Business Mediation—What You Need to Know* provides business professionals, practitioners, and neutrals with a solid working knowledge of the mediation process, the function of the mediator, and of how negotiation skills affect the outcome. The book presents four actual cases and describes how the parties were at loggerheads until they met with a mediator. The appendix contains AAA mediation rules, sample mediator standards, excerpts of training materials, and an extensive bibliography. A paperback, this book has 128 pages, costs $8, and is available from the American Arbitration Association's Department of Publications, 140 West 51st Street, New York, NY 10020–1203, (212) 484–4011.

Membership in the American Arbitration Association

The AAA administers more than 60,000 cases each year. Fees cover the major part of its administrative costs, but it requires further support to finance its membership services, research, and educational work. Foundations and major national organizations provide funds for special projects. AAA members include corporations, unions, trade associations, and law firms, as well as individuals interested in voluntary arbitration.

Members may consult with the AAA on special problems. Help can be given on design or administration of grievance and arbitration systems. The experience of the AAA's staff is unique in this regard.

Members also have access to the association's Eastman Arbitration Library, which houses one of the most comprehensive collections on dispute settlement, and you are invited to use the AAA educational facilities. Seminars, films, pamphlets, and programs are designed to meet specific needs. Discounts are available to members.

Association members receive the *Arbitration Journal* and *Arbitration Times* as part of their membership. Members also receive a choice of free subscriptions to award-reporting services or other publications, depending on the type of membership that they hold. Membership in the American Arbitration Association is open to all who are interested in voluntary out-of-court dispute settlement. Memberships range from individual to those for large companies and unions. Support for the association is important in order to accomplish the goals that have been set.

For further information about becoming a member, please contact the Membership Department, AAA, 140 West 51st Street, New York, NY 10020–1203.